MW01027388

Culture and Politics

Raymond Williams (1921–1988) was Professor of Drama at the University of Cambridge, where he worked from 1961 until his retirement in 1983. He previously taught for the University of Oxford Delegacy of Extra-Mural Studies and the Workers' Educational Association in East Sussex. His books include *Culture and Society* (1958), *Border Country* (1960), *The Long Revolution* (1961), *Modern Tragedy* (1966), *The Country and the City* (1973), *Keywords* (1976), *Marxism and Literature* (1977), and *Towards 2000* (1983).

Phil O'Brien is the author of *The Working Class and Twenty-First-Century British Fiction* (2020). He is on the editorial board of *Key Words: A Journal of Cultural Materialism*, secretary of the Raymond Williams Society, and has taught at the University of Manchester, Liverpool John Moores University, Edge Hill University, and the Open University.

Culture and Politics

Class, Writing, Socialism

Raymond Williams

Edited with an Introduction by Phil O'Brien

VERSO

London • New York

First published by Verso 2022
© Raymond Williams 2022
Introduction © Phil O'Brien 2022

1 3 5 7 9 10 8 6 4 2

Verso
UK: 6 Meard Street, London W1F 0EG
US: 20 Jay Street, Suite 1010, Brooklyn, NY 11201
versobooks.com

Verso is the imprint of New Left Books

ISBN-13: 978-1-78873-863-7
ISBN-13: 978-1-78873-865-1 (HARDBACK)
ISBN-13: 978-1-78873-867-5 (US EBK)
ISBN-13: 978-1-78873-866-8 (UK EBK)

British Library Cataloguing in Publication Data
A catalogue record for this book is available from the British Library

Library of Congress Cataloging-in-Publication Data
A catalog record for this book is available from the Library of Congress

Typeset in Minion Pro by MJ & N Gavan, Truro, Cornwall
Printed in the UK by CPI Group (UK) Ltd, Croydon, CR0 4YY

Contents

Acknowledgements

Five of the ten essays included in this book have never been published before in their current form, while a sixth ('British Working-Class Literature after 1945') was published for the first time in 2020 in *Key Words: A Journal of Cultural Materialism*. The essays were originally delivered as lectures, are held in the Raymond Williams archive, or have been published in edited collections and journals as follows: 'Herbert Read: Freud, Art, and Industry' is an unpublished chapter from *Culture and Society: 1780–1950* (1958), originally titled 'Sir Herbert Read' and held in the Raymond Williams Collection in the Richard Burton Archives, Swansea University (WWE/2/1/6/4/10); 'The Future of Marxism' was published in *The Twentieth Century*, 170.1010, July 1961, 128–42, and later in *New Left Review*, 114, Nov–Dec 2018, 53–65; 'The Meanings of Work' is from *Work: Twenty Personal Accounts*, ed. Ronald Fraser (Penguin with *New Left Review*, 1968), 280–98; 'Marxist Cultural Theory' is an edited transcript from an archive of recordings loaned by the Williams Estate – it is a re-recorded version of a lecture originally given in Montreal in April 1973; 'Popular Culture: History and Theory' is a talk delivered at the Open University on 23 May 1978 – the transcription by Tony Bennett was published in 'Popular Culture No. 2 Bulletin',

Open University, August 1978, and later in *Cultural Studies*, 32.6, November 2018, 903–28; 'British Working-Class Literature after 1945' is an edited transcript of a lecture given at Aarhus University, Denmark, 25 September 1979 – it was published in *Key Words*, 18, 2020, 45–55; 'Pierre Bourdieu and the Sociology of Culture' was co-authored by Nicholas Garnham and appeared in *Media, Culture and Society*, 2.3, July 1980, 209–23; 'Popular Forms of Writing' is an edited transcript of a talk given at Centerprise, Hackney, 8 January 1982; 'The Future of Socialism' was delivered at Heathlands Hotel, Bournemouth on a *New Socialist* panel (titled 'The Future of Socialism') at the Labour Party Conference fringe, 30 September 1985 – the transcript, titled 'Discussion between Raymond Williams and Tony Benn', is held in the Williams archive at Swansea (WWE/2/1/7/3/7); 'When Was Modernism?' is an edited transcript of a Lewis Fry Memorial Lecture delivered on 17 March 1987 at the University of Bristol. All ten of the essays have been revised – the previously published material, the archive papers and, particularly, the lecture transcriptions – but only lightly and where appropriate, in order to enhance yet preserve Williams's original work.

Merryn Williams, the daughter of Raymond Williams, has supported this project from the beginning and, by kindly loaning a treasure trove of lecture recordings following a memorable afternoon in Oxford in Spring 2019, her involvement transformed the collection. Many thanks to Merryn, her husband John, and the Williams family. This book is for them. Thanks to John Merrick at Verso whose unstinting support from the outset has made this book possible and to Leo Hollis for overseeing its publication. Ben Harker and Daniel Hartley generously offered their expertise and guidance on the introduction; John Connor, Daniel Gerke, and Ted Striphas aided with the sourcing of material; and Daniela Caselli gave much-needed advice on Antonio Gramsci. Thanks to Nicholas Garnham and SAGE for allowing the inclusion of the Bourdieu essay, Tony Bennett for approving the use of his transcription of the Open University talk, Ken Worpole for sharing his memories of Williams's visit to Hackney, and to the Barry Amiel and Norman Melburn Trust who provided funding to transcribe the lecture tapes. The Working Class Movement Library in Salford helped track down crucial information on Tony Benn, as did the trustees of the Benn estate, and the archivists at Swansea University and the University of Reading offered their invaluable expertise and helped with the publication of archival material. Along with thanking Merryn and the estate of Raymond Williams, I also express my gratitude to the trustees of the estates of Stuart Hall, E. P. Thompson, Pierre Bourdieu, and Tony Benn who have approved the use of personal papers held amongst Williams's own papers in South Wales.

Introduction: Raymond Williams on Culture and Politics

'It is as if a fixed point in the landscape has suddenly dissolved', wrote a distraught E. P. Thompson on the death of Raymond Williams in January 1988.[1] Stuart Hall, who described the shock of losing Williams at the age of sixty-six as 'irreparable', felt ill-equipped to know how 'to express or where to put our sense of the enormity of that loss'.[2] The 'our' registered by Hall was the beleaguered British left of the late 1980s, while the intense feeling of despair indicated a temporary defeat of the political possibilities Williams, as a committed socialist, represented; it was a 'confidence in the future' which Williams insisted he had 'often written to try to restore'.[3] The value of his complex thinking came with a comradely and collaborative approach to intellectual and political work. 'His presence was felt as a constructive and uniting pressure', wrote Thompson.[4] What remains of that presence and pressure

---

1   E. P. Thompson, 'Last Dispatches from the Border Country', *Cambridge Review*, June 1988, 52.

2   Stuart Hall, 'Only Connect: The Life of Raymond Williams', *New Statesman*, 5 February 1988, 20.

3   Raymond Williams, *Politics and Letters* (1979; London: Verso, 2015), 294.

4   Thompson, 'Last Dispatches', 51.

today, of that complex yet constructive position, more than three decades on? *Culture and Politics: Class, Writing, Socialism* brings together ten uncollected and unpublished essays, six of which are taken from public talks and lectures. They offer a compelling insight into what Terry Eagleton described as the 'extraordinary personal liberation' of hearing Williams speak.[1] This introductory essay contextualizes and critically examines his work by adopting a biographical mode, tracking Williams's thinking from his breakthrough year of 1958 up to his death in 1988. It is a necessary focus, given that the official biography, *Raymond Williams: A Warrior's Tale* (2008) by Dai Smith, ends at 1961, while the only other biography, *Raymond Williams* (1995) by Fred Inglis, offers a novelistic and at times contentious account of his life.[2] Crucially, the timely selection and publication in Williams's centenary year of what have been difficult to find essays and previously unavailable lectures is an attempt to draw out the opportunities contained in his writing for radical transformations in culture and society in the twenty-first century.

It is with his landmark book of that name – *Culture and Society* (1958) – that the collection begins, in the form of a 'lost' chapter on the critic and anarchist Herbert Read, unpublished and archived until now.[3] As first conceived, it should have been included in 'Part III: Twentieth-Century Opinions', after chapters on D. H. Lawrence and R. H. Tawney. The section is central to the purpose of a book which Williams described as 'a history and criticism of the ideas which have been concentrated in the modern meanings of "culture".[4] The original manuscript was submitted in March

---

1   Terry Eagleton, 'Introduction', in *Raymond Williams: Critical Perspectives* (Cambridge: Polity, 1989), 1.

2   For an insight into the contentious aspects, see Raphael Samuel's review of Inglis's biography: 'Making it Up', *London Review of Books*, 18.13, 4 July 1996.

3   The typescript text was stored amongst Williams's papers before being deposited in the archives at Swansea University in 2007. It has been proofread with annotations added in Williams's hand and was ready for publication when pulled from the manuscript of *Culture and Society* at the final moment.

4   Letter from Williams to Ian Parsons, 12 January 1956, Chatto and Windus Archive, University of Reading Special Collections (UoR), CW 174/5.

1956, receiving a favourable yet critical review from the publisher's reader Cecil Day-Lewis. Williams had worked with the future poet laureate and former Communist on *Drama from Ibsen to Eliot* (1952) and would work with him later, on his second novel *Second Generation* (1964). He produced a 'masterly condensation' of the latter, Williams remarked sardonically, 'which succeeded in reversing the whole meaning of the novel', before adding, '[t]he result was that I had to take the manuscript back and shorten it myself'.[1] The same problems of length had also been identified with *Culture and Society* but Day-Lewis was less certain what could be left out. 'Its length is formidable', he reported back to the publisher Chatto and Windus, 'but there's not much superfluous fat on it, and I don't see how the author could make any extensive cuts'.[2] But Williams did manage to make cuts, returning the manuscript in the winter of 1956, with a note to his editor Ian Parsons: 'I have given it four weeks hard labour and hope the pummelling has got it into better condition. I have followed the lines we agreed at our discussion'.[3] It would appear therefore – although one cannot be certain – that it was Parsons who suggested scrapping Read. Williams cut approximately 40,000 words in total from the original 170,000-word manuscript, including the 10,000 which would later form part of *Keywords: A Vocabulary of Culture and Society* (1976) as well as a section on Thomas Arnold, entries in the bibliography, and parts of his chapter on the industrial novels. Day-Lewis certainly did not express concerns over the Read entry, instead flagging up weaknesses in the introduction ('a heaviness of exposition'), the 'Marxism and Culture' chapter ('lack[s] impetus'), and

1   *Politics and Letters*, 285–6.
2   Day-Lewis, who as a senior figure at Chatto and Windus would also comment favourably on *Border Country*, added: 'The merits of the book are its learning, its good sense, its refusal to despair of modern civilisation, its willingness to "see the other side", its sturdy independence of mind [...] and above all its insistence on the interrelation of art and social developments'. Reader's Report by Day-Lewis for *Culture and Society* by Williams, UoR, CW RR/43, 16 April 1956.
3   Letter from Williams to Parsons, 1 December 1956, UoR, CW 174/5.

the *Keywords* 'appendix' ('of arguable value').[1] Tellingly, he saved his most withering criticism for the final section. '[T]his is clearly an important work', he admitted, before adding: 'whose findings are somewhat weakened by the lack of any original thinking in the conclusion chapter'.[2]

It was the conclusion to *Culture and Society* which also attracted the strongest condemnation from reviewers on its publication while signalling the way forward for the direction of Williams's thinking with its radical insights into class, democratization, and the importance of popular culture. Review after review from 1958 comment on the 'controversial' content of the final pages, suggesting, in contrast to Day-Lewis, that it did at least contain 'original thinking'. The most histrionic response came from that organ of liberal thought in Britain, *The Guardian*: 'The 40-page conclusion, in which he discusses our present discontents, is abominably muddled, and much of the muddle comes from his failure to define the word "culture" satisfactorily', wrote Anthony Hartley. The one-time deputy editor and poetry critic at *The Spectator* added:

> The bitter truth is that there can be no such thing as 'democratic culture' except in the most banal sense of there being cultural opportunities open to everyone. […] I have a feeling that both Mr Williams and anyone else whose profession, roughly-speaking, is thinking should stop lying awake at nights worrying about themselves, society, and democracy and try to work a little harder at their job.[3]

Williams saw *Culture and Society* as an oppositional book, and the extent to which he succeeded in rattling a reactionary intellectual establishment is reflected in the hostile tone of such reviews. As an outsider on the inside, a Welshman from a working-class

---

1   UoR, CW RR/43, 16 April 1956.
2   Ibid.
3   Anthony Hartley, 'The Loaf and The Leaven', *Manchester Guardian*, 7 October 1958, 4. A year later Williams wrote his first review for the paper and went onto become a prolific contributor across three decades, right up until a year before he died, publishing more than 200 book reviews and articles with the encouragement and support of *Guardian* literary editor Bill Webb.

family who went on to have a long association with Oxbridge, it was a position Williams repeatedly adopted: writing against established English culture and puncturing holes in the assumptions and constructions of official bourgeois English literary criticism via immanent critique and by enriching and expanding socialist cultural theory. In *Culture and Society* the starting points were interventions by F. R. Leavis and T. S. Eliot, and the reactionary positioning of culture as a highly selective, 'civilized' realm separated from the 'vulgarity' of democracy, socialism, popular education, the working class, and industrial society. There is a sustained yet developing and often transformational analysis of such key aspects, traceable throughout both Williams's life and this new volume of his writings. So where does Herbert Read fit in?

Williams described the 'lost' chapter, somewhat inaccurately, as being on 'the English Freudians and Herbert Read'.[1] Although he was disappointed to have to make other cuts, the decision to scrap Read was an easy one to make.[2] 'I was so hostile to Read that I was less distressed about that', Williams revealed in *Politics and Letters* (1979), 'although I regret it now because it would have been relevant in the sixties, when the whole question of Freud became so important in discussions of art'.[3] That this present book begins and ends with reflections on Freud should go some way to correcting that perceived absence in Williams's oeuvre.[4] His

---

1   *Politics and Letters*, 99. Ruth Benedict's work begins the Read chapter; she was from New York so not an English Freudian. Her mentee and lifelong friend Margaret Mead – together two of the leading North American anthropologists of the twentieth century – was a prominent figure in the 1960s debates alluded to by Williams.

2   He recalled cutting a section on William Godwin from part one of *Culture and Society* – 'I was very sorry to let Godwin go' (*Politics and Letters*, 99) – but that is not mentioned in his correspondence with Parsons nor is the typescript text in the archive at Swansea.

3   *Politics and Letters*, 99–100.

4   Alongside his discussions of Freud in *Politics and Letters*, 331–4, and *The Long Revolution* (1961; Harmondsworth: Penguin, 1965), 95–7, see Williams on psychoanalysis in 'Problems of Materialism', collected in *Culture and Materialism* (1980; London: Verso, 2005), 103–22, and John Higgins, 'A

patient critique of psychoanalysis and Freudian readings of art in the opening essay re-emerge in the concluding 'When Was Modernism?' lecture from 1987, published here for the first time in its entirety. Despite acknowledging that he was 'deeply impressed' when he first read *The Psychopathology of Everyday Life* (1901), he had reservations when critically approaching, as a trained literary analyst concerned with construction and composition, the way Freud as a writer – Williams likened him to a novelist – presented findings taken from his practical experience with patients.[1] Not only did Williams demand that the observations made by the founder of psychoanalysis be historicized, 'returned' to their 'social and historical period' and their class distinctions,[2] he also stressed the importance of recognizing that the 'emergence of conscious story-telling, the deliberately wrought articulation of an experience [...] are developments out of observable components of everyday discourse'.[3] Such a focus on the social and democratic formations of language – rather than the Freudian denaturalization of language in ordinary social life – is present across this volume: in 'Popular Forms of Writing', as a way of questioning the standardization of language and the dominance of Standard English, and in 'When Was Modernism?', where such social formations receive a more substantial articulation through an engagement with the problem of language in theorizations of an 'ahistorical' unconscious. But in 'Herbert Read: Freud, Art, and Industry', the central issue for Williams, representative of his broader thinking, is that the theories adopted by those discussed rely on universal and essentializing propositions about art and

---

Missed Encounter: Raymond Williams and Psychoanalysis', *Journal of Literary Studies*, 6:1–2, 1990.

1   *Politics and Letters*, 331–2.

2   Fredric Jameson makes a similar demand: 'To come to some ultimate reckoning with psychoanalysis would require us radically to historicize Freudianism itself, and to reach a reflexive vantage point from which the historical and social conditions of possibility both of Freudian method and of its objects of study came into view', *The Political Unconscious* (1981; London: Routledge, 2002), 47.

3   *Politics and Letters*, 331–3.

society; specifically, there is a lack of emphasis on 'making' and the contingencies of history which, in turn, results in the forms of observation and selection, which define and create what is observed and selected, becoming naturalized. There is one particular charge against Read which explains his initial inclusion in the book: as a critic and theorist, he sees art and taste, according to Williams, as a corrective to the ugliness of industrial society. The approach in *Culture and Society* was not one of direct, explicit attack, however. There is a partial sympathy throughout with those being critiqued and the Read chapter is exemplary of this approach. Williams's distaste for Read is not immediately apparent from the respectful tone and mild praise. The chapter is also representative of the book's general style: long quotations from the texts being analysed, gentle opprobrium, an extended engagement with Romanticism, and what Williams himself described as 'first-stage radicalism'.[1]

Culture and Society transformed Williams's life in several ways and, with *The Long Revolution* (1961), cemented his position as a founding figure of the British New Left, alongside Thompson and Richard Hoggart. While the former book was warmly received – despite the attacks on its conclusion – the latter initially earned Williams a reputation as a provocative writer of 'scandalous' and 'dangerous' works of sociological and theoretical advance.[2] However, it was Thompson – in a typically rambunctious takedown of what he saw as a culturalist tendency in the New Left – who provided one of the most hostile yet penetrating reviews. He attacked much of the tone in *The Long Revolution*, echoing criticisms also aimed at *Culture and Society* and Williams's earlier work, while centring his critique on what he saw as a 'determination to de-personalise social forces and at the same time to avoid certain terms and formulations which might associate [Williams] with a simplified version of the class struggle which he rightly believes to be discredited'. *The Long Revolution*

---

1   Ibid., 110.
2   Ibid., 134.

'evaded, and not circumvented, the problem'.[1] It is the book's lack of complex engagement with history as class struggle and an understanding of struggle as a dialectical relationship inside and outside culture, therefore, with which Thompson took issue. Perry Anderson reads 'The Future of Marxism', published the same year, as an indirect rejoinder, answering Thompson's challenge even before it had been made.[2] 'The texts of 1961 moved in parallel past each other, like ships in the night. The chance of a direct, sustained exchange between the two greatest minds of the New Left in Britain was missed', he laments.[3]

'The Future of Marxism' first appeared in the journal *The Twentieth Century*, a 'strange, misplaced destiny', according to Anderson,[4] who would oversee its republication in *New Left Review* fifty-seven years later. Did Williams send 'The Future of Marxism' to Thompson in 1961?[5] A letter sent by Thompson

1   E. P. Thompson, 'The Long Revolution (Part I)', *New Left Review*, I/9, May–June 1961, 26.

2   Williams also never responded directly to such challenges even after they had been made. See 'Notes on British Marxism Since 1845', first published in *New Left Review* in the winter of 1976, following Eagleton's infamous act of parricide in the same journal, attacking his former mentor's alleged reformism, idealism, and populism. 'Williams does not mention Eagleton by name', notes Daniel Hartley, 'but responds methodically to almost every accusation levelled against him', *The Politics of Style* (Chicago: Haymarket, 2017), 70. See also Terry Eagleton, 'Criticism and Politics: The Work of Raymond Williams', *New Left Review*, I/95, Jan–Feb 1976.

3   Perry Anderson, 'The Missing Text: Introduction to "The Future of Marxism"', *New Left Review*, 114, Nov–Dec 2018, 51.

4   Ibid., 46. Williams contributed two other pieces to *The Twentieth Century*. 'New English Drama' appeared in the Autumn 1961 issue, and then in 1963, alongside Hoggart and John Berger, he contributed to a section on undervalued books since 1958, Williams recommending *On Human Unity* (1961) by E. E. Hirschmann.

5   This is the question Anderson asks in 'The Missing Text', 45. He also assumes Stuart Hall (as editor of *New Left Review*) would have given Williams the opportunity to respond to Thompson. Anderson is correct, Hall asked Williams to reply but did so before *The Long Revolution* had even been reviewed by Thompson. Letter from Hall to Williams, 21 March 1961, Raymond Williams Collection, Richard Burton Archives, Swansea University (hereafter 'Williams Archive'), WWE/2/1/16/148.

to Williams more than a decade on would suggest not, if we are to read the essay as part of the same debate. 'I would like to ask you about a critique I once wrote, far too fast and far too long, of *The Long Revolution*. Much of it is worthless, much of it I would not now support', admitted Thompson, '[...] if it was your feeling that the criticism was loud, ungenerous, beside the point, then I'd better let it die'.[1] It is a revealing request for approval and a show of reverence – something he did not always receive in print while alive – which many adopted in correspondence with Williams. Stuart Hall wrote in March 1979, for example, asking if he should accept a chair in sociology at the Open University. 'I don't quite know why I'm writing', admitted Hall, who by the late 1970s was approaching fifty and had run the pioneering Centre for Contemporary Cultural Studies in Birmingham for a decade, 'I did feel I wanted you to know and I did think that if you had strong negative or positive reactions, they would weight in some important way with me in taking that decision'.[2] Hall explains in his memoir that he saw Williams as a father figure, as he did Thompson before a public falling out.[3] Similarly, '[y]ou are so magisterial you inhibit

---

1   Letter from Thompson to Williams, 29 May, Williams Archive, WWE/2/1/16/356. There is no year given on the letter but a reference to issue 67 of *New Left Review* dates it to after 1971. Thompson was compiling a book of political writings which would become *The Poverty of Theory* – notorious for its attack on Althusser – and he considered including parts of his *The Long Revolution* review, if Williams did not object. He was keen to use the middle section correcting the notion of culture as 'whole way of life', Thompson offering 'whole way of conflict' and 'struggle' to strengthen Williams's theory. *The Poverty of Theory* – which was being planned as early as spring 1976 – came out in 1978; it does not include the review of *The Long Revolution*. Thompson's archive in Oxford is closed until 2061, fifty years after his wife Dorothy's death at her request. It will be another forty years before we know how Williams replied or if he discussed 'The Future of Marxism' with Thompson.

2   Letter from Hall to Williams, 19 March 1979, Williams Archive, WWE/2/1/16/148.

3   Hall: 'I found Raymond incredibly approachable and, because of his intellectual interests, much closer to my own formation than Edward ever had been. They were my fathers'. However, he says of Thompson: 'At the infamous History Workshop conference held at Ruskin College in Oxford in December 1979 he ripped us up and set out to destroy one of his greatest devotees,

me from writing' is a remarkable line to find in a letter from Thompson, written in the winter of 1960 as he worked on *The Making of the English Working Class* (1963), informing Williams that he hoped Hall, as the journal's editor, would allow him to review *The Long Revolution* for *New Left Review*.[1] Whereas some on the left mirrored Thompson's forms of intellectual attack it was never Williams's style. As a 'socialist reviewer', and in describing Williams as the left's 'best man', Thompson felt 'released' to provide a direct critique because the 'reception of the book is so well assured'.[2] That was not how Williams read it. 'The onslaught from the right was so strong that I felt at certain critical moments an inability on the left to sustain theoretical differences and yet present a common front', he revealed.[3] In contrast, Williams preferred to focus on the critical arguments and theoretical differences themselves, considering how they may or may not advance the case for socialism. Later referring to the time of Thompson's review, he bemoaned: 'It was a period in which the left in general

---

Richard Johnson. This was a savage, savage attack, and it represented a parting of the ways. We never really got it together again', Stuart Hall, *Familiar Stranger* (London: Penguin, 2018), 265.

1   It is often described as Hall approaching Thompson to review *The Long Revolution* but, as implied from his letters to Williams, Thompson approached Hall. Letter dated 12 December 1960, Williams Archive, WWE/2/16/356. On receiving his copy of *The Long Revolution*, Thompson writes again thanking Williams for the acknowledgement in the book's foreword. Such encouragement inspired him to return with renewed energy to writing what became *The Making of the English Working Class* (1963). Letter dated 21 March 1961, Williams Archive, WWWE/2/16/356.

2   Thompson, 'The Long Revolution (Part I)', 24.

3   *Politics and Letters*, 134. Williams provides a direct response to Thompson eighteen years later: he suggests a limitation to the review and its romanticization of 'struggle', particularly during the 'unheroic' 1950s, stressing the important differences between 'class struggle' and 'class conflict'. Jim McGuigan also notes there is a tacit acknowledgement of Thompson's critique by Williams in *Culture* (1981), Williams accepting that there must be consideration of the forces outside of culture and the dialectical interaction between them. See *Politics and Letters*, 135, 412; McGuigan, *Raymond Williams: Cultural Analyst* (Bristol: Intellect, 2019), 104.

had difficulty in restraining itself from frustrated point-scoring'.[1]
As Anderson points out, the location for Williams's intervention
was a strange one, *The Twentieth Century* – a conservative journal
funded by the CIA until the late 1950s – being 'in a world as far
removed from that of *New Left Review* and its predecessors as
could be imagined'.[2] Through his choice of publication Williams
avoided direct confrontation but, whereas the thrust of the analysis
in *The Long Revolution* was dismissed as gradualist and reformist
by Thompson, what Williams wrote for *The Twentieth Century* was
avowedly and explicitly Marxist. It also affirms the 'consistency'
of Williams's thought, as noted by Daniel Gerke,[3] disrupting the
imposition of a convenient trajectory from a Left-Leavisism of
the 1950s to a revolutionary Marxism of the 1970s.

'The Future of Marxism' contains many of the abiding features
of Williams's political writing: the refusal of a fixed and mechanical version of Marxism, an insistence on the complex specificities
of actual conditions within a given society, and, from these two
positions, the development of a truly international socialism. 'The
peace movement, and the support of colonial liberation movements, are then the critical fields of our contemporary socialist
activity', he argued in 1961.[4] Here you have the Williams most
commonly associated with the mid-1980s – exemplified by 'The
Future of Socialism' (1985) in this collection – when he stressed
that the terrain for socialists must include ecology, feminism, and
peace.[5] '[T]he continuation, in Britain, of th[e] sense of an easy,
improving society, seems to me to depend on ignoring the facts

1   *Politics and Letters*, 134.
2   Anderson, 'The Missing Text', 45. See also Frances Stonor Saunders,
Who Paid the Piper?: The CIA and the Cultural Cold War (1999; London:
Granta, 2000), 109–10.
3   Daniel Gerke, 'Pearls before Swine: Raymond Williams and "The
Future of Marxism"', Raymond Williams Society Blog, 29 March 2019.
4   See below, p. 67.
5   For Williams's attempt 'to broaden the scope of the Marxist conception
of totality and to connect it to the new social movements', see Daniel Hartley,
'On Raymond Williams: Complexity, Immanence, and the Long Revolution',
Mediations, 30.1, 2016.

of international military struggle, which is changing us deeply from inside', he wrote,[1] following the Mau Mau Uprising in Kenya, during the Algerian War of Independence, at the height of CND's Aldermaston marches, shortly after the doomed Bay of Pigs Invasion of Cuba, and as John F. Kennedy expanded US involvement in the Vietnam War. So the consistency of Williams's radicalism, its complex international perspective, and, more broadly, its continuity with Marxism should be stressed in light of attempts to minimize such currents.[2]

One of the key moments in Williams's political life came in July 1966 when he resigned his Labour Party membership, as he explains in *Politics and Letters*: 'I decided to leave [...] and write some sort of a manifesto, stating very clearly that the Labour Party was no longer just an inadequate agency for socialism, it was now an active collaborator in the process of reproducing capitalist society'.[3] It was a decisive moment: his personal negotiations between the revolutionary and reformist traditions on the left clearly emerged and inevitably collapsed. 'When you have been pondering a decision for fifteen years, you can finally take it in two days without haste', he revealed.[4] It was a decision to leave but also an acceptance that reformism, in the final instance, was inadequate: within a month he started work on what would become the *May Day Manifesto* (1967/8).

---

1   See below, p. 67.

2   Francis Mulhern reveals his regret at minimizing such continuities with Marxism while maximizing the 'Left-Leavisite' aspects of Williams's writing. See Mulhern, 'Culture and Society: Then and Now', *New Left Review*, 55, Jan–Feb 2009, 31–45.

3   *Politics and Letters*, 373. Williams was a member of the Labour Party for five years from 1961. He had campaigned for the party as early as 1935 when, aged fourteen, he worked for the local candidate, Michael Foot. His father was local branch secretary and keen for his son to stand as the Labour candidate in 1945 but, having a 'very reserved attitude' to the party, Williams refused. In *Politics and Letters*, he records working for Labour during six general elections, from 1935 until 1974. He was also a member of the Communist Party from 1939 until allowing his membership to lapse during the war and, in 1969, joined Plaid Cymru for at least a year.

4   *Politics and Letters*, 415.

The manifesto's composition involved a reconstitution of the New Left, reuniting old friends (Williams, Hall, E. P. Thompson and Dorothy Thompson, for instance) alongside emerging radical voices (with Eagleton, Michael Rustin, and Robin Murray amongst them). 'Against an advanced capitalism, only an advanced social-ism offers any chance of the recovery of human controls', they proclaimed, with automation and technology playing a central role in their vision of liberation from the capitalist relations of work.[1] It is in these sections that one can clearly see the hand and mind of Williams, the conciliatory figure of the manifesto com-mittee. He would expand on such questions in 'The Meanings of Work', first published in 1968, the year of the *May Day Manifesto*'s second edition. It was a time of rebellion and revolution as well as a remarkable moment in the history of the freshly emboldened and expanded New Left. Wary of what could be the comforting simplicities of nationalization (that great emblem of the labour movement), in 'The Meanings of Work' Williams advocates for workers' control and the expansion of truly democratic, self-managing co-operatives. Amongst lines and phrases taken directly from the manifesto, he stresses the need for automation to be 'used to reduce not cost but labour' – this would 'relieve and release human energy for our own purposes' and be the 'means of a lib-eration which has often seemed only a dream'.[2] Characteristically refuting all forms of determinism, the task according to Williams was 'to use the machines, rather than to be used by them'.[3] 'The Meanings of Work' was part of a four-year project by *New Left Review*, led by one of its editors, Ronald Fraser. He commissioned fifty short essays on work from socialists and non-socialists which appeared between 1965 and 1969 in the journal as well as across two Pelican Originals. Williams's essay, an afterword to the first book, dates to a decade when his energies were often harnessed by the drafting of practical policy interventions: the radical proposals

---

1   Raymond Williams (ed.), *May Day Manifesto 1968* (1968; London: Verso: 2018), 32.

2   See below, p. 89.

3   Ibid.

for democratic control of the media in *Communications* (1962) followed by the detailed account of radical socialist transformation put forward in the *May Day Manifesto*, for example. But the 1960s ended with the breakdown of a left unity he had fought hard to maintain. The manifesto working committee called a National Convention of the Left and, with the support of Williams, considered running candidates in the 1970 general election who would have been a direct challenge to the Labour Party. 'A movement which had managed to sustain a significant amount of left unity disintegrated over the electoral process', regretted Williams, before adding, pointedly: 'A strategy of common activity could survive anything except an election'.[1] The frustrations of 1970 provided the platform for Williams's most important decade.

The Country and the City came out in 1973, followed by *Keywords* three years later, with *Marxism and Literature* a year after that – publications which cemented his status as a formidable intellectual of international renown.[2] The release of the first book coincided with 'Base and Superstructure in Marxist Cultural Theory', an essay which would form a central plank of the third. First appearing in *New Left Review*'s winter issue of 1973, it was based on a lecture given in Montreal seven months earlier. 'Marxist Cultural Theory', the fourth essay in this book, is a verbatim transcript of that talk. They are almost identical pieces but the small differences are deeply significant. Both versions of the essay capture Williams as he sets his work 'into a new and conscious relation with Marxism'.[3] It was new in the sense that it was an extension and expansion of a relationship which can be traced back to the Wales of his youth. Williams had first encountered Marxist literary theory at Cambridge in 1939, not within

---

1   *Politics and Letters*, 375.

2   Sandwiched between these three hugely important books was another significant intervention by Williams, his study *Television: Technology and Cultural Form* (1974), one of the earliest and arguably most important books on television and social change.

3   Raymond Williams, *Marxism and Literature* (Oxford: Oxford University Press, 1977), 6.

formal study but from discussions with fellow socialists. Yet
before that an informal and practical knowledge of and affiliation
with Marxist thinking was already part of his political education,
as the son of working-class parents and someone active on the
left as a teenager in the 1930s around his home village of Pandy
on the Wales–England border.[1] By the mid-1970s, the relationships between Marxism and literature had 'preoccupied most of
my working life', he revealed.[2] He felt the Marxism of his earlier
Cambridge years had been relatively narrow – what he described
as a radical populism – and, while maintaining a commitment to
its central currents, sought a more complex and dynamic Marxist
theory of literature and culture. As an undergraduate he witnessed
many of the arguments drift into deadlock, but the reopening of
the debates by Western Marxists in the 1970s through the work
of Lucien Goldmann, Louis Althusser, Antonio Gramsci, and
Walter Benjamin energized Williams, by then back at Cambridge
and about to be appointed Professor of Drama. '[M]y own long
and often internal and solitary debate with what I had known as
Marxism now took its place in a serious and extending international inquiry', he said, with some relief.[3] That refusal of a fixed and
mechanical Marxism – the imposition of a theory onto culture,
for instance, rather than a materialist reading of culture as a con-
stitutive social process – finds its greatest expression in 'Base and
Superstructure in Marxist Cultural Theory'. It is such an important
essay in both Williams's body of work and in the broader intellectual traditions of Western Marxism that its earliest exposition
warrants publication here for the first time. The differences that

1   In Pandy, Williams's socialist politics were international, rather than
local or national. As a teenager he found the 'traditional politics of locality and
parliament in the Labour movement […] boring [and] narrow'. *Politics and
Letters*, 32. He visited Geneva in 1937 for the League of Nations Youth Conference – making a stop in the French capital to buy a copy of *The Communist
Manifesto* from the Soviet Pavilion at the Paris Expo, reading Marx and Engels
for the first time – and spoke against the Munich Agreement at Abergavenny
a year later.
2   *Marxism and Literature*, 1.
3   Ibid., 4.

exist between the two versions, however slight, are substantial for their theoretical implications.

One of Williams's enduring contributions to cultural theory is the model of dominant, residual, and emergent which he first introduced in the 'Base and Superstructure' essay, before it came to form an essential part of his arguments in *Marxism and Literature*. It is therefore key to his own position within Marxist cultural theory, namely that of cultural materialism – what Williams described as 'a theory of the specificities of material cultural and literary production within historical materialism'.[1] And yet, compellingly, he switched one of the model's terms at the last moment. In the original Montreal lecture Williams uses 'corporate' rather than 'dominant'.[2] Why the change? 'Indeed I would call it a corporate system', he revealed, when describing the central interlocking practices, meanings, and values within a given society, 'but this might be confusing, since Gramsci uses "corporate" to mean the subordinate as opposed to the general and dominant elements of hegemony'.[3] It is a qualification which corrects a term he had

---

1   Ibid., 5.

2   There are also some minor editorial revisions made to the second version published in *Culture and Materialism*. Notably, however, Williams leaves in four uses of 'corporate' in quick succession in both published versions. See 'Base and Superstructure in Marxist Cultural Theory', *New Left Review*, I/82, Nov–Dec 1973, 10, and *Culture and Materialism*, 40.

3   Williams, 'Base and Superstructure', 9. Williams's comment on Gramsci is misleading. Gramsci uses 'corporate' when describing the process through which distinct subordinate groups are incorporated, rather than simply to mean 'subordinate'. In 'Analysis of Situations: Relations of Force' from the prison notebooks, for example, Gramsci describes a third moment in the political formation of various social groups and classes thus: 'one becomes aware that one's own corporate interests, in their present and future development, transcend the corporate limits of the merely economic group, and can and must become the interests of other subordinate groups'. This is a decisive moment, he notes, adding, 'it is the phase in which previously germinated ideologies […] come into confrontation and conflict, until only one of them […] tends to prevail […] bringing about not only a unison of economic and political aims, but also intellectual and moral unity, posing all the questions around which the struggle rages not on a corporate but on a "universal" plane,

been using in lectures at Cambridge since at least 1972. There is also something more forceful in the switch: 'dominant' implies agency, 'corporate' suggests process. And while 'dominant' gives an enhanced sense of commanding strength and oppressive control by one class over another, 'corporate' indicates, in abstract terms and in its direct English usage,[1] a body or group sharing common practices and values, albeit defined and enforced by a central organizational power. A change is also registered in the differing final lines from each version, yet here it is a shift of emphasis in the opposite direction. Whereas the *New Left Review* essay ends with a call for a new focus on the 'conditions of practice' to become 'the point of break and the point of departure [...] within an active and self-renewing Marxist cultural tradition',[2] the essay included in the present collection stresses the need for a 'radically new direction' in cultural theory: 'instead of asking about the components of objects, we ask about the conditions of practices'.[3] In placing the final emphasis on 'conditions of practices', it is more emphatic both in its call for renewal and in its Marxism. And while dominant, on the one hand, is more effective, corporate is, on the other, more exacting as an expression to capture what is at risk: the incorporation (a term Williams uses across both versions) of emergent cultural forms – as truly oppositional forces and processes of change within an active conception of hegemony – *into* the corporate (or effective and dominant) culture.

These slight yet significant differences are possible to trace because of the origins of such essays and the specific dynamics of Williams's thinking. 'Marxist Cultural Theory' is the first of four

---

and thus creating the hegemony of a fundamental social group over a series of subordinate groups', *The Antonio Gramsci Reader* (London: Lawrence and Wishart, 1999), 205.

1   In the English version, 'corporate' is translated from Gramsci's uses of 'corporativa', 'corporativi', and 'corporativo' in the original notebooks. In Italian, 'corporativo' refers to specific interest groups centred around economic preoccupations. The word has its roots in the medieval 'corporazioni', which means guilds. Many thanks to Daniela Caselli for this information.

2   Williams, 'Base and Superstructure', 16.

3   See below, p. 113.

edited transcripts included here which are taken from cassette tapes in the Williams family archive. The lecture was delivered to a conference in Canada; the recorded version is a recreation of that talk, from memory and notes. The tape and subsequent transcript capture what was an active and creative process for Williams: public speaking as critical thinking and intellectual discovery. It also marks a noticeable shift in the tone and style – partly registered by that dynamic between writing and speaking – used by Williams. He made a lifelong commitment to expand, extend, and redefine the uses and value of intellectual work, something which can be seen in the range of audiences addressed in the lectures contained in the present volume: Hackney Workers' Educational Association (WEA), for example, and the Open University. 'Popular Culture: History and Theory' is a talk from 1978 given as a seminar presentation at the latter. Again, it is a transcript of Williams speaking, exploring and making theoretical interventions into fields of study which his writing had made possible. Invited by sociologist and tutor Tony Bennett to address the influential Popular Culture module which was then being planned, Williams (who was an external assessor on the course) took the opportunity to reflect upon the challenges faced when devising a theory of what was still in the late 1970s an emerging educational discipline.[1] Complaining of an 'anti-theoretical culture' in England and a dismissive attitude towards popular culture, Williams characteristically demanded a focus on production, not effect, and on the rich, fertile, and varied novelty of popular cultural forms. He once again dismissed the mechanical Marxist position – that such forms uncritically reproduce capitalist society – and stressed the importance of uncovering emergent tendencies within popular culture which can provide critiques of capitalism. In a formulation reminiscent of his concluding remarks in 'Marxist Cultural Theory', he states plainly: 'production and conditions of

---

1   Williams's seminar presentation was followed a month later by Stuart Hall, who spoke on 'Popular Culture, Politics and History'. See Tony Bennett, 'Popular Culture 1978: History, Theory, Politics', *Cultural Studies*, 32.6, 2018, 897–902.

production, within a historically identifiable body of practices and cultural relations – that is what, I think, a popular culture course now needs to be'.[1]

The Open University offered the ideal conditions in which to create such dynamic new forms of educational and theoretical work. It could more readily break from the traditions and territories of the established universities, having been launched in 1969 by Minister for the Arts Jennie Lee and the Labour government from which Williams had so decisively recoiled. Despite strongly supporting its establishment, viewing the Open University as the most significant achievement of Harold Wilson's time as prime minister, he complained that the more radical elements of adult education had been overlooked.[2] Williams – awarded an honorary doctorate by the university in 1974 – heavily influenced its arts courses, as a leading architect of interdisciplinary study and one of the founders of cultural studies, while playing a direct role through the delivery of television lectures, papers, and talks such as the one below – the first in what led to a decade of collaboration with the Popular Culture module. 'The use of television for real education has barely begun, and most of the signs are that it will be a real expansion of our resources, not just as a transmission system but in actual modes of understanding', he enthusiastically predicted in his regular TV column for *The Listener*.[3] While Williams embraced the collaborative approach amongst tutors, he regretted that the Open University's formation was not used as a moment to reshape adult education; with 'no properly based tutorial organization, and little of our old educational democracy', he felt that, a decade after being granted its Royal Charter, an opportunity for transformative innovation within education had been missed.[4]

---

1   See below, p. 125.

2   For a collection of work written by Williams during his fifteen years as an adult education tutor, see *Border Country: Raymond Williams in Adult Education*, ed. John McIlroy and Sallie Westwood (Leicester: NIACE, 1993).

3   Raymond Williams, 'Open Teaching', *The Listener*, 6 May 1971, in *Raymond Williams on Television* (London: Routledge, 1989), 142.

4   *Politics and Letters*, 371. Williams was still hopeful in 1979 that a

Alongside his commitments in Britain towards the end of the 1970s, and as he approached a retirement from Cambridge which was taken in 1983, Williams continued to lecture overseas. Much of the work contained in *Marxism and Literature* stems from invited talks in North America, Italy, West Germany, and Yugoslavia.[1] In 1979, a year after completing the interviews for *Politics and Letters*, a punishing process which left him experiencing a deep personal crisis,[2] Williams embarked on an intensive tour of Denmark. He had recovered from the uncertainty and anxiety which made writing impossible for the first time in his working life. Delivering eleven lectures across ten days in five cities, the familiar expansive, interdisciplinary Williams was on full display as he ranged across topics including Marxist criticism, women's studies, the industrial novel, television, socialism and culture, literary theory, and cultural studies. His second lecture, given at Aarhus University in 1979 on a Tuesday morning in September, was on 'British Working-Class Literature after 1945'. It captures Williams as a theorist and author of working-class literature, reflecting on the formal problems he encountered when writing his debut novel *Border Country* (1960). There is a central focus on the fiction of his contemporaries from the late 1950s and early '60s and, by theorizing the work of Alan Sillitoe and David Storey (notably *Saturday Night and Sunday Morning* (1958) and 1961's *Flight into Camden*), he traces the emergence of two distinctive forms of working-class writing in the immediate post-war period,

---

'properly based tutorial organisation' could be established; see 'Television and Teaching: An Interview with Raymond Williams', in *Raymond Williams on Television*, 213. But shortly before he died, he complained that the Open University lacked 'that crucial process of interchange and encounter between the people offering the intellectual disciplines and those using them'. See Williams, 'The Future of Cultural Studies', *Politics of Modernism* (1989; London: Verso, 2007), 157.

1 As well as speaking in California, Montreal, and Bremen, Williams lectured on Marxism and literature in Rome, Naples, Bari, Belgrade, Zagreb, and Ljubljana in the spring of 1976 and, in December that year, went to Paris.

2 See Williams's letter to Perry Anderson in Fred Inglis, *Raymond Williams* (1995; London: Routledge, 1998), 260–2.

prompting a critical consideration of why and how certain forms of literature are defined as working class.[1]

Williams delivered the talk on post-'45 fiction before lunch and in the afternoon gave a seemingly lost lecture titled 'Women's Studies as an Academic Discipline'. While stressing the crucial role of feminism, remarking on what he saw as 'a remarkable and growing body of distinctively feminist scholarship and argument, shifting our intellectual perspectives in many fields',[2] Williams has been criticized for failing to place due emphasis on the experience of women. Sheila Rowbotham said of Williams, in an otherwise positive review of *Towards 2000* (1983), that 'he does not consistently see politics through the social experience of how change affects women in the same degree as it affects men'.[3] And Morag Shiach, whose Cambridge doctorate Williams supervised, notes that the 'cultural struggles of women are given little space' in *Culture and Society* and *The Long Revolution*.[4] He 'acknowledged the importance of feminist accounts of history', Shiach noted, following the death of Williams, 'but clearly felt they were, and were being, best produced by women. As someone engaged in this project, I found this mixture of support with strategic distancing both rare and admirable'.[5] He partially defended his work

1   Williams's concluding remarks were interrupted by the ending of the tape, just as he began to look at the work of Jim Allen and Alan Plater. For a detailed discussion of this premature ending, see Phil O'Brien and Nicola Wilson, 'Introduction: Raymond Williams and Working-Class Writing', *Key Words*, 18, 2020, 9–11.

2   Williams, *Towards 2000* (1983; Harmondsworth: Pelican, 1985), 249.

3   Sheila Rowbotham, 'Picking up the Pieces', *New Socialist*, 31 October 1985, 49. See Rowbotham, Lynne Segal, and Hilary Wainwright, *Beyond the Fragments: Feminism and the Making of Socialism* (1979).

4   Morag Shiach, 'Resources for a Journey of Hope', *The Cambridge Review*, June 1988, 60.

5   Ibid. Elsewhere, Shiach has been more pointed in her criticism: 'Feminists can find much of use to them in the work of Raymond Williams; they cannot, however, find many women'. See Morag Shiach, 'A Gendered History of Cultural Categories', in *Cultural Materialism: On Raymond Williams*, ed. Christopher Prendergast (Minneapolis: University of Minneapolis Press, 1995), 51.

by drawing attention to his novels – particularly the character of
Kate Owen in *Second Generation* – and the writing he published
on the fiction of that 'remarkable generation' of authors: Elizabeth
Gaskell, Charlotte and Emily Brontë, and George Eliot. A central
feature of his book *The English Novel from Dickens to Lawrence*
(1970), for instance, is an analysis of, as he puts it elsewhere, 'the
phenomenon of the women novelists of the English nineteenth
century carrying so much of the most questioning consciousness
in that culture and in that form'.[1] Such insight embodies both
the uses and the limitations of Williams's writing, according to
Cora Kaplan, who – in a skilful historical tracking of changes in
thought from *Culture and Society* in the late 1950s to 'Forms of
English Fiction in 1848' two decades later – notes the 'fundamental' influence his work had on socialist women intellectuals of the
twentieth century. His extended analysis of the previous century
'was remarkable', according to Kaplan, 'in that it brought the question of gender forward through the heightened attention he gave
to women's writing'. And yet, 'the overt themes of the novels –
sexuality, sexual difference, and gender – appeared for an instant
only, and then in the most gnomic reference possible, before they
were abstracted to a generic plane where they virtually represented the universal human condition – "man alone"'.[2] This is the
type of complex reading – locating useful resources and moments
of advance whilst simultaneously identifying the limits of such
analysis to push and extend critique and understanding – which
the work of Williams requires.

Tellingly, the industrial novel of the mid-nineteenth century,
which Gaskell in particular did much to define, was a form Williams returned to with renewed focus in the late 1970s and early
'80s, producing a series of essays on class, Wales, and Marxism.[3]

1   Raymond Williams and Edward Said, 'Media, Margins and Modernity',
in *Politics of Modernism*, 195.
2   Cora Kaplan, '"What We Have Again to Say": Williams, Feminism, and
the 1840s', in *Cultural Materialism: On Raymond Williams*, 225.
3   For example, 'The Welsh Industrial Novel' from 1978 (although he
delivered the first lecture with that title a year earlier, coinciding with the

This was also the period in which he formed an intellectually productive and enriching relationship with Pierre Bourdieu. While
the work on the industrial novel represented a new engagement
with a sociology of literature,[1] his work on and with his French contemporary was also an extension of previous interests, captured in
'Pierre Bourdieu and the Sociology of Culture'. It appears to have
been Thompson who first alerted Williams to Bourdieu, writing
excitedly – after a visit to Paris in the mid-1970s – of a group of
scholars in the French capital seeking to 'make contact with the
English tradition of "cultural" historical work'.[2] Bourdieu provided
a useful antidote to the structuralist turn taken by socialist intellectuals in Britain, according to Thompson, who described the
research being produced by Hall's celebrated Birmingham centre
as 'too Althusserian'.[3] While Hall and Eagleton initially embraced
Althusser (before parting from the work of the philosopher who
dominated and divided Marxist thinking in the 1970s), Thompson
hoped his old comrade could be steered towards Bourdieu.

   Williams subsequently made his own trip to Paris in December
1976, delivering a series of lectures on Thomas Hardy at the École
Normale Supériore where Althusser taught and where Bourdieu
had studied. Here he first met and collaborated on a seminar with

publication of *Marxism and Literature*), 'Region and Class in the Novel', 'The
Ragged-Arsed Philanthropists', and 'Working-Class, Proletarian, Socialist:
Problems in Some Welsh Novels', all from 1982. See *Who Speaks for Wales?
Nation, Culture, Identity* (2003), ed. Daniel Williams, for the definitive collec-
tion of Williams's writing on Wales.

1   'Forms of English Fiction in 1848' was originally delivered at a conference in Essex with the title 'Sociology of Literature'. Kaplan also gave a paper
as part of the Marxist-Feminist Literature Collective.

2   Postcard from Thompson to Williams, undated, Williams Archive,
WWE/2/1/16/356. Thompson's note from Paris appears to be from 1975. See
Luiz Carlos Jackson and Ugo Rivetti, 'Pierre Bourdieu and Raymond Williams:
Correspondence, Meeting and Crossed References', *Tempo Social*, 32.1, 2020,
205–25.

3   Postcard from Thompson to Williams, undated, Williams Archive,
WWE/2/1/16/356. See Thompson's famous polemic against Althusser in *The
Poverty of Theory* (1978). For Williams on Althusser, see 'Crisis in English
Studies', *Writing in Society* (London: Verso, 1983), 192–211.

the latter – Williams writing a year later of 'deep differences' which
gave way to 'an extraordinary convergence of themes and interests' and 'an exceptionally productive theoretical revaluation'.[1] 'It
gives a basis for genuine uses of comparative method in research',
enthused Williams, 'by going beyond the barrier of "irreducible
national culture"'.[2] For Bourdieu, their intellectual exchanges represented a meeting of minds. 'I feel so isolated here', confessed the
author of *Distinction* (1979), echoing how Williams had often felt
during his career, 'that the extent of our agreement seems to me
somewhat miraculous'.[3] What interested Williams was Bourdieu's
work on education and on what he began to see, more broadly, as
the establishment of a sociology of culture, situated around their
own distinctive yet overlapping positions. It was an approach
requiring 'new kinds of social analysis of specifically cultural
institutions and formations, and the exploration of actual relations between these and, on the one hand, the material means of
cultural production and, on the other hand, actual cultural forms'.[4]
A year before he wrote of such new directions in *Culture* (1981),
Williams collaborated with Nicholas Garnham on what was the
first extended introduction in English of Bourdieu's landmark
work in *Distinction*. They had previously worked together on the
BBC documentary film *Border Country* (1970), with Garnham
as director. Appearing in a special edition of the journal *Media,
Culture and Society* (July 1980), which included three newly translated Bourdieu contributions,[5] 'Pierre Bourdieu and the Sociology

---

1   Raymond Williams, 'French Connection', *New Society*, 5 May 1977,
240.

2   Ibid.

3   Letter from Bourdieu to Williams, 7 September 1977, Williams
Archive, WWE/2/1/16/33.

4   Raymond Williams, *Culture* (Glasgow: Fontana, 1981), 14.

5   Two of these were from *Distinction*, first published in English in 1984,
after originally being released in France in 1979. 'The Aristocracy of Culture'
was taken from Part I of Bourdieu's classic study, while 'A Diagram of Social
Position and Life-style' is from the 'Reconversion Strategies' section in Part II.
A third essay, 'The Production of Belief: Contribution to an Economy of Symbolic Goods' – translated by Richard Nice who would also produce a masterly

of Culture' found alliance with the French sociologist in his resolute commitment – as Williams and Garnham saw it – to a
materialist theory of class struggle alongside an unpatronizing
assessment of working-class culture, an analysis which resisted
naïve glorification.

Media, Culture and Society took a stance against Althusserian
Marxism, while Garnham believed that an engagement with Bourdieu's work was a way of thinking from and beyond what Hall had
identified – in an earlier issue of the journal – as the 'structuralist
and cultural enterprises' prevalent in but not wholly adequate for
the contemporary formations of cultural studies.[1] The Williams-
Garnham essay was an attempt to build and expand upon the links
forming between Bourdieu and his group (including Jean-Claude
Passeron and Jean-Claude Chamboredon) and the first New Left
in Britain, partly through the publication of work by Williams,
Thompson, Hoggart, and Eric Hobsbawm in translation in *Actes
de la Recherche en Sciences Sociales*.[2] Although Garnham – as

---

translation of *Distinction* – had appeared in *Actes de la Recherche en Sciences
Sociales* in 1977.

1   Stuart Hall, 'Cultural Studies: Two Paradigms', *Media, Culture and
Society*, 2.1, January 1980, 72; Nicholas Garnham, 'Editorial', *Media, Culture
and Society*, 2.3, July 1980, 207–8. Later, Williams would offer an indirect
response to Hall's historical critique, stressing – in contrast to Hall – that cultural studies began in adult education and not with texts such as *The Uses of
Literacy* (1957) by Hoggart or his own *Culture and Society* (1958). See 'The
Future of Cultural Studies', *Politics of Modernism*, 151–62. For an account of
the journal's 'stance against Althusserian Marxism', see 'An Interview with Professor Paddy Scannell', *Westminster Papers in Communication and Culture*, 4.1,
2007, 5.

2   The journal was established by Bourdieu in 1975. It published part
of Williams's *The Country and the City* in 1977 and first introduced French
readers to *The Uses of Literacy*, while Thompson (in 1976 with 'Modes of
Domination and Revolutions in England') and Hobsbawm (with 'Man and
Woman in Socialist Iconography' in 1978) both contributed. Such an exchange
of intellectual ideas around culture and politics between France and Britain –
originating in the pages of *Actes de la Recherche en Sciences Sociales* – can be
seen in the work of Didier Eribon – author of *Returning to Reims* (2009) – who
was introduced to Williams's writing in 1979 by his mentor Bourdieu. A year

editor of the special issue – took the lead on writing the essay, Williams's specific thinking comes through; not only is it recognisable by the reference to his then forthcoming book *Culture* but also in the ways the critique draws back to what was described earlier as one of Williams's most significant and resonant interventions: the model of residual, dominant, and emergent.

The complex exchange of ideas across these various sites of Marxist thinking either side of the English Channel was productive for Williams, who held onto a more hopeful theory of cultural production than Bourdieu, someone he saw as unable to conceptualize change within and of society. Williams also had what Bridget Fowler describes as a 'more lively sense of the dynamics of popular and high art' than Bourdieu,[1] by placing due emphasis on the capacity for creative, contingent, oppositional forms and recognizing the importance of working-class and popular writing, both published and unpublished, celebrated and ignored.

He takes up such concerns in 'British Working-Class Literature after 1945' before expanding his historical analysis of creative processes and practices in 'Popular Forms of Writing', the third previously unpublished talk included below. Williams was invited by Ken Worpole to deliver a guest lecture for Hackney WEA to raise money for Centerprise, a radical bookshop and community centre in Dalston. Hackney Council and Greater London Council (GLC) were its two main sources of funding; by 1982, after eleven years as a vital cultural space in one of the poorest parts of England, Centerprise was under serious threat from Thatcherite attacks on local government. Located in an ethnically diverse working-class area, the centre – run as a co-operative rooted in the community arts movement – established a publishing project in order to give space to those marginalized from and unrepresented within dominant culture. Along with Williams, the likes of

---

later he interviewed Williams for *Libération* and, to conclude his bestselling memoir, reflects on the significance of reading *Border Country* as a shared experience of class mobility.

1   Bridget Fowler, 'The Cultural Theory of Bourdieu and Williams', *Key Words*, 3, 2000, 126.

Thompson, Ngũgĩ wa Thiong'o, Nawal El Saadawi, Linton Kwesi Johnson, and Andrea Levy also delivered guest lectures over the years, before the centre was forced to close its doors in 2012. Rosa Schling, in documenting the history of Centerprise, notes: 'it was hoped that readers of books by local authors would find recognisable representations of their own experiences and interests, and thereby feel enabled to write and publish themselves'.[1] Such writing outside of formal practices and established institutions was, for Williams, an essential part of cultural production. It allowed for an expansion of cultural democracy through adult education – something Williams committed fifteen years of his teaching career to as a WEA tutor. 'Centerprise embraced autobiography, creative writing workshops and writing by adult literacy students', says Tom Woodin. 'These various practices were held together in an exploratory tension and the result was to be a cross-fertilisation of forms for the expression of working-class experience'.[2] It was such questions of form which Williams addressed in his lecture to the writers at Centerprise and Hackney WEA, stressing the necessity of writing about working-class life not for the amusement of the dominant class but against the standards of a monotonous, mainstream literary culture.

The penultimate essay in this collection is another public talk delivered by Williams, three years later and with Thatcherite attacks on local government once more providing the backdrop. 'The Future of Socialism' was Williams's contribution to a panel with Tony Benn, held as a fringe event at the 1985 Labour Party Conference in Bournemouth. Organized by the magazine *New Socialist*, it took place on Monday 30 September, the second day of the annual gathering by party members and on the eve of Neil Kinnock's infamous Militant speech. Benn and Williams had their considerable disagreements – over the then cabinet minister's plan in the 1960s to set up a network of commercial radio stations,

---

1   Rosa Schling, *The Lime Green Mystery: An Oral History of the Centerprise Co-operative* (London: On the Record, 2017), 124.

2   Tom Woodin, *Working-Class Writing and Publishing in the Late Twentieth Century* (Manchester: Manchester University Press, 2018), 106.

for example – but they found common ground in support of democratic constitutional party reforms and against the party's rightward shift under Kinnock. Williams wrote to wish Benn a speedy recovery from Guillian-Barré syndrome in the autumn of 1981, in the middle of his deputy leadership campaign. 'Bless you for your card', replied the MP for Chesterfield. 'I am on the mend and am preparing for an active September. The tide is on the turn for socialism now'.[1] The pair had first met in 1978 when Benn was invited to speak at the Tawney Group in Cambridge and then again four years later at the launch of the Socialist Society. Williams was a founding member and on the society's arts policy sub-committee. 'Without seeking to create a new party or faction,' the group's founding statement proclaimed, 'the society would encourage socialist renewal inside the labour movement and help those fighting for socialist ideas in the Labour Party'.[2] Benn, after hearing Williams speak, described the society's first conference as 'a great initiative to bring all the socialist groups together on a non-sectarian, comprehensive basis to publish works about socialism'.[3]

The launch of *New Socialist* a year earlier was part of this socialist resurgence amid the onslaught of Thatcherism: Michael Foot was Labour leader, Benn the 'outstanding representative' of the socialists in the party, and the Labour left had control of the GLC.[4] In the Labour-funded magazine, Williams, who was on the advisory board, made what was a persistent call of his during the 1980s for a new politics – uniting the peace, women's, and ecology movements alongside political education programmes and trade

1   Letter from Benn to Williams, undated, Williams Archive, WWE/E/1/16/22. The letter, in Benn's hand on Houses of Parliament headed paper, is undated but he was hospitalized in June 1981 so, with the reference to being 'on the mend', it is likely to be from that year.

2   Raymond Williams, Lynne Segal, and Martin Jacques, 'Founding of a Socialist Society', *Morning Star*, 23 January 1982, 3.

3   Tony Benn, *The End of an Era: Diaries 1980–90* (London: Hutchinson, 1992), 192.

4   *NLR*, 'Foreword', in Tony Benn, *Parliament, People and Power: Agenda for a Free Society – Interviews with New Left Review* (London: Verso, 1982), vii.

union research departments – which would 'shift the popular ground on which we have in fact been defeated: not to adapt to it or to manoeuvre around it, but to go out and try to transform it'.[1] One of the many problems identified was the unwillingness of distinctive anti-capitalist movements to formulate socialist responses to the ongoing crises in order to bring about social and structural transformation, what Williams described in *New Socialist* in 1986 as 'hesitations before socialism'.[2] This was also the theme of his contribution to the magazine's Bournemouth event a year earlier when, as the second day of the party conference drew towards midnight, Williams urged the left to seek to understand what he saw as reasonable and principled hesitations. With Benn – who was resistant to significant electoral reforms – on the panel,[3] Williams took the opportunity to criticize and argue against what he insisted were fundamental stumbling blocks: representative democracy, characterized as an alternative to direct democracy, and an unwillingness to think beyond such received forms, for example. The posing of difficult questions to the left – rather than simple condemnations of Thatcherism and the Labour right's response – are a hallmark of Williams's essays on socialist strategy from this period. As an early proponent of ecosocialism, he challenged the labour movement on its perennial commitment to production, highlighting the problems of maintaining an industrial social order which reproduced poverty inside growth. His comments on that late September evening are published here for

---

1   Raymond Williams, 'Socialists and Coalitionists', in *The Future of the Left*, ed. James Curran (Cambridge: Polity Press and *New Socialist*, 1984), 193. Originally published as 'Splits, Pacts and Coalitions', *New Socialist*, 16, March–April 1984, later collected in *Resources of Hope* (1989).

2   See Raymond Williams, 'Hesitations before Socialism', *New Socialist*, 41, September 1986.

3   See Benn's comments to *New Left Review* in *Parliament, People and Power*, 62–8. Benn and Williams would have found more common agreement on the latter's analysis and critical yet qualified praise of self-management within industry – the second block identified as causing hesitations before socialism.

the first time but we do not have Benn's contribution or reply.[1] 'He is an old and distinguished socialist who has written some marvellous books and his views are well worthwhile', recorded Benn in his audio diary immediately after the event.[2] Commenting later in the *Morning Star* on the death of Williams, Benn echoed the sentiments of Thompson and Hall: 'He was a humane man who inspired people in their own capacity to shape their future, which is what socialism is all about'.[3]

Shortly after this appearance in Bournemouth, and embarking on what became his last and unfinished project, Williams returned with renewed focus to modernism: an interest first sparked by an undergraduate enthusiasm for James Joyce, surrealist cinema, and jazz. 'When Was Modernism?' was one of Williams's final public lectures, delivered in March 1987 at the University of Bristol. As was typical, he lectured from brief notes. Fred Inglis then used the notes, alongside his own, to reconstruct the talk. An incomplete, abridged version was subsequently published posthumously as the first essay in *Politics of Modernism* (1989) – its editor Tony Pinkney adapting rough plans for such a study made by Williams shortly before he died. 'When Was Modernism?' can be thought of as a draft of the first chapter but, until now, we have only had Inglis's much shorter reconstruction.[4] The version included here is an edited transcript of the complete recorded lecture, the fourth

1   There may be a record of these in Benn's papers which were deposited with the British Library in 2019. However, at the time of writing, they are in the process of being catalogued and unlikely to be made available before 2024.

2   Unpublished transcript from Benn's audio diary, courtesy of the Trustees of the Tony Benn Estate and the British Library.

3   Benn quoted in David E. Morgan, 'Raymond Williams, Socialist Writer, Dies', *Morning Star*, 28 January 1988, 5. Inglis in his biography attributes Williams's obituary in the *Morning Star* to Benn, saying it was 'no accident' that he 'wrote the obituary in the house daily of the old CP', and describing Benn's writing as 'good prose'. Inglis, *Raymond Williams*, 13. It was, in fact, written by Morgan, a day after the original *Morning Star* story which quotes Benn, on 29 January 1988, *Morning Star*, 4.

4   Inglis's reconstructed version is approximately a third of the length of the original lecture.

in this collection taken from the family archive. It enhances our understanding of Williams's work on modernism as well as adding a newly expanded analysis to the research area which has become *the* boom industry of contemporary British academia. In offering a materialist critique, Williams historicized the ideologies of modernism (and postmodernism) and the construction of what became – in its most limiting uses – a cultural orthodoxy, deploying one of his familiar critical frameworks to question the processes of retrospectively selecting, grouping, and excluding certain figures and specific works which feed into the designation (and subsequent formal and institutionalized reduction) of a 'new' form of art and artistic practice. The demand issued by Williams – one which returns us to the political premise of *Culture and Society* – is that cultural forms and practices must be understood as social and historical processes. From there, one can identify the ideological uses of specific forms as well as the politics behind and embedded within the adoption of complex words like culture, society, modern, and modernism. Or, as Williams puts it in this context, 'the appropriation of "modern" for a selection of what have in fact been the modern processes is an act of pure ideology'.[1] Inglis's version – widely read and cited – captures the outline of Williams's analysis but misses the fully extended scope of his critique while including lines not said on that spring day in Bristol.[2]

It is exhilarating to now read the original as it was delivered by Williams less than a year before his death; this overdue publication warrants, and will hopefully lead to, new research on the politics of modernism. Complicating the simplistic characterization of

---

1   See below, p. 217.

2   For example, the line 'without Dickens, no Joyce' is Inglis's. He compiled his version using a single page of skeleton notes prepared by Williams for the Bristol lecture. Some of those figures not discussed in the original lecture but included in the notes are T. S. Eliot, W. B. Yeats, Filippo Marinetti, Wyndham Lewis, Vladimir Mayakovsky, Pablo Picasso, and Ignazio Silone, while Édouard Manet, D. H. Lawrence, Ernest Hemingway, and Ezra Pound are neither in the notes nor in the original lecture so have been added by Inglis.

Williams as the 'British Lukács' by describing his 'simultaneously modernist and anti-modernist' tendencies, Pinkney has stressed the centrality of modernism to his writing.[1] 'The *modernism* that is Williams's almost by instinct is locked in combat', he argues, '[…] with a politico-intellectual decision in favour of a realism that thwarts many of his own deepest political energies'.[2] This illustrates something of Williams's persistent probing and questioning of form: his extended and sustained attempts to analyse, push forward, and redefine categories and classifications, as they pertain to his own writing as a novelist, cultural analyst, literary theorist, and socialist intellectual. From form we again get the move to ideology, in that a formal technique – identified here as modernist – was taken to be a universal condition – that of modernism. It is this, for Williams, which is ideological. And, as Daniel Hartley elucidates, 'abstract universality pertains to the lived and representational modalities of capitalist abstraction; it is an extension of, rather than a challenge to, the rule of capital'.[3] So there are significant problems with the ways in which modernism – as both a highly selective historical category and an aesthetic technique – becomes the experience of a universal alienation of a modernity which is subsequently declared over, or to have been 'just now', in Williams's phrasing, a situation in which we become stuck. That way lies political destruction, he predicted. In one sense the foreboding which ends 'When Was Modernism?' is uncharacteristic. And yet, it is a warning which comes with an acknowledgement that alienation and incorporation by the logics of capital can be overcome. 'I say we must speak for hope', Williams insisted, 'as long as it doesn't mean suppressing the nature of the danger'.[4] Such

---

1   Tony Pinkney, *Raymond Williams* (Bridgend: Seren, 1991), 16.

2   Tony Pinkney, 'Raymond Williams and "The Two Faces of Modernism"', in *Raymond Williams: Critical Perspectives*, 28.

3   Daniel Hartley, 'Anti-Imperial Literacy, the Humanities, and Universality in Raymond Williams's Late Work', in *Raymond Williams at 100*, ed. Paul Stasi (Lanham: Rowman and Littlefield, 2021), p. 96.

4   Williams interviewed by Terry Eagleton, 'The Practice of Possibility', in *Resources of Hope* (London: Verso, 1989), 322.

a comment – made the same year as his modernism lecture, in one of his final interviews – is a fitting epitaph to Williams's writing. He was of one of the twentieth century's great intellectuals: his work and this centenary collection provide moments of oppositional force and help us identify opportunities for social transformation amid the developing pressures of the present century.

Phil O'Brien
Salford
January 2021

1

Herbert Read: Freud, Art, and Industry

In our own century, certain new disciplines of learning, and developments within existing disciplines, have deeply affected our general attitudes to our common life, and hence our attitudes to culture.[1] In certain fields, while the new emphasis is marked, the continuity is evident. In history, for instance, as was observed in the study of Tawney,[2] there has been minute and scholarly investigation of many aspects of the great changes which nineteenth-century writers had identified from general experience. In the study of literature and language, a wide academic extension has had great effects on the content, if not the form, of the inherited ideas: the names which immediately spring to mind are I. A. Richards and F. R. Leavis.[3] In political and social theory, we have,

---

1   An unpublished chapter from *Culture and Society: 1780–1950* (1958), held in the Raymond Williams Collection, Richard Burton Archives, University of Swansea, WWE/2/1/6/4/10. All references – including page numbers with corrections made to quoted material when necessary – and new explanatory notes added by the editor.

2   R. H. Tawney (1880–1962) – who like Williams was a committed socialist and, as a leading figure in the WEA, held a deep belief in adult education – is the subject of Chapter 2 in 'Part III: Twentieth-Century Opinions' in *Culture and Society*.

3   I. A. Richards (1893–1979) and F. R. Leavis (1895–1978), as proponents

essentially, been continuing a nineteenth-century debate, but over large areas of new social experience. In contrast with these kinds of discipline, where the continuity, if also the change, is marked, there are the highly important twentieth-century developments of psychology, anthropology, and sociology, which have, on occasion, been more difficult to assimilate to the established tradition. Sociology, however, has both applied and tested the observations on industrial society made by the nineteenth-century critics. If its methods are characteristically those of an industrial society, and hence, of a certain kind of mind, it is nevertheless true that the co-existence of dynamic ideas with uncertain areas of fact was, in the constructions of both past and present, extremely dangerous. History, on the one hand, and sociology, on the other, are proving, in practice, extremely useful and indeed essential controls on our quick, general constructions of experience. It is, as a result, becoming easier to separate assertions of value, which for good or ill are always indestructible, from the assertions and conjectures of fact which have so frequently accompanied them. This will have an important effect on our attitudes to the creators of our general ideas, although we do not of course escape these by instituting an investigation, or by assuming an indifference to general theory, or until we have different, and comparable, ideas of our own. The life of a factual investigator is busy and absorbing; but no man can reduce himself to an investigator, however much, in an image of practical usefulness, he may try.

Sociology, then, has been useful, and refining, as a supplier and an inspector. Anthropology, one might say, has been similarly useful and refining, but it is evident, in addition, that it has created new ways of social thinking. A work like Ruth Benedict's *Patterns of Culture* (1934), for example, has been of wide importance in general thinking, although, among anthropologists, it is, I believe,

---

of practical criticism and for their roles in shaping Cambridge English, were two men who Williams radically disagreed with but deeply respected. See Williams's 1983 retirement lectures published as 'Cambridge English, Past and Present' and 'Beyond English' in *Writing in Society* (1983).

controversial.[1] The most observable effect of anthropology upon general thinking can be indicated in two questions from Benedict:

> In culture [...] we must imagine a great arc on which are ranged the possible interests provided either by the human age-cycle or by the environment or by man's various activities. A culture that capitalized even a considerable proportion of these would be as unintelligible as a language that used all the clicks, all the glottal stops, all the labials, dentals, sibilants, and gutturals from voiceless to voiced and from oral to nasal. Its identity as a culture depends upon the selection of some segments of this arc. Every human society everywhere has made such selection in its cultural institutions. Each from the point of view of another ignores fundamentals and exploits irrelevancies.[2]

If this point of view has given, as it were, a new kind of purchase on one's own society, the idea that it is but one segment of a great arc being obviously welcome in a time of unrest and fundamental criticism, the related idea of the nature of change has been equally encouraging:

> Such a view of cultural processes calls for a recasting of many of our current arguments upholding our traditional institutions. These arguments are usually based on the impossibility of man's functioning without these particular traditional forms. Even very special traits come in for this kind of validation, such as the particular form of economic drive that arises under our particular system of property ownership. This is a remarkably special motivation, and there are evidences that even in our generation it is being strongly modified. At any rate, we do not have to confuse the issue by discussing it as if it were a matter of biological survival values. Self-support is a motive our

---

1   Ruth Benedict (1887–1948) was a leading American anthropologist and Columbia professor whose books – alongside her most well-known work *Patterns of Culture* (1934), which Williams draws on – include *Tales of the Cochiti Indians* (1931), *Zuñi Mythology* (1935), and *Race: Science and Politics* (1940). Williams returns briefly to Benedict's work in *The Long Revolution*, 98–9.

2   Ruth Benedict, *Patterns of Culture* (1934; London: Routledge, 1968), 17.

civilization has capitalized. If our economic structure changes so that this motive is no longer so potent a drive as it was in the era of the great frontier and expanding industrialism, there are many other motives that would be appropriate to a changed economic organization. Every culture, every era, exploits some few out of a great number of possibilities. Changes may be very disquieting, and involve great losses, but this is due to the difficultly of change itself, not to the fact that our age and country has hit upon the one possible motivation under which human life can be conducted. Change, we must remember, with all its difficulties, is inescapable. Our fears over even very minor shifts in custom are usually quite beside the point. Civilizations might change far more radically than any human authority has ever had the will or imagination to change them, and still be completely workable.[1]

On the whole, this emphasis has been valuable, in particular in its promotion of tolerance, as against the dominative element in imperialism. It will be remarked, however, that its criterion is abstract, and that there is an essential neutrality (at once interesting and dangerous) in such a concluding phrase, for the description of a civilization, as 'completely workable'. The difficulty is real, for intolerance and the fear of change can only be met, for most people, by some such reassurance; and if in fact, in a society like ours, there is not stability but a tension perhaps too great to be ultimately borne, this kind of reassurance is human and positive. This, indeed, is Benedict's position:

The sophisticated modern temper has made of social relativity, even in the small area which it has recognized, a doctrine of despair. It has pointed out its incongruity with the orthodox dreams of permanence and ideality and with the individual's illusion of autonomy. It has argued that if human experience must give up these, the nutshell of existence is empty. But to interpret our dilemma in these terms is to be guilty of an anachronism. It is only the inevitable cultural lag that makes us insist that the old must be discovered again in the new, that there is no solution but to find the old certainty and stability in the

---

1   Ibid., 25–6.

new plasticity. The recognition of cultural relativity carries with it its
own values, which need not be those of the absolutist philosophies.[1]

This is reasonable, and it is certainly true that 'modern thought
[...] about our changing standards is greatly in need of sane and
scientific direction'.[2] The observation, however, still leaves quite
open the vital question of the agency of such direction, in social
practice. In the world of ideas, the habit of relativity is liberating;
but its values have to reckon, not only with 'absolutist philosophies', but, if the phrase can be used, also with 'absolutist lives'. I
mean that while other situations, other patterns, other commitments, are of course theoretically possible, and in fact, elsewhere,
exist, it remains as a primary fact that any actual life, as a condition
of its coming to being, is shaped in a particular situation, a particular pattern, and by certain commitments. These can of course be
separately valued, as an intellectual process; and further, while in
one sense they are and must be absolute if the life is to be carried
on, they are never static or final. A commitment to an actual life
has to precede its criticism, or else there is no experience, but
merely observation. The 'sane direction', and re-direction, has then
to be carried out *within* this experience; if it is merely carried out
on it, it may, as a procedure, be 'scientific', but it will, as practice,
be dominative and arbitrary. The danger is at least as much to the
directors as to the directed.

The point has to be made, for the dominative element is visible
in current social practice that has been affected by such thinking. Yet a social anthropologist like Benedict teaches an essential
control. From social anthropology generally, as from certain
kinds of sociology, the valuable emphasis is received of ways of
life as social wholes: whole configurations, necessarily integrated,
which are not to be understood by any process of reduction to
their parts, as if these were separate. The term culture is used to
put this emphasis on 'a whole way of life', and this whole trend in
social thinking depends, in certain essentials, on the meanings

1   Ibid., 200.
2   Ibid.

previously given to 'culture', in the attempt to maintain attention to the whole life of man. The development of social anthropology has in fact tended to substantiate the ways of looking at a society and a common life which had earlier been wrought out a general experience of industrialism. The emphasis on 'a whole way of life', as a value, is continuous from the emphases of a Samuel Taylor Coleridge or a John Ruskin: a personal assertion has become, most valuably, an intellectual method. We can add, in good faith, that although in our own century the earlier constructions of a different way of life, in terms of an idea of the Middle Ages, or of the eighteenth-century village, have continued to exercise some sway, they have been reinforced, and in some cases replaced, by the different ways of life made actual to us through the work of the anthropologists. These are more substantiated than the historical constructions, but they are, of course, no nearer to us in experience. Their function, in our general thinking, is constant: to give reassurance that the human categories of industrialism or the version of life which industrialism urges on us, and which we might otherwise only personally doubt, are not in fact either universal or everlasting. Such reassurance is always a kind of gain.

The impact of the new psychology has been quite different in character. In its social bearings, the difficulty has been clearly put by Morris Ginsberg:

> The relations between psychology, including psychopathology, on the one hand, and sociology on the other are [...] extremely complex. The function of social psychology is, it seems to me, to show how the social structure and the changes in this structure affect the mentality of the individuals and groups composing the society, and conversely how the mental condition of the members affects the social structure. The present condition of social psychology suggests that the most promising field of inquiry is the study of small groups. The strength of psycho-analysis was in part due to its concentration on the interpersonal relation within the family. The study of crime also suggests that, where it is possible to make detailed case histories of individuals in their social setting, the psychological approach is enormously helpful.

Yet concentration on small groups has its dangers. There is a tendency to forget that the tensions within these groups may well reflect the strains and stresses of the larger social structure of which they are a part, and that the character of the group is determined not merely by the interplay of the personal qualities of its members, but also by the traditions of the larger society. The latter, however, is not open to direct inspection by psychological methods. Herein lies the difficulty of social psychology. Its future development depends in the first place on improvements in the methods for observing group behaviour. But it also depends upon whether better ways can be found for linking its work with history and sociology than have so far been available.[1]

These observations are of the greatest importance, for it seems to be true that the gains of psychoanalysis – the real, if still properly controversial, personal illuminations – have to be set against a certain loss, in their consequences upon our social thinking. Sigmund Freud's *Civilization and its Discontents* (1930) is a work of extreme interest which amounts, it seems to me, to a substitute for history as we have known it; and this is not, at its present stage, a substitute that we can accept. Freud has already been usefully criticized by anthropologists for offering as a universal sexual pattern what they insist to be a specific pattern, in a particular culture. The point can be usefully extended when his theory of culture is in question. Indeed, much of the effect of psychoanalysis, on general thinking, has been the abstraction of the individual, or the small family group, from society as a whole; and the abstraction of a particular kind of society – a known and properly observed reality – from the whole flux of human settlement and commitment. The value of psychoanalytic theories of the individual remains to be considered, in its own proper terms; but its contribution to general ideas of culture remains uncertain and unsatisfactory, for the reasons which Ginsberg indicates.

1   Morris Ginsberg (1889–1970) was a professor of sociology at the London School of Economics and the author of *The Psychology of Society* (1921), *Studies in Sociology* (1932), and *The Idea of Progress: A Revaluation* (1953).

It is of course still very early to look for the full results, in general thinking, of these new sciences of man. The work is necessarily very specialized, and it is right that we should go to it to see if we can learn, rather than, from older positions, to controvert. On the other hand, it is the way in which a specialism can be assimilated into general experience and thinking that finally determines its importance. We have reason to be grateful to those writers who have attempted this process of assimilation; and one of the most interesting of these writers is Herbert Read, to whom (if the case were not as it is) I should have to apologize for making so general an introduction.[1] Read's work has been of very great interest, and his theories of art and the artist, and of their social functions, are already of practical importance in our contemporary ideas of culture. The point of particular importance to me is that in Read's work one finds at once a continuation of the tradition hitherto examined and, in the process of this continuation, the attempted assimilation of the new sciences.

In *Art and Society* (1936), Read discusses Benedict's views on the integration of cultures, and continues:

> The world has probably never exhibited such a lack of cultural integrity
> as now exists in the capitalist form of modern society. At times – when,
> for example, we see a typical suburban development – it would seem
> that the aesthetic instinct itself has atrophied; that men are no longer

---

1   Herbert Read (1893–1968) was an influential art and literary critic, philosopher, poet, theorist of modernist design, and anarchist. His books include *Art Now* (1933), *Art and Industry* (1934), *Art and Society* (1936), *The Philosophy of Modern Art* (1952), and *The True Voice of Feeling: Studies in English Romantic Poetry* (1953). He was knighted in 1953. Henry Moore – a lifelong friend – described Read's book *Education through Art* (1943) as transforming the British educational system, demonstrating the importance of art to young people, while Walter Gropius found a kindred spirit in Read, someone equally concerned with art, architecture, and society. See *Herbert Read: A Memorial Symposium*, ed. Robin Skelton (London: Methuen, 1970) for more reflections on the importance of Read to leading figures in twentieth-century art and literature such as Moore, Gropius, Ben Nicholson, Barbara Hepworth, Roland Penrose, and Stephen Spender.

sensitive to form, but content to live in a chaos of styles, or rather, in a complete aesthetic nullity. But on analysis it appears that these developments are inherent in the methods of production; they are determined, that is to say, not by free choice, but by economic necessity – by the direct necessity of profit-making implied in the methods of production and distribution, and in any case by the ultimate lack of cultural unity implied in the structure of a society organized on a competitive rather than a cooperative basis. There is no escaping the patent fact that the degradation of art during the last two centuries is in direct correspondence with the expansion of capitalism.[1]

Such an attitude is quite evidently continuous from Ruskin and William Morris, although in its expression there is also another element – the influence of Karl Marx – evident in the important change from the description of modern society as 'industrialist' to its significant description as 'capitalist'. Yet Read's general position is not the Marxist one, nor would it be received easily by that large body of English socialists who are in the utilitarian tradition. Taking his instance from a point made by Benedict ('All the miscellaneous behaviour directed towards getting a living, mating, warring, and worshipping the gods, is made over into consistent patterns in accordance with the unconscious canons of choice that develop within the culture'[2]), Read continues:

The process of integration is instinctive, and it may be doubted whether a great civilization was ever consciously planned. It is an unconscious growth, and is killed by rationalization. At the present moment we have a civilization which has suffered such a fate. We are at the dead end of a process of rationalization, and by a supreme effort of consciousness we are trying to recognize the fact. Consequently we live in an age of transition, in which a whole way of life and thought is breaking down, never to recover, and if civilization is to continue we have to discover a new way of life.[3]

1   Herbert Read, *Art and Society* (1936; London: Faber and Faber, 1967), 128.
2   Quoted by Read, ibid., 114.
3   Read, ibid.

The continuity here is from Robert Southey, Coleridge, or even Thomas Carlyle. In particular, the mode of discovery of a new way of life has to be sharply distinguished from the modes which the way we are leaving promoted and sustained. In practice, Read's emphasis is on the recovery, and integration, of that mode of discovery which is art. A social reformer like H. G. Wells is dismissed for explaining art as an aspect of leisure:

> an outlet for mankind's surplus energy. What energy man can spare from war, commerce, science, and other practical activities, he expends in these useless but quite delightful occupations – painting, sculpture, poetry, music, dancing, cricket, football and other forms of mental and physical gymnastics.[1]

On the contrary, Read insists:

> Art is a mode of knowledge, and the world of art is a system of knowledge as valuable to man as the world of philosophy or the world of science. Indeed, it is only when we have clearly recognized art as a mode of knowledge parallel to but distinct from other modes by which man arrives at an understanding of his environment that we can begin to appreciate its significance in the history of mankind [...]. [W]e still treat art as an aid to thought, or as an interpretation of thought, instead of as a mode of thought in itself [...]. The necessity for the future [...] is a reintegration of art as an independent mode of apprehension and expression; as the sensuous correlative, equal and opposite, of intellectual abstraction.[2]

Read's examination of this 'mode of knowledge' takes its starting-point, on the one hand, from Romantic literary theory (about which he has written most effectively in *The True Voice of Feeling* [1953]), and on the other hand from Freudian psychology. He glosses a famous, but most unsatisfactory, comment on the artist from one of Freud's *Introductory Lectures on Psychoanalysis* (1917),

---

1   Ibid., 6.

2   Ibid., 7, 134. Although Williams presents this as one quote, it is taken from different sections of Read's book: the first part is from the introduction while the set of elliptical quotes are from a later discussion of socialist realism.

and seizes on the point that art is a way back from phantasy to reality – an externalized, universalized, pleasing embodiment of such phantasy. Read accepts this, but sees the need to concentrate on the psychology of the way back: the nature, that is to say, of the motives and skills of such embodiment, and of their reception by other minds. On these points he concludes:

> If we picture the regions of the mind as three super-imposed strata (we have already noted how inadequate such a picture must be), then continuing our metaphor we can imagine in certain rare cases a phenomenon comparable to a 'fault' in geology, as a result of which in one part of the mind the layers become discontinuous, and exposed to each other at unusual levels. That is to say, the sensational awareness of the ego is brought into direct contact with the id, and from that 'seething cauldron' snatches some archetypal form, some instinctive association of words, images or sounds, which constitute the basis of the work of art [...]. With such a theory we could then go on to explain the social function of the artist. His primary function, and the only function which gives him his unique faculties, is this capacity to materialize the instinctual life of the deepest levels of the mind. At that level we suppose the mind to be collective in its representations, and it is because the artist can give visible shape to these invisible fantasms that he has power to move us deeply. But in the process of giving these fantasms material shape, the artist must exercise a certain skill lest the bare truth repel us. He therefore invests his creation with superficial charms; wholeness or perfection, a due proportion or harmony, and clarity; and these are the work of his conscious mind, his ego. [...] In that further process art, as art, has always suffered – simply because in such a case the message will always appear more important, more insistent, than the mode of conveyance, and men will forget that in art it is the mode which finally matters. But by the mode we mean more than the externals of beauty; we mean above all the driving energy, the vitality of the forces which well up from the unconscious.[1]

---

1   Ibid., 94–5. Williams would later use part of this same quote in the opening chapter to *The Long Revolution* during a short analysis of Freud, reality, and the creative mind. See page 30 of *The Long Revolution*.

It is fair to say, I think, that this is as far as a distinctively twentieth-century theory of art has gone; although it must be remarked, in parenthesis, that it seems quite unacceptable as it stands. In particular, the concept of the 'fault', and that of 'a certain skill lest the bare truth repel us', seem unnecessary. It is a theory that posits disintegration and fragmentariness, for it is perfectly possible to seek an explanation of the power and vitality of art in terms of a greater attention to wholeness: a capacity for a certain whole attention to experience, which should include, in its very process, a mode of embodiment that is again controlled by the whole experience. Certainly, I do not think we have yet to subscribe to an idea of the constitution of the artist as one of valuable derangement, not to the meagre version of his embodying skill as a matter of suasion, reassurance, and charm. May it not be that this rare capacity for holding a whole experience in a particular and communicable form is a more adequate hypothesis 'to explain that access, that lyrical intuition, which is known as inspiration'?[1]

In the matter of demonstrable psychology, our theories of art are still almost wholly speculative. But if Read's theory, like certain aspects of Romantic theory, seems in a certain sense a type of the particular disintegration which followed industrialism, it yet remains capable, as did Romantic theory, of drawing important attention to the kinds of experience which industrialism neglects. Art, as he insists, is a mode of knowledge, and one which the utilitarian assumptions leave little room for. The room which is in fact left is the function of decoration: that decoration of life which is leisure, or that decoration of useful objects which is industrial art. On these points, Read has much that is extremely valuable to say.

Art and Industry (1934) is a fine and deservedly influential book. Again beginning, in certain respects, from Ruskin and Morris, Read succeeds in completing, and in effect replacing, their ideas of art and industrialism. He begins with a most useful discussion of the distinction between 'fine' and 'applied' art, which he

---

1   Ibid., 94. This is another quote used later in *The Long Revolution*, 30.

traces from the Renaissance, and sees as having been widely and
damagingly emphasized by the industrial revolution:

> a complete distinction was henceforth to be made between the artist
> who made things to satisfy a practical purpose, such as the builder
> and the architect, and the artist who made things (essentially non-
> utilitarian) for the delectation of individuals. Then round this cabinet
> or private art, and fed by the type of learning which the Classical
> Revival encouraged, there sprang up a tradition of connoisseurship or
> dilettantism, based on the knowledge and appreciation of such works
> of art. This tradition is known to us as *Taste*, or *Good Taste*, and to it,
> I think, we owe all the confusion of values that has existed since the
> sixteenth century until the present day. Taste, in all its incompleteness
> and exclusiveness, has been made the measure of industrial art, of the
> art of the machine age.[1]

It would be difficult to over-emphasize the value of this observation, which, in its general outline, seems to be certainly true. It
can valuably be compared with William Wordsworth's remarks
on taste, in relation to poetry. It is true, of course, that the tradition of cultivated taste was responsible for some valuable early
criticism of the ugliness produced in the industrial revolution.
But the result of this criticism, in the long term, was chaos. Either
there was a blind rejection of the new instruments of production –
'you cannot have a tasteful industry'; or, worse, 'you can have a
tasteful industry, if you apply to these new methods the kind of
thing which has been hitherto recognized as beautiful'. Both solutions remain to plague us: the theoretical rejection of machine
production, with a nostalgia for, and a pastiche of, pre-machine
work; and the attempted taming of industry by taste – 'make the
thing and then make it tasteful'; Read should compare the latter,
however, with his own theory of the psychology of art.

Read, in admirable detail, exposes both these solutions, and
their failure. His own position he puts thus: 'The machine has

---

1   Herbert Read, *Art and Industry* (1953; Bloomington: Indiana University Press, 1961), 12.

triumphed, and only now are we beginning to accept that inevitable fact, and to work out an aesthetic and social philosophy based on that fact.'[1] Such a philosophy, Read continues, will emphasize the distinction between 'humanistic art', the product of 'man's innate desire to create an art expressive of his individuality', and 'abstract art', the genuine, formal art of the machine.[2] The former is what we are used to, and since,

> industrialism promises a life spent in a more leisurely and contemplative fashion […] [i]f the necessary adjustments can be made in the monetary system so that the capacity to consume bears a relation of approximate equality to the power of production; if the age of plenty, already potential, can be realized in fact.[3]

Humanistic art, then, which is the product of such leisure, will not only survive, but flourish. If, however, we insist that this is the only kind of art, we condemn ourselves to remain in the world of ugliness and 'tasteful' decoration which is our present environment. The new emphasis that is necessary is on the art of design, abstract art. The appeal of useful objects, as art, can moreover be intuitional as well as rational. The machine, evidently, can produce the latter, satisfying 'all the canons of beauty which have a basis in numerical proportion.'[4] But the machine can also, Read argues, produce objects of an intuitional aesthetic appeal; in fact, he adds, and by illustration seeks to prove, it already does. Perhaps his most valuable point, in this context, is his comment on standardization:

> Naturally such forms will be standardised and uniform. That does not seem to me to be an objection, if they conform to all other aesthetic requirements. The quality of uniqueness must obviously be sacrificed in the machine age. But what is the worth of such a quality? It is certainly not an aesthetic value. The sense of uniqueness – is it not rather

---

1   Ibid., 30–1. Here Read is discussing William Morris, machinery, and art.

2   Ibid., 33.

3   Ibid., 34, then 33.

4   Ibid., 37.

a reflection of the possessive impulse, an ethically unworthy impulse typical of a bygone individualistic phase of civilization? If there were any danger of a shortage of machines, so that all diversity disappeared from daily life, there would be some cause for alarm. But actually machines multiply and change rapidly, and their products are of far greater diversity than those produced by handicraft.[1]

It is therefore no longer necessary, Read continues, to assume an opposition between aesthetic values and the machine. The opposition, rather, is between such values and the 'present industrial system'. His consequent proposals are immediately practical, in the way that proposals based on a rejection of machines could not be. He declares, in general terms, against capitalism, and against a competitive society. But his stress is on 'the wider recognition of art as a biological function, and a constructive planning of our modes of living which takes full cognisance of this function'.[2] He conceives such planning over a wide range of social activities, but his first stress is on education, on which he makes detailed proposals both in *Art and Industry* and *Education through Art* (1943). In summary, he sees an education of the senses and the feelings (now neglected) as the basis for any radical redirection of society.

In general, this work has been so useful that one does not want to make difficulties over it. Yet one cannot help feeling that the application of Freudian psychology to Romantic theory has limited the usefulness of a general case, which does not seem to have to depend on anything of that kind. It is worth adding, as a footnote, a comment by Eric Gill,[3] in a letter to Read: 'Your idea of

---

1   Ibid., 37–8.

2   Ibid., 44.

3   Eric Gill (1882–1940) was a sculptor, engraver, designer, and inventor of the typeface Gill Sans, whose work connected the Arts and Crafts Movement with modern British art and design, often imbued by his own Catholicism. He was a friend of David Jones – author of *In Parenthesis* (1937) – and in the 1920s settled at Capel-y-ffin in the Black Mountains, just north of Williams's boyhood home in Pandy.

the artist as an abnormal man is what revolts me'.[1] 'I want to keep the word "art" down to the level of ordinary making & I want to exalt the workman to the high level of the imaginative maker', Gill added later.[2] Gill's whole position is, indeed, extremely interesting. Beginning, as this quotation suggests, from Ruskin and from Morris (whom temperamentally he so much resembled), he reached, in his maturity, a position very much like Read's in his acceptance of the value of machines: 'Our trouble is not primarily the *existence* of machines but their ownership and control by persons whose one concern is profits'.[3] Industrialism is bad, not because all its material products are bad (many of them are good), but because 'it is bad for men'.[4] Gill then defines this badness very much in Ruskin's terms. What is particularly interesting, however, and in a sense the basis of his difference with Read, is his distrust of aesthetics as a separate province of human experience:

> Mr Penty says aesthetics cannot be explained in the terms of morals. I did not say they could. I said aesthetics were to be explained in terms of the mind. I said that the faculties of the mind are the intelligence and the will and that therefore, the object of intelligence being the truth and that of the will being the good, aesthetics were to be explained in terms of truth and goodness [...]. 'The public must be educated', said the leaders of the arts and crafts movement, meaning educated in aesthetics; I say rather that the public should be educated in faith and morals [...]. To me it is clear that commercialism, dishonesty, avarice, self-will and self-esteem, conceit, vanity, love of luxury and ostentation on the one hand (i.e. moral failings) and stupidity, blindness and every

---

1   Letter from Gill to Read, 20 August 1934, in *Letters of Eric Gill*, ed. Walter Shewring (London: Jonathan Cape, 1947), 292.

2   Letter from Gill to Read, 27 August 1934, in *Letters of Eric Gill*, 293. In the original typescript text, Williams runs this quote into the previous one from Gill but they are from two different letters, dated a week apart, so have been separated here.

3   Letter from Gill to Miss Hall, Librarian of the Catholic Library, Johannesburg, 27 August 1934, in *Letters of Eric Gill*, 295.

4   Letter from Gill to *The Criterion* in response to Arthur Penty, October 1934, in *Letters of Eric Gill*, 303.

kind of silliness on the other (i.e. intellectual failings) are more damaging to civilization and culture and therefore to art (i.e. the making
of things – for art is not merely the making of paintings and sculptures
and buildings) than any lack of art-school training or *ad hoc* cultural
education […]. Mr Penty yearns for a revival of art patronage. But
every man who spends money on things made by men is a patron of
art. Again, it is precisely the artificial division of human works into art
and not art which compels us to return to first principles.[1]

This is a point of view so useful, and so rarely now argued, that
one can only feel grateful to Gill for it, as indeed one feels grateful
on almost everything he touched. He was not a very thorough
thinker, but his extraordinary vitality, sympathy, and honesty
made him – as they make his *Autobiography* (1940) and his *Letters*
(1947) – one of our major points of contemporary reference. He
would not have supposed that he had solved very much, but his
spirit is worth recalling as we ponder the more detailed, more
learned, and very valuable teaching of Herbert Read.

1958

---

1   Ibid., 299–307. The long, elliptical quote used by Williams is not in the
correct order, but each section is taken from the Gill letter in response to Penty,
see pages 301, 299, and 307, in that sequence. Arthur Penty (1875–1937) was
a writer and architect and, like Gill, associated with the Arts and Crafts Movement and the ideas of Morris and Ruskin. He wrote on architecture, Guild
Socialism, and Christianity – notably in *The Restoration of the Gild System*
(1906) and *Towards a Christian Sociology* (1923) – and set up the short-lived
Fabian Arts Group while offering a sustained critique of industrialism in *The
Criterion*, *Guild Socialist*, and *G. K's Weekly*.

2

The Future of Marxism

There are two dimensions of politics.[1] There is the dimension in which, because of living pressures, men try to understand their world and improve it. This dimension is persistently human. But besides it, always, is that parading robot of polemic, which resembles human thinking in everything but its capacity for experience. If you step into the robot's world, you get your fuel free, and you can immediately grind into action, on one of the paper fronts, where the air stinks of pride, destruction, malice, and exhaustion. Men need a good society and they need food, and further, in our own time, we know that we are living on the edge of destruction. But the slip into the robot world, so easy to make, is against these needs even when it claims to satisfy them. As I look, now, at the greater part of our political campaigns and periodicals, I recognize, reluctantly, the cancer of violence in them, which is our actual danger. And it is no use, after that, turning away. We have to fight to recover the dimension in which people actually live, because it is only there that any good outcome is possible.

The first characteristic of the robots is that the world exists in terms of their own fixed points. Are you a Marxist, a revisionist,

---

1   Originally published in *The Twentieth Century*, 170.1010, July 1961, 128–42. New references and explanatory notes added by the editor.

a bourgeois reformist? Are you a Communist, a Left radical, a fellow-traveller? What answer can a man make to that kind of robot questioning? 'Go away', I suppose. It seems the only adequate thing to say.[1] For we have had it before. Are you Protestant, Catholic, Free Churchman, free-thinker, atheist? If you try to say what you feel and know, you have to fight off the mechanical hands trying to stick their own labels on you or get your voice on one of their recordings. They do this because, once the labels are on, they can fight, show you your enemy, throw you into one of their prepared campaigns. But in the intensity of human need the first struggle is to know the difference between experience and that robot world, to know rice and schools and human speech from that demented, airless pseudo-political dimension. The current robot campaign is to get men to join the camp of democracy to fight for survival against the camp of democracy. 'Accept no substitutes; ours is the only *genuine* camp; we will prove it by engaging in relentless struggle'. And robots do not die; only men die.

The real difficulty is that, in order to think at all, we have to use ideas and interpretations which the robots have already recorded. Somewhere, in the world of human thinking coming down to us from our predecessors, the necessary insights, the fruitful bearings, exist. But to keep them where they belong, in direct touch with our experience, is a constant struggle. I am reminded of this, once again, as I try to sort out my thoughts after reading George Lichtheim's *Marxism: An Historical and Critical Study* (1961) – a book that is evidently the result of years of patient work and thought. I am not a scholar of Marxism, and I cannot accurately judge whether Lichtheim's detailed analysis is correct. But his conclusions are interesting, and directly relevant to our actual world. Lichtheim sees Marxism disintegrating as a system of thought and guide to action:

> its accomplishments are shown to be incompatible with its ultimate aims, which thus disclose their essentially metaphysical – i.e.

---

1 Williams had more to say on labelling as a form of control in 'You're a Marxist, Aren't You?', collected in *Resources of Hope*, 65–76.

transcendental and unrealizable, nature. What remains is, on the one hand, the travestied fulfilment of these aims in a reality which is their actual negation; and on the other, the *caput mortuum* of a gigantic intellectual construction whose living essence has been appropriated by the historical consciousness of the modern world; leaving the empty husk of 'dialectical materialism' to the ideologists of a new orthodoxy. In the sunset of the liberal era, of which Marxism is at once the critique and the theoretical reflection, this outcome confirms the truth of its own insights into the logic of history; while transferring to an uncertain future the ancient visions of a world set free.[1]

The sweep of this judgement is very much like actual Marxist argument. Lichtheim is in no way a robot, but this tone raises disturbing echoes. Ways of thinking get old and become irrelevant, but not often, it seems to me, in quite this cataclysmic way. That image of the sunset worries me; it has been, for so long, one of the robots' stage effects. And when they have not been actually tearing at each other, one of their most complicated games has been that of putting one another in the dustbin of history, which they always seem very certain about. Lichtheim may be right, but I find myself drawing back and wondering what, in our actual world, the future of Marxism is likely to be. For this is the irony: that a lot seems to go in these dustbins of history. The number of systems that are officially dead but won't lie down is extraordinary. A book called *Karl Marx and the Close of his System* was published in 1898, and look what has happened since then.[2] This doesn't prove anything,

---

1   George Lichtheim, *Marxism: An Historical and Critical Study* (1961; New York: Columbia University Press, 1964), 406. Lichtheim (1912–1973) was an historian of Marxism and socialism; he wrote a book on Georg Lukács in 1970 for the Fontana Modern Masters series (to which Williams contributed *Orwell* in 1971) as well as penning several important studies of Marxist scholarship, including *The Origins of Socialism* (1969) and *From Marx to Hegel* (1971).

2   Here Williams is referring to a book by classical liberal economist and staunch critic of Marxism, Eugen von Böhm-Bawerk (1851–1914). A leading theorist of the Austrian School of Economics, his work influenced Ludwig von Mises and Friedrich Hayek.

either way, about the validity of Marxism, but it does suggest that the relation between systems of thought and actual history is both complex and surprising.

What I keep coming back to, after the force of Lichtheim's arguments, is that Marxism, or its surrogate in Marxism-Leninism, is now the official doctrine of about a third of the world, actively taught and propagated by powerful political and economic systems, and on any possible estimate likely to be active for as far ahead as we care to think. Well, of course, that is provided for, in the argument: the systems are really a travesty of Marxism, their official thoughts are simply empty husks and dead heads. This could be true, and we ought to consider its possibility when we hear that argument very common among the small number of Marxists in Britain: that 1,000 million people, stretching from the Baltic to the Pacific, can't be wrong. But we ought to check every stage of the argument quite carefully. Are the systems created and projected by the Russian, Chinese, and other Communist revolutions really a travesty of Marxist intentions? If they are, to any substantial extent, what will be the relation, in the growth of these societies, between the widespread teaching of a doctrine equivalent to a great national religion, and the reality which this teaching might theoretically or practically question or condemn? I don't, with any confidence, know the answer to either of these questions, but at least I am much less sure than Lichtheim both that the systems are travesties and that, even if they were, the doctrines would be merely empty and dead. I will try to express my doubts about each of these points.

The widespread disillusion, among thinkers in the West, over the course of the Communist revolutions is very easy to understand. Two charges stand examination: first, that the revolutions have been disfigured and perverted by the use of terror for political aims; second, that the common people have in fact not been liberated, but have simply passed from the rule of aristocrats, landlords, and bankers to the rule of bureaucrats and a party apparatus.

On the first charge, there must be no more equivocation, no more convincing talk about 'revolution and rosewater', no more reduction of men who died to mere errors and mistakes. The Communist societies themselves will have to face this reality, in depth, sooner or later; human beings cannot grow without facing that kind of truth about themselves. Political terror was used, on a vast scale, both for political ends and, it would seem, by a monstrous kind of extension, for its own sake. The facts, so often disputed, so often still the matter of argument, but now at least admitted by everyone at a minimum level which is still revolting, have lodged deeply in our minds, and we would be less than human if they had not.

I remember feeling, in the late 1930s, when political terror was being used both in the Soviet Union and in Nazi Germany, how much strength there seemed to be in the argument that these were really the same kinds of society: the new kind of totalitarian state. But I eventually rejected this conclusion then, and still reject it now. It seems to me to be a very common error, in judging societies, to abstract one element which they share, and then go on to assume that as whole societies they are identical. The use of political terror is so important that, in the case of Fascism and Soviet Communism, the resemblance in this respect was taken as a total resemblance: our eyes were often closed by this wholly good emotion – the repulsion from terror as such. Yet it now seems perfectly clear that any such total identification between Fascism and Communism is absolutely misleading. I would not go as far as George Orwell once did, in saying that the resemblance was really the resemblance between rats and rat-poison.[1] But it is perfectly clear that Fascism had little to offer but terror, at home

---

1 'The socialist movement has not time to be a league of dialectical materialists', wrote Orwell, 'it has got to be a league of the oppressed against the oppressors. You have got to attract the man who means business, and you have got to drive away the mealy-mouthed liberal who wants foreign fascism destroyed in order that he may go on drawing his dividends peacefully – the type of humbug who passes resolutions "against Fascism and Communism", i.e. against rats and rat-poison. Socialism means the overthrow of tyranny, at home as well as abroad. So long as you keep *that* fact well to the front, you will never be in much doubt as to who are your real supporters', *The Road to Wigan Pier* (1937; London: Penguin, 2001), 206.

and abroad: it was a blind explosion of hatred and frustration. Soviet Communism, on the other hand, not only carried through the industrial revolution necessary in a backward country, but much more crucially, carried through a cultural revolution which is not only an absolute human gain but which seems, still, in its achievements and its weaknesses alike, a specific product of a particular system. I am of course not saying, in this argument, that terror becomes good or bad according to what else is happening in the society; it is evil always and everywhere. But if you want to make a true judgement of the society, you have to look at all the forces active in it.

The comparison between Soviet Communism and Fascism is now heard less often, because Fascism seems dead except in two or three marginal nations and because the Soviet Union claims to have rejected Stalinism, in this respect. The disillusion of Western intellectuals has not, however, visibly decreased, although this is difficult to estimate because prominent intellectuals are still, in majority and in positions of influence, of the generation formed by the reaction to Fascist and Stalinist terror. Still, there is a recognizably new formulation: that the Soviet Union is a negation of the hopes of the revolution because it has become a society ruled by a directing elite, which controls all sources of power and controls men's minds by indoctrination and censorship. An interesting version of this formulation is now common among academics: that, *really*, the political aspects of the cold war are old hat (indeed most political aspects of everything are old hat). The facts are, we gather, that the Soviet Union and the United States are getting visibly more like each other: societies dominated by organization men through giant corporations, dependent on and interlocking with a military elite, and conditioning their populations through the mass media. Here, again, many of the facts are in dispute, but I would myself accept that there are important resemblances of this kind, and that it would be quite plausible to assume, even, that this is a universal pattern of future society.

Once again, however, I find I have to reject this conclusion. I would do so simply on the grounds that these organizations are

formally dedicated to quite different ideological ends, though this
is a part of the argument to which I must return, as it needs separate treatment. In more immediate terms, I find the resemblance
unconvincing, or merely partial, because it seems to me undeni-
able that the elites are, finally, serving quite different functions. It
is not only that the Russian elite has been the agency of quite new
social forms, whereas the American elite is essentially an agency
of rational stability within an existing system. This could be coun-
tered by arguing that increasingly the function of the Russian
elite is the maintenance of a system that was once new but is now
established. What is much more important, surely, is that the kind
of society each elite is aiming at is quite different. The American
version of a commercial democracy, with the individual consumer
as sovereign, is very different indeed from the Russian version of a
directed modern state, with the community as sovereign. I do not
live in either, and I share the values of neither. But the differences
in practical policy do seem to me quite plain. In such a func-
tional economic field as transportation, for example, the two elites
reach opposite conclusions, both in the attitude of public transport systems and the use of private cars; and these then visibly
change the societies. Because bureaucracies often resemble each
other in their methods of working, and their immediate attitudes
to people, it does not follow that their basic habits of thought are
similar. It would be unjust to both societies to argue that, through
sometimes comparable means, they are pursuing wholly comparable objectives. The feel of the local evidence about bureaucracy
is convincing, but the feel of the general evidence, about the kind
of society that is resulting, argues all the other way. You can prefer
one or the other, and most people actively do. But whatever you
feel about the Soviet Union, it is difficult in the end to argue that
the kind of society being created there is a negation of what is
usually understood as the Marxist ideal. The nationalization of
the means of production and distribution, the creation of new
social, legal, and political forms, are there, for admiration or rejection. The Soviet bureaucracy serves them, and is crucially different
from the American or British power elite simply because it has

these wholesale versions of society, so that it can operate much more directly and tightly through the organization of a political party which is at once government and administration.

Still, the comparison of power elites may not be the most substantial criticism. People who remember the radical and liberating emphasis in early Marxism are not concerned with the fact that there is power-elite control elsewhere, however similar or dissimilar. They insist that the real negation, in Soviet society, is that what was intended to be a workers' state has become a party-bureaucratic state; the liberation of the working people is as far away as ever. This, as I understand him, is Lichtheim's position, though he seems also to subscribe (the two positions are not incompatible) to the 'power elite' version, dismissing the Soviet Union as 'simply another instance of modern planned and bureaucratized industrialism'.[1] I find this the most difficult thing of all to make up my mind about. By the standards of the British working-class tradition, I cannot feel that the working people of the Soviet Union, and still more of China, have been liberated in any practical sense. I do not mean that the British working class is free, whereas the Soviet or Chinese is not. I mean that the disciplines imposed on working people by the demands of a more modern industrial system still operate, and operate more harshly in the Soviet Union and China just because their industrial growth is still either in a dynamic or early stage.

At this point, the most difficult theoretical questions arise. The most convincing alternative, as an explanation of the historical process, both to Marxism and to the interpretation I began in *The Long Revolution* (1961), is, quite simply, that industrialization is the real key, the real dynamic.[2] Certain imperative demands of a system of industrial production remake human societies,

1   Lichtheim, *Marxism*, 398.

2   See Perry Anderson, 'The Missing Text: Introduction to "The Future of Marxism"', *New Left Review*, 114, Nov–Dec 2018, for more on *The Long Revolution* and Williams's Marxism. Also E. P. Thompson's review 'The Long Revolution (Part I and Part II)' in *New Left Review*, I/9, May–June 1961, 24–33, and I/10, July–August 1961, 34–9.

imposing new kinds of discipline and stress but offering enough, in the way of consumption and in substitution of mechanical for human labour, to get the disciplines and stresses accepted, in a continual and restless balancing of cost and reward. Then the industrial revolution is primary, and capitalism and socialism are simply alternative ways of organizing it: capitalism at first centred only on production and profit, at whatever cost, but later developing continual consumption and mass culture as ways of keeping the system going and the people willing to work; socialism directing production differently, but compelled to introduce both labour discipline and social discipline of new kinds to command the necessary channelling of energy. There is a good deal of evidence for seeing the thing in this way, and certainly, from the Communist leaders and their foreign representatives, we hear more about the achievements of socialism in these terms than in any other. The present world struggle is often presented as a direct competition between capitalism and socialism to see which can best make industrialism work.

But then, of course, at this point we are bound to ask what are the factors which lead societies into these alternative courses, if their overall industrial aims are basically the same. Well, we say, actual historical conditions, and Marxism was attractive because it offered a fundamental analysis of these conditions. It is at this point, however, that all the difficulties return. We are always in danger of taking too short a view – history is much slower than any of us can bear – but it certainly does now look as if the Marxist thesis of passing, by a recognizable historical process, through various stages of capitalism to the establishment of socialism, is not the way the world is going. The socialist revolutions have occurred mainly in industrially backward countries, often seeming to skip the capitalist stage in any important sense, while in the countries of mature capitalism the likelihood of socialist revolutions is small, and programmes of radical change have increasingly taken on a reformist character which affects not only the method of establishing socialism but the kind of socialism that would be established.

Of course this has been pointed out many times, but what are the real conclusions we should draw from it? That Marx himself was wrong in this respect seems comparatively unimportant, because it is the movement he generated, rather than his own absolute formulations, that we must now be concerned with. And it seems to me we are usually much too limited in our view of the world, when we now pronounce Marxism outmoded and out of date. It is true that Marxism, in any of its orthodox forms, seems to have comparatively little to say about the present situation within Western capitalist societies; or rather, what it continues to say sounds like a wilful and simplifying dogmatism, which reality is continually contradicting. At the same time, however, what it says about imperialism, and in theory and practice about the economic liberation and progress of now [industrially] backward countries, seem to me to make better sense than any other version of this now commanding issue. The general trend of Communist success, in these areas of the world, seems to be due not primarily to clever power politics but to the formulation of a theoretical and practical programme which in general the realities confirm.

The successful revolutions have occurred where there has been a strong peasant movement of revolt against impossible condi-tions, and where this has been allied with or directed by Marxist or Marxist-influenced intellectuals and sometimes elements of the urban working class. The two most significant recent cases are China and Cuba: the former under Marxist direction from the beginning; the latter increasingly taking on a Marxist character as the revolution unfolds. It is important to see this as an organic development of Marxism rather than a mere contradiction or abandonment of Marx. Lenin's fundamental change of direction certainly altered the whole character of Marxism, but is it enough to say that in cutting it off from its former Western European context, and putting it in a new context, Lenin was simply per-verting its ideals? It is a matter of political judgement, but my own judgement is that this change of direction has in general served the cause of human liberation in a decisive way, and in a way essentially compatible with the original impetus of Marxism.

What we have then to look at is the effect on Marxist thought of this change of context. There seem to me to be two major and related effects. First, that since the revolutions have occurred in societies without mature democratic forms, the emphasis on a small, highly organized directing party has necessarily changed the whole previous conception of the working class taking power. Second, that the impetus of these revolutions, from the people, has been primarily the long peasant demand to break landlordism and exploitation of the labourer, while at the same time the necessary future of the country – not only as Marxist intellectuals see it but as economic survival and growth dictate – is an industrial future. The contradiction between noble but limited peasant aims and the demands of this industrial future has been the major problem of each of these revolutions as they develop, and in this situation the directing party has to some extent taken over from all immediate class interests. The major human suffering in the development of Soviet Communism was of precisely this character. In China and Cuba there have been differences, but in each we can see the same combination of a generalized liberation with an actual directing party. The immense cost to its first generations of any forced industrial revolution is exacted by the directing party from a people which the party can be seen in the long term to be liberating, but in the short term to be controlling with exceptional and often inhuman rigour. While this critical stage lasts, any threat to the ruling party, or to its definitions of policy, is mercilessly repressed.

It is not my purpose to defend these developments in Marxist theory and practice, but I think we have to make an effort to understand them, in the context in which they are actually operating. A Chinese or Cuban peasant is bound to see this process in ways different from any we can really imagine. At the same time, there is something ludicrous in the practice of Western Communist parties imitating the habits of thought and theories of organization deriving from wholly different social situations. Not only because they will then seem right out of touch with the reality of their own societies. But also because if they underwrite these developments as the twentieth-century version of Marxism as a whole, they lose their capacity, as Marxists, to define the course of these revolutions. For, even on the most favourable view, we are bound to recognize that the exercise of control by the directing party is always in danger of becoming an end in itself, in detail if not in general. The aim of social revolution can easily be perverted to the creation of a powerful industrial and military state: a perversion of which the elements of chauvinism in each of these revolutions give continual warning.

Yet it is not only Western Marxists who have this duty to keep their analysis clear. It is also, obviously, the capable Marxists within the directing parties themselves. And it is here that we must turn again to the relation between an ideology and the society in which it operates. I think we have a possible parallel in our own history. If we follow Christianity through the many and varied societies within which it has operated as an officially directive set of fundamental beliefs, we find, at first, no possible basis for optimism. For it seems to me clear that in many respects Christianity has survived as an official belief by adapting itself to the changing ideals and practices of the society which contains it. In its attitudes to class divisions, to moneymaking, and to love and the family, it has often changed like water, taking on the convenient colouring of the time. Will not the human ideals at the roots of Marxism similarly change, in Communist societies? Are not men and ideologists capable of endless self-deception, endless intellectual twisting, to achieve this marriage of convenience? It would be stupid to say, after the history of Marxist argument in the forty years of Soviet Communism, that the self-deception and the twisting have not occurred, in major ways: sometimes to a point where we want to give the whole thing up in disgust. It has seemed to make no difference that Christianity is other-worldly, and Marxism this-worldly. Christianity could gloss war and class-rule and materialism; Marxism has glossed terror and actual dictatorship. At this point it is easy to fall back, as Orwell fell back,[1]

---

1   While Anderson reads 'The Future of Marxism' as an indirect response to Thompson's criticisms of *The Long Revolution*, the essay is also a rejoinder to

on the feeling that all ideology is hypocrisy, to cover the realities of convenience and power.

Yet does this answer to our experience, in the end? It seems to me that in the history of Christianity, for example, alongside every example of official perversion and hypocrisy, there has been challenge of a Christian kind, based not on new beliefs but on the original beliefs. While the gospels are there, a basic kind of human feeling, relevant at any time and in any situation, is always potentially active. We have had uncountable thousands of cases of men moved by this feeling to challenge and sometimes to change the complex of dross and perversion which has been set over them. I see no valid reason why this will not also hold true of Marxism. Indeed it seems to me that already, in elements of the Polish and Hungarian revolutions, and also within the Soviet Union itself, this kind of challenge has been made and has not been wholly defeated. Many Christians would say that the underlying beliefs are of a different order: Christian values are timeless, Marxist values are limited and temporal. I cannot, myself, accept this distinction. The teaching of love is fundamental but so also is the teaching of freedom. I find it interesting that in Poland and Hungary, and in the writers of 'the thaw' in the Soviet Union, there was no significant turning to the values of a wholly alternative system; no turning, for example, to capitalist versions of freedom. The power of the challenge, in fact, was that the societies were being criticized in terms of their own system of values. Whenever this happens, there is a real dynamic, and a real possibility of change.

Orwell's writing on socialism. 'In the Britain of the fifties, along every road that you moved, the figure of Orwell seemed to be waiting', comments Williams in *Politics and Letters*. 'If you tried to develop a new kind of popular cultural analysis, there was Orwell; if you wanted to report on work or ordinary life, there was Orwell; if you engaged in any kind of socialist argument, there was an enormously inflated statue of Orwell warning you to go back. Down to the late 1960s political editorials in newspapers would regularly admonish younger socialists to read their Orwell and see where all that led to' (384). For an extended analysis of Orwell, see Williams, *Orwell* (1971), and the subsequent discussion of the book in *Politics and Letters*, 384–92.

Of course the governors and the high priests will do all they can to contain or suppress it, and their all is much. But I would say, against Orwell, that the evidence is that you cannot finally suppress a challenge of this kind: you can destroy those who make it, but not the ideas they embody. For the nominal source of the power of the rulers, the doctrine by which at worst they rationalize their controls, has to be disseminated. The gloss will go with it, of course, but I do not honestly see how anybody could go on disseminating the fundamental beliefs, aspirations, and images of Marxism, and successfully conceal from everyone that they compose a continually revolutionary doctrine. Nor do I myself believe that the ruling parties are engaged always and only in deception. At certain critical points, elements of the basic ideology emerge very clearly, not only to define the directions of the society, but also as the ground for conflict between groups within the parties. Communist politics has this evident difference from the kind of politics we see in our own ruling parties. Even in the sometimes bloody disputes, there are theoretical and absolute elements which suggest that it is still a basic doctrine that is being fought about, rather than a gloss for personal rule. Further, it is not, in my view, the worst of these groups that always wins. In the Soviet Union, for example, in recent years, it has been quite clearly one of the better groups.

For all these reasons, I think it is wrong to assume that Marxism as a set of active doctrines is finished. I am continually struck by the view of the world that has become orthodox among Western intellectuals in the years since the last war. The real world, as they see it, is the United States and Western Europe; the rest is divided between 'enemies' and 'neutrals': the former too evil to matter, the latter too backward to count. If Marxism seems irrelevant in the United States and Western Europe, it becomes, in this view, totally irrelevant – an 'old' idea. But even while they are saying this to each other, with almost incredible complacency, movements deriving from Marxism are decisively changing the shape and balance of world society.

The usual corollary of this North Atlantic viewpoint is that capitalism, while not exactly liked, has proved itself able to contain the socialist challenge in its own societies, which are consequently moving into a new post-capitalist stage: the open welfare state. People who go on using Marxist or even socialist arguments are then seen as merely sentimental fundamentalists, or cases of historical lag. Two things are overlooked by this new and confident orthodoxy. First, that whatever is happening within Western societies, our lives are in fact dominated by the spread of revolution elsewhere: not only as a matter of international relations, but as a matter of international economics and trade. As a socialist, I have to live within an alliance which exists either to destroy Communism (if it could be safely done) or to contain it. And all socialists in Western countries have to live with colonial policies which either seek to destroy or delay colonial revolutions (if either can be safely done) or seek to direct them into 'moderate' paths. With these issues at the centre of our political life, the struggle between socialists and others, in Western societies, becomes inevitably, in the first instance, a struggle over international issues. The peace movement, and the support of colonial liberation movements, are then the critical fields of our contemporary socialist activity. And it is not only that the struggle, in these fields, is still evidently alive and undecided. It seems also that the shape of Western society is itself being primarily determined by this international struggle, to which the open welfare state seems merely a marginal accompaniment. Indeed the continuation, in Britain, of this sense of an easy, improving society, seems to me to depend on ignoring the facts of international military struggle, which is changing us deeply from inside, and also on ignoring the facts about the changing nature of the world economy, which will hardly leave us to go comfortably on as we are.

I will not fight in the cold war, in either camp, and I do not want to replace it by some kind of economic war – a popular argument for economic change in Britain. Instead, I want to work out relations of a living kind, both with the Communist societies and with those parts of the world now losing their dependent status. The temptation, for some people here, is to go over to those other 'camps', but that would be an act of treason of a very deep kind. If what I have said about the actual political results of Marxist movements elsewhere is right, it is as impossible for me to underwrite their definitions and systems as it would be for me to join the reactionary forces which are trying to destroy them. This is not just a matter of national and political loyalties (though to lose them, for me, would be to lose everything). It is also, quite directly, a matter of theory. In fact in the older industrial societies the course of political development has been quite different. We who live in them have to interpret our own social experience, and it may be that certain traditions we have managed to keep alive, certain interpretations of new problems only encountered in mature industrial societies, will be critically important in the development of international socialism.

The independent Marxists of the West have been turning, recently, to the early thought of Marx, in particular to the concept of 'alienation'. At the same time, many non-Marxist socialists have been looking at the same set of problems: the relation between work and leisure; the nature of community; the problems of resisting manipulation within the expansion of culture. I do not know how far we have got, though I think we have made some progress. I cannot say that I myself find in early Marx anything more than a series of brilliant hints and guesses, but I may be wrong, and in any case the area of concern is common. I feel certain that this work can benefit our own societies, and I believe it may be of critical importance to the Communist societies as they develop. In any case, it will serve to define our relations to them. What we can offer is a tradition of critical independence and a tradition of active democracy, which in themselves do not compose socialism, but which are essential to any mature form of it. It we chuck those traditions, in the name of solidarity, we are chucking a great part of the future.

Perhaps the moral of all this is that the future of Marxism depends on a recovery of something like its whole tradition, and that this could happen in practice in the course of defining relations between our own socialist movements, the liberation movements of the industrially backward countries, and the developing Communist societies. The name of 'Marxism' will of course be fiercely claimed by each of these historically separate movements, and for my own part I would prefer to drop the struggle over the inheritance, and see the thing in a broader way. Marx was a great contributor to socialism. Inevitably, in actual history, his influence has been joined to other forces. The only thing that matters is the reality of socialism: the achievements of peace, freedom, and justice. Marx and many others, Marxists and many others, can contribute to this reality in many different ways. If Lenin took Marxism in one direction, because of the actual problems he faced, many Western socialists have taken socialism in another direction, because of their own actual problems. Neither movement has a monopoly of the truth; neither can dismiss the other as having no future. In the present world crisis, everything depends on the search for understanding, between varying traditions and peoples. The robots do not want this, but men want it.

1961

3

The Meanings of Work

It is surely necessary to talk about our work, in any society and at any time.[1] Of course, it's sometimes called talking shop: in some minds, almost a social crime. But we get the perspective on that from shop. The shutters up for the night; the man back in the parlour with his family; willed separation of this life at the table from what went on during the day, just the other side of that green baize door. Actually most of us have to talk about our work, just to get it done. To talk among ourselves, about what needs to be done and how it can best be done, is so natural that when it fades away into an uneasy silence we can usually be certain that something is wrong. This is the meaning of human work, as distinct from the energy of animals: an articulation of need, a definition

---

1   Originally published in *Work: Twenty Personal Accounts*, edited by Ronald Fraser (Harmondsworth: Penguin, with *New Left Review*, 1968), 280–98. New references and explanatory notes added by the editor. 'The Meanings of Work' is an afterword to the twenty accounts collated by Fraser, twelve of which are discussed by Williams in his essay. Those not covered by Williams include 'The Nightwatchman' by Tom Nairn, 'Producing the News' by Ronald Freeman, 'The Research Scientist' by John Playfair, 'The Solicitor' by David Chancery, 'The Copper' by Robert Bradley, 'The Programmer' by Keith Chesterton, 'The Croupiere [*sic*]' by Krii Ackers, and 'The Accountant' by Richard Fry.

of co-operative means, in what is felt and known to be a common condition.

Yet what is a common condition, or one known as common? In hardly any society is all people's work the same or even similar. If the men are all shepherds or fishermen, still the women's work is usually different. And as societies become more complicated, and the range of work extends, any simple community of situation becomes harder to realize and to talk about. At the same time, though, communication becomes necessary in new ways: since doing different work we are still involved with each other, affecting each other's lives. The older communication will continue, within a particular social or occupational group: a discussion of this work that we are doing, because it is our job. But between groups, or between individuals moving out of their groups, the character or the communication changes.

Some part of it, always, will be simply informative: how our kind of work is done. But even here, as a rule, this is different from the simple description that occurs within a working group. Sometimes the work has to be simplified, if what we think of, temporarily, as an outsider or a layman or the general public, is to understand it. Sometimes, again, we think that the man we are talking to, or his kind of man, or people in general, have the wrong idea about us and our work: we see our reflection in the other's eye, and we often don't recognize it or think it fair; we talk to make it a real reflection, of who we are and what we are doing, as opposed to a casual stereotype.

This is very complicated, because in addition to the obvious difficulties there are tensions between different groups, and what we say is affected by them. I have noticed often that people give different accounts of their jobs, take up different attitudes towards them, when they are talking among themselves and when they are talking to outsiders. This can range all the way from a kind of idealization – 'It's the greatest job in the world; just look at me' – to an extreme kind of deprecation – 'It's a shocking job, but don't think the worse of me for it'. Or we tell people what lousy work ours is, but would not like it if they agreed too wholeheartedly;

back in our own group we have come to some sort of terms about it. Or, again, we tell people what is wrong with the work and its conditions, as a way of altering them. This is often from the heart, but a good negotiator, for example, may learn it in the end as a matter of routine, just as a public relations officer, putting out some glamorized version of a job as a way of getting new people to do it or everyone to regard it more favourably, could switch accounts and do tomorrow for probation officers what he is doing today for the modern army.

In a complex society some kind of talk about work is inevitable, but it can range all the way from simple propaganda to actual exchanges of experience, and even within these actual exchanges it can range from the truth as we see it to the truth as we want others to see it. The most interesting area is in fact the relations between these kinds of truth: what we have felt and settled as our own experience, and what we can make common, with others, by talking to them.

It is certain that we shall only understand work, in any depth, if the discussion goes on long enough to get beyond public relations and simple bargaining, or their personal equivalents. If it goes on, that is, to the point where we can begin to talk about work, the common experience, in ways that make sense of our own experience of it and yet also extend to connect with the working experiences of others. In our own society this is, I believe, very difficult. It is not only the sheer variety of jobs and working conditions. It is also that in the conventions of the society (conventions which have a quite solid material base) we come to the discussion with certain built-in divisions: workers and members of staff, for example; or working-class jobs and middle-class jobs. The lines of division may be vague here or there, in an altering social structure, but we have to recognize that this is one conclusion of the discussion so far: that we can draw a rough line between some kinds of jobs and others, and go on to think of the people doing them, not just as distinct occupational groups but as social classes.

Thus for all the differences between four jobs – say, being a miner, a doctor, a bus driver, a solicitor – we tend as a matter of habit to offer, as our first common experience, a conventional grouping in which it seems self-evident that the miner and bus driver have something in common, and the doctor and the solicitor something else in common. This common experience of class division may seem a paradox, but it is so settled and pressing an experience that we have to go on talking about it until all its elements are clear. This is, I think, most likely to happen when we start from the working experience and go on from there, to some kind of common description, instead of starting from the conventional descriptions and trying to fit experiences in and to them. That is why I am glad that the arrangement of the essays in *Work* does not follow conventional lines;[1] that it is very different men and women, taking their turn to talk from their own experience outwards. I don't mean by this that radical questions about class differences, in different kinds of job, don't arise. They jump at one, consciously and sometimes unconsciously. But if, as I believe, the conventional class description conceals and is sometimes meant to conceal as much as it illuminates, then to start from actual men and women is right.

What the class description illuminates is surely evident. We can all compare the typical days of these men and women, and add in our own. As we come together in one day, this day, in different parts of Britain, we know we are faced with something more than technical differences in the jobs being carried out. We are faced with extraordinary differences in the money we are getting, in working conditions, in social atmospheres, in attitudes to the future. If we came together not in print but in a room, what else would be said, and what would be left unsaid? What groups would be formed? Who would drift across to whom? How long would this or that contact last? How much agreement would there be, given the information so far recorded, that this existing distribution of money, time, comfort, security, and respect is right or tolerable?

---

1   The essay has been given a light edit to enhance its reading as a stand-alone piece while minor changes have been made to avoid confusion. For example, 'this book' has been changed to *Work* in this sentence.

I can only guess at these answers, but I know I don't find the distribution right or tolerable myself, and this not only on class lines. I find myself asking questions about the relative importance of this or that kind of work, and the way this is now practically assessed in a continuing social structure. I imagine an incomes policy, an incomes board, which has taken this real evidence in public, following the human consequences through, and I am sure that this is enough to make what is now called an incomes policy, shuffling its familiar counters of norms and percentages and conventional rates, a caricature of what it should be. We are faced here with real men and women, and not with anonymous categories. What the class description confirms in real inequalities it also usually hides, by making them differences between groups when the differences actually occur between people. There's the need for equity, and for that, of course, we need classifications. But there's also the need for meaning and there the classifications won't help us: we're at the point where we're not only workers, the usual stereotype, but through this, before and after it, there while the work is being done, men and women.

Take, for example, a very simple test of meaning: whether we do work so obviously useful that we have only to describe it, not justify it. I don't think that division comes on class lines. And I'm sure this is right. Of course some unfamiliar jobs have as yet no settled valuations; we can't assume that our habitual responses, about useful and less useful work, are always right, though it's right to compare them, in an open-minded way, with the conventional responses of our actual society, as expressed in rewards and respect. Nobody in his senses, I'd assume, would then believe that usefulness, in its most general human sense, is what decides our social order. But even if it did, that isn't the only question. To be useful is also to be used. The problem of meaning isn't only between how we see the job and how others see it. It's also between how we see the job and how we see ourselves: a question of how much of what we are goes into, gets a chance in, our work; does it diminish us or confirm us, in our own deepest feelings? And these answers needn't correspond to what pass for general answers, about being useful and respected. What we're asking, there, is about the deepest meaning of work. It seems like a personal question, as it's usually put. It's only when we discover that many of us are asking it, in comparable ways, that we can make it what in the end it must be: a social question. I'll give my own answers, as a way of continuing the question: answers as arguments.

What in Britain we usually mean by class are the surface differences: important enough, but not in the end decisive. We ask what renumeration we get, for doing this or that job. We ask much less often how it came about that we are doing this job and not that: how this direction of our energy was actually arrived at. There's the relation between jobs and education, which of course isn't only between our work and the education we wanted, but between the work and the education we were able to get. There are many variations in these histories: no simple correlation, for example, between early leaving and the sort of work eventually done, though a general relation of that kind quite clearly exists. What we see, I think, in and through these examples, is a particular social order, providing different kinds of education, at a period in our lives before we are really conscious of it and its consequences. It's deeply influential, the way it's distributed, but not mechanically determining: there are recoveries, new starts, changes of direction, opportunities and checks. The way these come, though, is also a social order: the chances are given, to do this or this, in precise ways. Only a few of these histories are in any real sense made; most, it is recognized, are determined by others.

But if and when we realize this we have to look again at what work now ordinarily means. In its most general sense, it is the process of giving human energy to a desired end. Yet we have only to say this to know that, in our kind of society, there is a gap, sometimes very wide, between this general meaning and what we actually do. This can be seen in two ways. The woman bringing up children and keeping a house going, often in bad conditions and for very long hours, isn't generally said to be *working*. She is only said to be that, a working wife or mother, if she goes out and does something else. And this distinction isn't made by a criterion of either usefulness or fulfilment. She may go out to teach children or to help to make something she and others need. She may be following an interest or a vocation that fulfils her. But it is just as likely that she has gone out to carry tea or write letters for somebody who finds it convenient to have her there: some of the old domestic service, which is supposed to have disappeared, has been simply transferred from homes to offices, and then called a career.

Or consider the man who comes home from a factory and goes out to his garden for two or three hours: the factory is work, but the garden is a hobby. Though there's no necessary difference, in the energy he applies, and if there's a difference about the desirability of the end, it's often in the garden's favour. Or the man who comes home from what he thinks of as work and goes out to give his time and energy to running a society or a trade union or a political party: that exhausting effort is called, of all significant names, voluntary work. There's a point made by Bill Jones towards the end of his essay ('Driving the Bus') that is surely true about many thousands of other people. Of the job itself – the *recognized* work of driving the bus – he says: 'If I were twenty-four years of age today you could stick this job on the buses where the monkey is reputed to stick his nuts.' But he at once adds: 'In the meantime there is still plenty of work to be done for the lads.'[1] And he has already said: 'To say that I have enjoyed every moment of my trade-union activity would be an understatement.'[2] When we look at that trade-union work, at the struggle and exposure it led to as well as the long organizing effort, we find that it answers better to the most general meaning of work than the conventional job; yet it was clearly a hard fight even to get it recognized as work at all.

---

1   Jones, 'Driving the Bus', *Work*, 217. An autobiographical note is included at the end of each of the twenty accounts. Jones recounts how he served in the First World War, joined the Communist Party in the 1930s (leaving after the crushing of the Hungarian Revolution in 1956), founded the London Busmen's Rank and File Movement, and led the 1937 Coronation strike before being expelled from the Transport and General Workers' Union, to which, by 1968, he had returned as vice-president.

2   Ibid.

The examples could be multiplied, but the main point is clear. A great deal of energy, given to the most ordinary human needs, is not, in our kind of society, given sanction as work; it is dismissed as voluntary, a spare-time or even an unofficial activity.

This point is related to the second way in which we can see the gap between what we call work and its most general definition. Even when we are doing what is socially recognized as work, in the conventional sense, many of us would hesitate before calling it giving human energy to a personally desired end. Or rather, if we had to say what the desired end was, we would often simply say money: not the work itself, but that by-product of doing it. As Dennis Johnson ('Factory Time') says, quite fairly:

> People who speak grandiosely of the 'meaning of work' should spend a year or two in a factory. The modern worker neither gives anything to work nor expects anything (apart from his wages) from it. Work, at factory level, has no inherent value. The worker's one interest is in his pay-packet.[1]

He adds, also fairly: 'The accent on money is understandable – after all, we are shorter of it than most.'[2] But the same sort of emphasis can be found where it isn't a case of low wages. As Jill Neville ends her essay ('Writing the Ads'):

> The fact is, I earn my living as a copywriter. I can't possibly be proud of it. But I must stop feeling so ashamed. 'I'm a copywriter', I say in a ringing voice. And if I'm drunk I add: 'I just have not got the moral strength to refuse all that lovely money.'[3]

---

1   Johnson, 'Factory Time', *Work*, 12. Johnson was from a Nottingham-shire mining family and worked as an electrician's mate in a cigarette factory for seventeen years. In 1968, he was studying literature at Ruskin College, Oxford.

2   Ibid.

3   Neville, 'Writing the Ads', *Work*, 165. Neville was an Australian author who moved to London in 1951. In 1968 – living with her brother Richard, the editor of *Oz* – she had already published her first novel (*Fall-Girl* in 1966) and would go on to publish another six, alongside writing poetry and a play, before her death in 2011.

There are ambiguities in the reduction of the meaning of work to money, over the whole range of personal tones from assured and justified complaint to a wry, half-meant apology. But the problem of the absence of other meanings is persistent. As Philip Callow ('The Clerk') puts it:

> The basic fact remains though that, in common with the other jobs I've had, it has no value as work. It is drudgery done in congenial surroundings. You feel dispensable, interim: automation will take it over one day, the sooner the better. You are there for the money, no other reason. You begrudge the time.[1]

Or Bryan Slater ('On the Line'):

> My work comes to me in a completely automatic way, in the gestures of an automaton. With a rag wrapped round my eyes I could still do it, and could do dozens before I realized that I had done any at all. But underneath this my mind never stops working. It lives by itself. Some call it dreaming, and if so, I am dreaming all day long, five days a week. The whole bench dreams like this. It is a galley of automatons locked in dreams. Someone who has something to say to you has to come right up to your ear and scream into it before you can wake up or answer. If you aren't working – or dreaming – in this way, you say you aren't in the swing of it, and you do less of your stint [...]. If you didn't dream at work it would send you mad.[2]

---

1   Callow, 'The Clerk', *Work*, 58–9. Callow, born in Birmingham, was living in Cornwall when 'The Clerk' was published and – after penning eight books, including works of fiction, short stories, essays, and poetry – had just started working full-time as a writer following an Arts Council bursary. He would go on to write more than a dozen novels and a series of biographies of writers and painters such as D. H. Lawrence, Walt Whitman, Paul Cézanne, and Vincent Van Gogh.

2   Slater, 'On the Line', *Work*, 97–8 and 99. Slater was born in Nottingham and worked in the Raleigh factory. In 1968, he was living in a council flat in Shropshire and was a member of both the Amalgamated Engineering Union and the Labour Party, while harbouring ambitions to paint.

This experience is obviously more true of some jobs than others, though it is worth emphasizing that it is not – as is sometimes suggested – confined to repetitive work on a factory line. But to the degree that it is a general experience, it is necessary to insist that we then look at the work and not, in a stereotyped way, at the workers. Feeling like this about their own work, and its lack of connection with more important parts of their lives, some people can feel that it's different for others; it doesn't affect them so much. We can't tell, of course. We would need the whole general experience on record. But as we limit ourselves at work, performing only an external role, it is very easy for us to see each other – to see the generalized others – as limited and external. The part of our own life which is not available and manifest is well known to us, even though it is not communicated; but then it is obviously difficult to have this kind of private information about others. What then often happens is that they are seen in a way in which we would never see ourselves: as typically limited workers, who ask no more than they are getting. The whole problem of meaning in work can then be evaded, in the same way that the problem of meaning in leisure is evaded by quick phrases about the bingo-happy masses. That is why it is useful to have Bryan Slater reminding us, from his experience, that:

> A man isn't just born to be a worker, like the bees, and nothing else. I'm sure every man can do something good for his life, apart from just slave all the time. You might not think so though if you listen to people who have never put their heads inside a factory gate.[1]

What happens, really, as men and women begin to speak, is a breaking down of many of the conventional class images about workers. The bus driver, the uniformed figure just glimpsed as part of the machine that is stopping for us, becomes Bill Jones ('Driving the Bus') who has just said, in a connecting language: 'Because it's early and passengers are few and far between, it's possible to take a second look across the bridge to the Tower of

---

1   Ibid., 103–4.

London – a great grey mass in the early light.'[1] Or, from another direction, we find Suzanne Gail ('The Housewife') acknowledging just the shock – the necessary shock – that comes when we ourselves are in the position of men and women whom we had conventionally reduced to workers. After her first experiences of the difficulty of housework, she was, she writes, 'humbled by the discovery that what I had considered work fit only for fools was beyond my capacity.'[2] And we can turn this recognition round, to look at it another way. There may, indeed, be work fit only for fools, but it is being done, at an unknown cost, by actual men and women, many of them aware of this situation, though to make this awareness common, and to carry the response right through, would be to revolutionize a whole social order.

On the other hand many people get satisfaction from their work, or from parts of it. In advertisements, of a recruiting kind, everybody seems delighted with his work; we all know, by now, that familiar and come-hither beam. And this makes it difficult for us to get past what is now a widespread suspicion of flannel. Even some actual accounts have a tinge of public relations, or of that personal equivalent when we are presenting, for rather distant others, a carefully composed self-portrait. But many of us would respond, I think, to what Robert Powley ('Selling for a Living') says: 'Like most people, I enjoy working wholeheartedly when I work.'[3] Though we would then have to notice that he says this when he is making up his mind to get out of a particular job, where such wholeheartedness wouldn't really be possible. Or look again at Matthew Raison's ('The House-surgeon') description of his job as a houseman as 'the nearest thing to voluntary slavery I

---

1   Jones, 'Driving the Bus', 206.

2   Gail, 'The Housewife', *Work*, 141. Gail was a university graduate who had just given birth to her second child when 'The Housewife' was published; she had subsequently resumed her postgraduate research.

3   Powley, 'Selling for a Living', *Work*, 136. Powley, born in Islington, worked in sales after leaving Holloway Grammar School before training to become a teacher and working as a lecturer at a teacher training college in London.

can think of'.[1] 'Done properly' it is so,[2] he says as a necessary qualification; but then that whole criterion – the essential meaning
of the work in an understandable tension with its objective difficulties – is the substance of what he tells us, and satisfaction and
dissatisfaction are parts of the same process, as the meaning and
the available conditions interlock, with a man in the middle. Or
consider what Hope Wise ('The Signalwoman') has to say about
her job on the railways: the satisfaction and the pride, against the
physical difficulties of that morning when everything is frozen
solid; and her observation of the engine driver getting down for
the last time, or the signalman breaking his nonchalance in a
sudden shared excitement.[3] If work did not include meanings and
experiences like this, there would be no problem: only a total and
common nullity. This comes out very clearly in the experience of
being deprived of a job, by some decision made elsewhere and by
others. Jock Keenan's moving description of being made unemployed ('On the Dole') is also a record of the gap in the meaning
of work. The bitterness is wholly justified, a man's voice breaking
through that other conventional stereotype of a lovely idleness,
the sheer absence of hard work: 'Lovely life if you happen to be a
turnip. But I am not a turnip, mate. I am a thoughtful, sensitive,
widely read man.'[4] In that whole account, we get the full complexity of this problem of meaning:

---

1   Raison, 'The House-surgeon', *Work*, 80. Raison was an Oxford graduate who qualified as a doctor in 1965, following in the footsteps of his father.
Three years later he was working as a GP in the Midlands with ambitions to
go into teaching.

2   Ibid.

3   Wise, in 'The Signalwoman', offers an account of life on the railways
which would be familiar to Williams, whose father was a signalman in Pandy.
Wise was born in Lancashire in 1934 and – after leaving school at fourteen –
had also worked as a housemaid, shop assistant, nurse, and bus conductress.

4   Keenan, 'On the Dole', *Work*, 274. Keenan was an unemployed miner,
originally from Fife, who had served in India during the Second World War
and was a member of the Communist Party until 1955.

> Frankly, I hate work. Of course I could also say with equal truth that
> I love work; that it is a supremely interesting activity; that it is often
> fascinating; that I wish I didn't have to do it; that I wish I had a job at
> which I could earn a decent wage. That makes six subjective statements
> about work and all of them are true for me.[1]

True, also, I think, for many others. It is how the gap is experienced. At just this point, if we are not careful, we could fall back on what we find available in an ordinary social mode: worldly-wise observations about the contrariness of human nature. But this won't do. The contradictions are in the real situation. It is a fact that most men and women want to make their own living: to do something that gives meaning, a way of making a life, and to get back from the activity not only the physical means to live but also a confirmation of significance, of the process of being oneself and alive in this unique way. The ordinary and inevitable kind of complaint, as the effort tires us or as the factual problems and difficulties appear, is a kind of energy, really: a way of dealing with fatigue and obstacles by talking about them if only, at first, to oneself. This is radically different, though in experience it can be made to seem the same, from the exhaustion and frustration which are not there in the work process itself but in the way it is organized.

Look at what Robert Doyle ('The Print Jungle') says, near the beginning of his essay, about the change in the feel of his work, as well as the more obvious changes of actual daily routine, when his firm was taken over.[2] There is no idealization of the earlier

---

1   Ibid., 273.

2   Doyle, in 'The Print Jungle', describes his job at a printing company – formerly the Amalgamated Press before it was bought out by the Mirror Group – as being in constant peril. 'For the unthinking there was some justification in believing that this new and formidable concentration of capital offered certain security for all time', he notes. 'But the latent fears of many, including my own, were soon to be justified by closures, rationalizations, streamlining and automation' (*Work*, 22). Dublin-born Doyle, known as Bob, joined the IRA as a teenager and then the Communist Party before signing up to fight with the International Brigades in Spain. He was captured by the

work, but what he says about demoralization is closely related
to a sharper perception, from just this experience of takeover, of
what he calls the jungle. The same point is clear in Clint Forsyth's
remarkable account ('The Technician'), where a quite unidealized
meaning and satisfaction, itself significantly related to the admis-
sion of difficulties and shortcomings, is shown in detail in the
process of being eroded and finally destroyed, again in a takeover;
a quite different conception of what the work really is – a suppres-
sion of its real content in favour of profit and public relations, in
the selling policy of the new controllers – slowly discloses itself
and is recognized as governing.[1] In cases like these we see the gap
actually opening, and this is especially important.

From almost every account of work we come to see that there
is never only a work process, of the kind that is usually abstracted:
a set of operations on things. There is also, whether recognized
or not, a set of social relationships, which in experience are quite
inextricable from the work. In organizing the work, these real
relationships have defined it; a change of social organization can
change the definition. It follows that we can only properly explore
the meanings of work if we explore this kind of organization:
whether by asking how we come to be doing a particular job, or
by asking why it is being done in this way and not that.

Take the first question first. If work often means that we have
to do what we would never freely choose to do, what kind of fact
is that? There are obvious cases where there are unpleasant jobs
to be done, that all other things being equal we wouldn't do, and
we do them, sometimes, because we see in the end that it isn't a

Italian army and held captive for a year. He later joined the Royal Navy – and
fought in the Second World War – but was dismissed after being arrested at
an anti-fascist rally in the East End, demonstrating against Oswald Mosley. He
died in 2009, aged ninety-two.

1   In 'The Technician', Forsyth describes a long process through which
his ambitions were thwarted and his spirit crushed by the manoeuvring of
management at the farm machinery manufacturers where he worked. '[D]isil-
lusioned about loyalty, convinced that sales techniques now took precedence
over quality', he concludes, 'I finally indulged my boredom and resigned to set
out on my own' (*Work*, 230).

conflict between desire and reality, but that the desire and the reality include each other: clearing up a mess, getting something out of the way, saying something difficult that absolutely has to be said. All of us do jobs like this, not because we want to do them as such, but because we see them as necessary, if the desire and the reality are to meet. But then what is characteristic of our kind of society is that the relation between desire and reality has been specialized and, as it seems, set beyond us. This isn't just that we can only do what we want if we do at least some other things that other people want. Such a fact is a condition of any society: the basis of any co-operative effort and common responsibility. But it can be specialized, and interpreted in particular ways, until it becomes a travesty of itself: a rhetoric surrounding an absence of meaning. What the rhetoric covers, in our own society, is the actual source of the decisions about what work is to be done and how it is to be done. To discover this real source, to follow the questions right through, is to see the reason for the gap between what work means and what much of it has been made to mean.

What is the reason why the woman bringing up her children, the man digging his garden, the men and women running societies, are not said conventionally, to be workers? They are *working* but not *workers* while they are doing that: a strange paradox. But the explanation is simple. They are not, though working, engaged in wage-labour for another; or in the performance of services for a salary or a fee. Some women, it is true, are in effect employed by their husbands; what they get, as housekeeping, is even spoken of as a wage by the husband. Yet that only brings this most immediate and personal of activities within the larger and dominant system: what most men and women would do anyway, looking after their children and their house, is specialized to the woman and reduced, by analogy, to the habits of thought of the impersonal system outside. This is a common and persistent degradation, in which a real desire is exploited and made to conform with an imposed and external reality. The weakness and exposure of women, while they are bearing children, has been used to impose what is not reality but a particular method of organization. Yet as such it is only a dramatic example of a common condition, in which both men and women are exposed and then used. The man who treats his wife as a special kind of wage- or fee-servant is only doing to her what has usually already been done to him. His work, springing from his desire to make his living in the world, has been accepted only on terms set by others. What he wants to give his energy to has to fit in with that system. Anything else he devotes his energy to will not, in such a society, be socially recognized as work. It will be what he does in what is called his own time.

Once again, the decision about what needs to be done, about what is worth giving his energy to, is usually not made by him, or by co-operation with others. It is made by those who, as it is usually put, have work to offer. Who are these people and how do they come to be in such a position, that they can decide what work there is and how it is to be done? The simple answer used to be the rich: if you have money, you can employ others. This is still often true, and it ranges all the way from the really rich, who can employ a houseful of servants, to the man or woman who sets aside a part of their own personal income to get some part-time service. But it isn't the possession of money, as such, that decides work. It is the possession of a very different thing: capital, not a store of currency to be dipped into to get some service done, but a store, an organization, of labour, and of the means of labour. Most work can only be done if its means are provided: tools, materials, workplaces, outlets. But then the decision about what work will actually be done, and how, falls to those who own or control these means. This, fundamentally, is capitalism. The means of work have passed into the hands of the minority who own this necessary capital and who are alone in a position, in a developing society, to begin new major enterprises. What is really social capital – the product of generations of co-operative work – has passed into the hands of a small group who then, as they say, have work to offer to others; or, as they more often say, have a need for an abstract thing they call labour (the labour market – that is, the energy of other men and women – is treated factually on the same level as that other requirement for the things which are raw materials).

This is the real root of the class system. What is often called a protest against class is no more than a secondary protest, about opportunities or treatment or attitudes within this system. This is an important area of tension and complaint but it must be seen as secondary to the basic process, which settles what work and what conditions of work are available at all.

The meaning of work, in such a system, is reduced, against all other human interests, to a profitable return on the investment of capital. Labour is wage-labour, and to find meanings of work in wages alone is a shadow – a real shadow – of this command-ing fact, by which men's freedom to direct their own energies has been practically limited for so long that it can pass as a fact of nature. There has, of course, been an important and widespread revolt against such a system. Generations of men and women have fought for the recovery of the means of labour, by a system of common ownership. In some areas – education, and the social services – work has been defined as a public service, subject to democratic direction and control. This was also one of the mean-ings of the demand for the public ownership of industry, and it is said that this has happened in our nationalized corporations. But we have only to look at the experience of anyone working in edu-cation or the social services or in one of the nationalized industries to know that in practice the alienation is still real: this is not, all the way through, free and co-operative effort, but is still subject, sometimes grossly, to external and seemingly arbitrary controls.

The reasons for this are important. It is not only that the nationalized industries have been instructed to fit in with a capi-talist economy, and to conduct their operations on what are called ordinary commercial lines, which is to say, choosing work accord-ing to whether it is profitable rather than whether it is, on general grounds, necessary. It is also that the basic organization of work – in these new services as in the old – has been made to conform with the kind of relationships that were so deeply learned when the power to direct other men's work was factually, by the possession of capital, in minority hands. Thus an authoritarian structure – what is euphemistically called the chain of command – is imposed on areas of work which are supposed to be and in fact often are socially owned and subject to open democratic decision. Because nowadays people usually resent authoritarian methods there is, of course, a constant attempt to disguise this reality. There is talk of human relations in industry but these, characteristically, are the human relations that are possible – information, politeness, outings, sports fields, office parties, speeches – after the decisive human relations, of who decides what is to be done and how, have been settled and built in. It is even called, in the trade, man-management, which means, quite frankly, keeping people happy while they are working for you.

If we are ever to recover effective control over the direction of the energy that we call work we shall have, it is clear, to call for more than common ownership, though we shall certainly have to call for that. Common ownership will only mean anything, in practice, if it is experienced where it matters, when decisions are being made: first-order decisions, not merely their second-and-third-order consequences. Because so much work is necessarily co-operative, many of us have some experience of the process of making decisions co-operatively: often, indeed, in a sort of under-world, before head office or 'they' get to know about it, or after they have gone home and left us to get the job done. It is never an easy process; it is often quarrelsome; sometimes it even releases disturbing emotions that an authoritarian system had appeared to avoid or to control. But then what comes out is what is at stake, all the time, in the actual direction of our energies.

Men can learn to live with their frustration, at a cost that has never been reckoned because the consequences appear so often as personal breakdown or degeneration, which are not easily referred, in our orthodox thinking, to their real social causes. It can be hard to break from this built-in frustration or from the resigned habits of cynicism directed at others and at oneself. The kind of courage that is necessary, to break the mould and start taking full responsibility for everything we are doing, everything we are giving our energy to, is bound at first to be rare. Yet it has in fact come as often from men already physically driven and exhausted, with a living to lose and a family at stake, as from men with more time, more ease, more immediate freedom to stand up as themselves. And because this is so there are good grounds for hope. Nothing is now more important in British society than the detailed thinking and practice of workers' control: the key idea of the self-managing co-operative enterprise, which is now the most living part of the socialist movement, and which has already passed from the simpler ideas appropriate to small-scale institutions, to complex and far-reaching ideas which explore the practices of control in large-scale and technically complicated industries. There is very much yet to be done, but these advanced ideas are the necessary response to a technically advancing economy. Men can gain more control, not less, when the jobs that demean or exhaust them can quite practically be mechanized or automated. If these techniques are used to reduce what is called the cost of labour – a typically capitalist interpretation that is now very prevalent – there is no hopeful future in them, only unemployment and still further loss of meaning. But if they are used to reduce not cost but labour, that is to relieve and release human energy for our own purposes, they are the means of a liberation which has often seemed only a dream.

This will only happen, though, if we are all making the essential decision, and to get to that point is a very hard and long fight. What is now called Luddism, or wildcat militancy, is very often, at root, a fight of this kind: to use the machines, rather than to be used by them; to impose a new social organization, where decisions are made by the men actually doing the work, as against an old organization in which decisions are invariably made elsewhere; to learn, if only in the first instance by the co-operative revolts that we call strikes, the means of a new human order. It is all hard and confused, consistently misrepresented by those with a stake in the present system and by all their associates who have converted most other men into workers, and ask only how they may be persuaded, induced or cajoled into continued production on the terms set by a minority. This conflict of ideas and actions is now at the centre of our history.

As we follow through the meanings of work we come, necessarily, to these major issues and decisions. But we have always to
remind ourselves that they run back, in detail, to quite ordinary
days, to quite local issues, to problems of feeling and description
that have to be lived through where we are. To have the chance to
work with and for people, rather than with and for things or bits
of paper: that chance is what our technology now gives us, though
under its present direction it takes the techniques as primary and
only then considers what it absurdly calls the human element.
Back where we live and work, in our only element, as whole
human beings, the choices and conflicts are often far from clear;
there is too much to do, of an immediate kind, whether we look
forward to it or kick against it or just quietly curse. Back where
we live and work, this very day, in Britain, it is hard to know and
agree on a common situation. That is where we start and end, on
our own, easily impatient of that general world we both glimpse
and draw back from: that we have got in touch, with ourselves
and with others, in new ways; that we have started to talk, on our
own behalf, about these crucial experiences; that work is not only
the bus, the computer, the print-shop, the hospital, the signal box,
the assembly line, the office, but through these very particulars is
an experience we are sharing, valuing, trying to clarify. We have
come this far, that we are talking about work: our own work and
yet not just our own work; a social fact made out of our personal
accounts. It is an important step forward, and it is clear that we
must try to go on talking and listening.

1968

4

Marxist Cultural Theory

Any modern approach to a Marxist theory of culture must begin
by considering the proposition of a determining base and a determined superstructure.[1] From a strictly theoretical point of view
this is not, in fact, where we might choose to begin. It would be
in many ways preferable if we could begin from a proposition
which originally was equally central, equally authentic: namely
the proposition that social being determines consciousness. It is
not that the two propositions necessarily deny each other or are
in contradiction. But it is the case that the proposition of base and
superstructure, with its figurative element, with its suggestion of
a definite and firm and fixed spatial relationship, constitutes, at
least in certain hands, a very specialized and at times unacceptable version of the other proposition. And it is the fact that in

---

1 'This is a re-recorded version of a lecture originally given in Montreal
in April 1973', wrote Williams on the sleeve of a recording of the lecture held
in the Williams family archive. 'It is a summary of 6 lectures given in Cambridge and Stanford in 1972 and 1973, and these will be the basis of a volume
on Marxism and Literature to be published by Oxford in 1975.' The lightly
edited transcription and explanatory notes are by the editor. First published as
'Base and Superstructure in Marxist Cultural Theory', *New Left Review*, I/82,
Nov–Dec 1973.

the transition from Marx to Marxism, and in the development of mainstream Marxism itself, the proposition of the determining base and the determined superstructure has been held to be the key to Marxist cultural analysis.

Now it is important, as we try to analyse this proposition, to be aware that the term of relationship which is involved, that is to say 'determines', is of great linguistic and real complexity. The language of determination, of determinism, is in fact inherited from idealist and theological accounts of the world and of man. It is in one of his familiar inversions, his contradictions of received propositions, that Marx uses the word 'determine' from an ideology that had been insistent on the power of certain forces outside man. Now that implication does not of course have to be taken over, indeed Marx's proposition explicitly denies it, and puts the origin of determination in man's own activities. Nevertheless, the particular history of the term serves to remind us that there are, within ordinary use – and this is true in most of the major European languages – possible, quite different, meanings and implications of the word 'determine'. There is, on the one hand, from its theological inheritance, the notion of that external cause which totally predicts or prefigures, totally controls, a subsequent activity. But there is also, from the experience of social practice, and from a wide range of experience, the notion of determination as setting limits, exerting pressures in very firm ways.[1]

One is not withdrawing the kind of claim that Marx had in mind but there clearly is a difference between a process of setting limits and exerting pressures, which is one meaning of determination, and a process in which a subsequent content is essentially prefigured, predicted, and controlled by a pre-existing external quality. We cannot fail to observe, looking at some applications of Marxist cultural analysis, that it is the second sense, the notion of prefiguration, prediction, and control, which has often, explicitly or implicitly, been used.

---

1   See Williams's entry for 'Determine' in *Keywords: A Vocabulary of Culture and Society* (1976; Glasgow: Fontana, 1988), 98–102.

The active relationship then is the first thing that we have to examine in this proposition, but then we go on to look at the terms themselves. Superstructure in fact has had a good deal more attention. People talk of *the* superstructure, although it is interesting that originally the term could be plural. People have talked of the different activities 'inside' the superstructure or superstructures. In fact already in Marx himself, in the later correspondence of Engels, and at many points in the subsequent Marxist tradition, qualifications began to be made about the nature of certain superstructural activities. The first kind of qualification had to do with delays in time, with complications, and with certain indirect relationships. The simple notion, which is still by no means entirely abandoned, of a superstructure had been the reflection, the imitation, the reproduction of the reality of the base in the cultural superstructure in a more or less direct way. Positivist notions of reflection and reproduction of course directly supported this. But since there are many real cultural activities in which this relationship cannot be found, or cannot without effort or even violence to the material be found, the notion was introduced of delays in time, the famous lags, of complications, of indirectness, as certain kinds of activity in the cultural sphere found themselves at a greater or lesser distance from primary economic activities. That was the first stage of qualification of the notion of superstructure. And the second stage was related but more fundamental, in that the relationship itself was more substantially looked at. This is the reconsideration which gave rise to a notion like mediation, that in the cultural process something more than a simple reflection or reproduction occurs. Or in the twentieth century with the notion of 'homologous structures', there may be no direct or easily apparent similarity, certainly no case of reproduction, between the superstructural process and the reality of the base, but there will be an essential homology of the structures which can be discovered by analysis. This is not the same as mediation but it is the same kind of amendment in that the relationship between the base and the superstructure is not supposed to be direct, not only that it's subject to lags and complications and indirectness, but almost and of its nature it is not direct reproduction.

Now of course, these qualifications and amendments are important but it does seem to me that what has not been looked at with equal care is the notion of the base. Indeed it seems to me that the base is the more important concept to look at if we are to understand the notion of cultural process. For it is quite clear that in many uses of this proposition, uses of the proposition as a formula, *the* base has come to be considered virtually as an object, or in less crude cases, it has come to be considered in essentially uniform and often static ways; the base is the real social existence of man; the base is the real relations of production corresponding to a stage of the development of material productive forces; or the base is a mode of production at a particular stage of its development. Now the difficulty about this is that while such a stage can be properly discovered and made precise by analysis, it is never in practice either uniform or static, except for the purposes of an essentially abstract analysis. It is indeed one of the central propositions of Marx's sense of history that there are deep contradictions in the relationships of production and in the consequent social relationships. There is not only deep contradiction but in relation to this a continual possibility of the variation of forces. And these again, when they are considered, as Marx always urged, as the activities of real man, amount to something very much more active, more complicated, and more contradictory than the developed metaphorical notion of *the* base could possibly allow us to realize.

So we have to say that when we talk of the base, we are talking of a process and not a state. And we cannot ascribe to that process certain fixed properties for subsequent deduction to the variable processes of the superstructure. Most people who have wanted to make the proposition more reasonable have concentrated on refining the notion of superstructure. I would say that each term of the proposition has to be revalued in a particular direction. The revaluation of the notion of determination to the notion of the setting of limits and the exertion of pressures. The revaluation of the notion of superstructure to the notion of a range of cultural practices, but crucially the revaluation of the notion of the base to the specific activities of man in real social and economic relationships, which contain fundamental contradictions and variations and which are therefore always in a state of dynamic process.

Now it's worth observing a further implication behind the customary definitions. The base has come to include, especially in certain twentieth-century developments of theory, a strong sense of basic industry. The emphasis on heavy industry, even, has played a certain part. And a particular way in which this emphasis can be picked up is to consider the notion of productive forces, because clearly what we are examining in the base is primary productive forces. Now I think that some very crucial distinctions have to be made here, they would take more time than I have in this present lecture, but these to begin with. It is true that in his analysis of capitalist production Marx considered productive work in a very particular and specialized sense corresponding to that mode of production. There is a difficult passage in the *Grundrisse* (1857–58) in which he argues that the man who makes a piano is a productive worker, but in which there's a real question whether the man who distributes the piano is a productive worker.[1] And

---

1   Included as an extended note in the third of his notebooks, Marx writes: 'What is *productive labour* and what is *not*, a point very much disputed back and forth since Adam Smith made this distinction, has to emerge from the dissection of the various aspects of capital itself. *Productive labour* is only that which produces *capital*. Is it not crazy, asks [Nassau William] Senior, that the piano maker is a *productive worker*, but not the *piano player*, although obviously the piano would be absurd without the piano player? But this is exactly the case. The piano maker reproduces *capital*; the pianist only exchanges his labour for revenue. But doesn't the pianist produce music and satisfy our musical ear, does he not even to a certain extent produce the latter? He does indeed: his labour produces something; but that does not make it *productive labour* in the *economic sense*; no more than the labour of the madman who produces delusions is productive. *Labour becomes productive only by producing its own opposite*', *Grundrisse* (1973; Harmondsworth: Penguin with *New Left Review*, 1993), 305. Written during the winter of 1857–58, Marx's notebooks were first translated into English in 1973, the year of Williams's lecture on 'Marxist Cultural Theory'.

there is really no question at all about whether the man who plays
the piano, whether to himself or to others (these are crucially different), is a productive worker at all. The point in that particular
application is perhaps hardly worth pursuing but it is very important to recognize that when Marx was engaged in an analysis of a
particular kind of production, namely commodity production,
he had to give to the notion of productive forces a specialized
sense of primary work on materials in a form which produced
commodities, which is narrowed remarkably, and in this context
very damagingly, from the original notion of productive forces,
in which, just to give brief reminders, the most important thing
a worker ever produces is himself, himself in the fact of that kind
of labour, or the broader historical emphasis of men producing
themselves, themselves and their history. Now when you talk of
the base, and you talk of primary productive forces, it matters
very much whether you are referring, as in one degenerate form
of this proposition became habitual, to primary production in
an economic sense or whether you are referring to the primary
production of society itself through the means of material production and reproduction of real life. If we have the broad sense
of productive forces, then we look at the whole question of the
base differently, and of course we are less tempted to dismiss as
superstructural, as merely secondary, certain vital productive
social forces, which are in that sense, from the beginning, basic.

Now, because of the difficulties of this ordinary proposition,
the practical difficulties of applying the crude formula which in
some hands the proposition of base and superstructure became,
you got an alternative and very important development, the
emphasis associated primarily with Lukács, on a social totality.[1]

---

1   Occasionally described, somewhat reductively, as the 'British Lukács',
Williams shared the Hungarian Marxist's approach to the realist novel and its
relationship to notions of social totality while often reaching different conclusions, notably on twentieth-century literature. See Williams's response to
a question on such affinities and divergences in *Politics and Letters* (349–50)
and, for an extended critique of the relationships between the thinking of
the two men, see Tony Pinkney, 'Raymond Williams and the "Two Faces

The totality of social practices as opposed to this layered notion of a base and a consequent secondary superstructure. The totality of practices which would be compatible with the notion of consciousness determined by social being, but which would not understand those processes in the development of limited senses of base and superstructure. Now the language of totality has become common, and is in many ways more acceptable than the notion of base and superstructure but with one very important reservation. It is very easy for the notion of totality to empty of its essential content the original proposition. I mean that if we come to say that society is composed of a large number of different social practices which form a concrete social whole, we give to each practice a certain specific recognition, we know that they interact, relate, and combine in very complicated ways, and so on, we are at one level much more obviously talking about reality, but we are at another level withdrawing from the claim that there is a process of determination. And this I, for one, would be very unwilling to do. Indeed, the key question to ask about any notion of totality in cultural theory is this: whether the totality includes the notion of intention.

That is to say if totality is simply concrete, if totality is simply the recognition of a large variety of miscellaneous and contemporaneous practices, then it is, it seems to me, essentially empty of any content that could be called Marxist. Intention, the notion of intention, restores the key question, the key emphasis that, while it is true that a society is a complex whole of such practices, it has nevertheless an organization, a structure, and that the principles of this organization and structure can be directly related to certain social intentions, intentions by which we define the society, intentions which in all our experience have been the rule of a particular

---

of Modernism'", in *Raymond Williams: Critical Perspectives*, ed. Eagleton, 12–33. Along with the substantial work carried out in *Marxism and Literature*, Williams expands on questions of social totality and what he identifies as significant advances in the work of Lukács and Lucien Goldmann during 'Literature and Sociology: In Memory of Lucien Goldmann', *New Left Review*, I/67, May–June 1971, 3–18.

class. In other words, one of the consequences of the crudeness of the base-superstructural model has been the too easy acceptance of models which appear less crude – models of totality or of a complex whole – but which, however, exclude the facts of social intention, the class character of a particular society and so on. And this is the more important to say because it reminds us how much we lose if we abandon the superstructural emphasis altogether. I have great difficulty in seeing certain processes of art and thought as superstructural in the terms of the formula as it is commonly used. But in many areas of social and political thought – certain kinds of ratifying theory, certain kinds of law, certain kinds of institutions, which after all in Marx's original formulations were very much part of the superstructure – all this kind of social apparatus in all this area of social and political and ideological activity and construction, if we fail to see a superstructural element we fail to recognize reality at all. That is to say that laws, constitutions, theories, ideologies, which are claimed as natural, or as having universal validity or significance, have to be seen as expressing and ratifying the domination of a particular class. And the difficulty of revising the formula of base and superstructure has had much to do with the perception of many militants – who have to fight these institutions as well as to fight economic battles – that if such institutions and their ideologies are not perceived as having that kind of relationship, if their universal validity or legitimacy is not denied and fought, then, in a sense, the class character of the society is no longer seen, and that has been true of some versions of totality as the description of cultural process. And I think that we can properly use the notion of totality only when we combine it with that other crucial Marxist concept of hegemony.

Indeed it is Gramsci's great contribution to have emphasized hegemony, and to have understood it with a depth which is, I think, rare.[1] Because hegemony supposes the existence of some-

---

1   As Daniel Gerke notes, 'Williams adapted Gramsci's concept of hegemony to refer to a culturally and psychologically saturated sense of what is possible, a reified "common sense" derived from the daily experience of living in capitalist society'. Gerke, 'The Long War of Position: Williams and Gramsci,

thing which is truly total, which is not merely secondary or superstructural, like ideology, but which is lived at such a depth, which saturates the society to such an extent, which, as he put it, constitutes the limits of common sense for most people under its sway, that it corresponds to the reality of social struggle very much more clearly than the notions derived from the formula of base and superstructure. One can put it perhaps in this way. If ideology were merely the abstract imposed notion, if the social and political and cultural ideas, the ideas over a very wide range of human experience which a majority of the population in society hold, were merely the result of manipulation, the result of a kind of overt training which one might suppose might be easily ended or withdrawn, then the society would be very much easier to move and to change than in practice it has ever been or is. The notion of hegemony as deeply saturating the consciousness of a whole group and a period seems to me fundamental. And hegemony has the advantage, when it is combined with the notion of totality, of emphasizing the facts of domination.

And yet there are times when I hear discussions of hegemony and feel that it too, as a concept, is being dragged back to the relatively simple, uniform and static concept which, for example, the superstructure in ordinary use had become. Because it seems to me that we have to give a more complex account if we are talking about any real social formation. And above all we have to give an account which accounts, first, for the elements of real and constant change in a hegemony and, second, for something that reminds us that it is not singular, indeed that its own internal structures are highly complex, and have continually to be renewed, recreated, defended, and by the same token, can be continually challenged and in certain respects modified. That is why instead of speaking

Culture and Crisis', in *Key Words*, 17, 2019, 29. Perry Anderson describes how Williams 'endorsed and developed Gramsci's conception of hegemony', establishing the Italian theorist's thinking as a major influence on socialist intellectuals in Britain. See Anderson, 'The Heirs of Gramsci', *New Left Review*, 100, July–Aug 2016, 73; and Williams's chapter on hegemony in *Marxism and Literature*, 108–14.

simply of *the* hegemony or *a* hegemony, I would wish to propose a model which seeks to allow for this kind of variation and contradiction, sets of alternatives and processes of change.

Because one thing that is very evident in some of the best Marxist cultural analysis is that it is very much more at home in what one might call epochal questions than in what one has to call historical questions. That is to say, it is very much better at distinguishing the large features of different epochs of society, as between feudal and bourgeois, or what may be, than between, as very often is for us quite the most urgent task, the distinction between different phases of bourgeois society, and different moments within the phases: the true historical process which demands a much greater precision and delicacy of analysis than the always striking epochal analysis which is concerned with main lineaments and features.

Now the theoretical model which I am trying to work with is this. I would say first, that in any society, in a particular period, there is a central system of practices, meanings, and values, which we can properly call corporate.[1] This implies no presumption about its value. All we are saying is that it is central. It is corporate, it is the true expression of what is dominant in our society and thus far the notion corresponds with that of hegemony; it is a system which is not to be understood at the level of mere opinion or mere manipulation. It is a whole body of practices and expectations, assignments of energy, ordinary understandings of the nature of man and of his world. The set of meanings and values which, as they are experienced as practices appear to confirm them and as in turn they give rise to new practices, constitutes a sense of reality for most people in a society, a sense of reality beyond which it is difficult for most members of the society to move. And yet it is clear that this is not, except by the operation of a moment of abstract analysis, in any sense a static feature. On

---

1   Here marks the beginning of a key difference between this original lecture and the version first published in the winter of 1973: the subsequent use of 'dominant and effective' instead of 'corporate'. See 'Base and Superstructure', *New Left Review*, I/82, 9.

the contrary, we can only understand a corporate culture if we understand the process, the very real process of incorporation, indeed of a constant incorporation. The modes of incorporation are of great social significance, and incidentally have in our kind of society great economic significance. The educational institutions are always the main agencies of the transmission of a corporate culture, and this is now a major economic as well as cultural activity, indeed it is both in the same moment. Further, at a philosophical level, at the true level of theory, at the level of the history of various practices, there is that process which I have called the selective tradition, which is always, within the terms of corporate culture, passed off as *the* tradition, the significant parts. The selectivity is the point; the way in which from a whole possible area of past and present, certain works, practices, meanings are chosen for emphasis, certain are neglected and excluded. Certain, even more crucially, are reinterpreted, diluted, put into forms which are meant not to contradict other elements within the corporate culture. The processes of education, of a much wider social training within institutions like the family, the practice of the organization of work, the selective tradition at a theoretical level: all these forces are involved with the continual remaking of a corporate culture on which its reality depends. Because if a corporate culture were merely an imposed ideology, as it is sometimes spoken of, if it were merely the property of the ruling class, or of a section of the ruling class, which is imposed on others, which occupies merely the top of their minds, it would be – and one would be glad – a very much easier thing to overthrow.

It is not only the depths to which it reaches, it is also the sense that it is continually active and adjusting that we have to emphasize if we are to understand its reality. Then we do have to ask the question, if we are talking about the real world in our kinds of society, about the degrees of alternative meanings and values, the degrees of alternative opinions and attitudes, even alternative senses of the world, which can be tolerated within a particular corporate culture. I think this has been much under-emphasized in notions of a superstructure, certainly, and even in some notions of hegemony. We have to recognize that in the practice of politics, for example, there are certain truly incorporated modes of what are nevertheless, within those terms, real oppositions, that a corporate culture can quite properly contain, as alternatives and variations within itself. Their existence within the incorporation has been recognizable always by the fact that, whatever the degree of internal conflict or internal variation, they do not as such surpass, or go beyond the limits of the central corporate definitions. This would be true, for example, of the practice of parliamentary politics, it would be true of certain kinds of debate about human value, which are quite real and which must not be reduced to ideas of an ideological cover, but which can nevertheless be properly analysed as corporate, if we find in practice that, whatever the degree of internal controversy and variation, they do not exceed the limits of the central corporate definitions.

But if we are to say this, we have to think again about the sources of that which is not corporate; of all those practices, experiences, meanings, values which are not part of the corporate culture. I think that we can express this in two ways. There is clearly something that we can call alternative to the corporate culture, and there is something else that we can call oppositional, in a true sense. And the degree of existence of these alternative and oppositional forms is itself a matter of constant historical variation in real circumstances. In certain societies it is possible to leave certain areas of social life in which quite real alternatives are at least left alone. If they are made available, of course, they are part of the corporate organization. The existence of the possibility of opposition, of articulated opposition, its degrees of openness, and so on, again depends on very precise social and political forces. The facts of alternative and oppositional forms of social life and culture, in relation to the corporate culture, have then to be recognized as subject to historical variation, and as having sources which are very significant, as we begin to examine them, because we find that there is a further distinction we might use between residual and emergent forms, both of alternative and of oppositional cultures.

Residual, in this sense, means that experiences, meanings, and values which cannot be verified, cannot be accepted in the terms of the corporate culture, are nevertheless lived, practised on the basis of some previous social formation. There is a real case of this in certain religious values, by contrast with the very evident incorporation of most religious meanings and values as a system. The same is true, in a culture like Britain, of certain notions derived from a rural past, which have a very significant popularity. The residual culture is in a way at some distance from the corporate culture, and one has to recognize that, in real cultural activities, it may get incorporated into it. Both because some part of it, some version of it, will in many cases have had to be incorporated if the corporate culture is to make sense in those areas. But also because at a certain point a corporate culture cannot allow too much of this kind of practice and experience outside itself, at least without very considerable challenge.

And the same is true of an emergent culture; that new meanings and values, new practices, new significances and experiences, are continually being created. And that there is in this case a much earlier attempt to incorporate them, indeed it is significant in our own period how very early the attempt is, how alert the corporate culture is to anything that can be seen as emergent. The case is then both that we have to see this relation in time between a corporate culture and on the one hand a residual and on the other hand an emergent culture. But also that we have to see that within residual and emergent culture we can make distinctions; they often require very precise analysis, between residual-incorporated and residual not incorporated, and on the other side emergent-incorporated and emergent not incorporated. It is a fact about the nature of a particular society, how far it reaches over the whole range of human practices and experiences in this attempt at incorporation. I think it was true of earlier phases of bourgeois society, for example, that there were many areas of experience which it was willing to leave alone, which it was prepared, for example, to call the sphere of private life, or as having no particular business of society or of the state. And this went along with certain kinds of political tolerance, even if the reality of that tolerance was benign neglect. Now, I believe it is true of the society which has come into existence since the last war, that progressively it finds itself, because of developments in the social character of labour, the social character of communications, and the social character of decision, extending much further than ever before in capitalist society into these areas of experience and practice and meaning. And therefore that the decision, as to whether a practice is alternative or oppositional, is often made within a very much narrower scope. Because, although there is a theoretical distinction between alternative and oppositional, between someone who simply finds a different way to live and wishes to be left alone, and someone who finds a different way to live and wants to change the society in its light – and this is usually the whole range of difference between individual and small-group solutions to social crisis and the solutions which properly belong to political and ultimately revolutionary practice – it is often a very narrow line, in reality, between alternative and oppositional: whether the thing is simply tolerated as a deviation or persecuted as a deviation, where it is simply seen as another way to live or oppositional in the true sense, where it is the core of the corporate culture that is not simply being disregarded or despised but is quite centrally being challenged.

Now it is crucial to any Marxist theory of culture that it can give an explanation of the sources of those practices and meanings which are alternative or oppositional. And this is particularly relevant of course to the question of emergent practices and meanings. We understand, from an ordinary historical approach, the source of residual meanings and practices. These are the results of earlier social formations, where certain real meanings and values were generated, and where in the default of a particular phase of a corporate culture there can be a reaching back to those meanings and values which were created in a real society in the past, which still seem to have some significance because they represent areas of human experience, aspiration, achievement, which the corporate culture either does not recognize, or undervalues, or even actively opposes. What we have to give more precisely is a non-metaphysical, a non-subjectivist explanation of emergent cultural practice.

We have, indeed, one source to hand from the central body of Marxist theory, that is to say the formation of a new class, the coming to consciousness of a new class.[1] And this remains quite centrally important. It is, incidentally, the fact which complicates any simple model of base and superstructure and the fact which complicates some of the more ordinary versions of hegemony, although it was of course Gramsci's purpose precisely to see and to create by organization the hegemony of a proletarian kind which was capable of challenging the bourgeois hegemony. So we have one area, in the emergence of a new class. But I think that we have also to recognize certain other areas and that, in cultural practice, some of these are of particular importance. And we can recognize them on the basis of this proposition: that no mode of production, and therefore no dominant society or order of society, and therefore no corporate culture, in practice exhausts human practice, human energy, human aspiration. Indeed it seems to me that this emphasis is not merely a negative proposition, so that we can allow for certain things happening outside the dominant mode. On the contrary, it is a fact about the modes of domination that they select from and consequently exclude the full range of human practice. The difficulties of human practice outside or against the dominant mode are, of course, real. It depends very much whether they are in an area in which the dominant class and the corporate culture have an interest and a stake. If the interest and the stake are explicit, these will be reached for, if possible extirpated with extraordinary vigour. But in certain areas, there will be in certain periods practices and meanings which are not reached for. Or there will be areas of practice and meaning which, almost by definition in its own limited character, in its profound

1   As Williams writes in *Keywords*: 'The main tendency of Marx's description of classes was towards formations' and, thus, 'Class consciousness clearly can only belong to a formation'. See 'Class', in *Keywords*, 60–9 (67 and 68).

deformation, the corporate culture is unable in any real terms to recognize. I think that this gives us a bearing on the observable difference between, for example, the practices of a capitalist state and a state like the contemporary Soviet Union in relation to writers.[1] Because from the whole Marxist tradition literature was seen as an important and crucial activity, the state is very much sharper in investigating areas where different versions of practice, different meanings and values, are being expressed. In capitalist practice, if it is not making a profit, if it is not being widely circulated, then it can for a time be overlooked, at least while it remains alternative. When it becomes oppositional in an explicit way it will of course be attacked.

But in any case the position is that from the full range of human practice at any one time, the dominant mode is a conscious selection and organization. Or at least in its fully formed state it is a conscious selection and organization and there are always sources of real human practice which it neglects or excludes. And these are different in quality from the developing and articulate interests of a rising class. The relations between the two are by no means necessarily contradictory, at times they can be very close, and on the relations between these areas, much in political practice depends. But culturally, and as a matter of theory, the areas can be seen as distinct.

Now if we go back to the question in its most usual form – what are the relations between art and society, literature and society? – in the light of the preceding discussion, we have to say first that there are no relations between literature and society in that abstracted

---

1   In 1946, editors at the literary journal *Zvezda* were removed while another periodical, *Leningrad*, was shut down by the Communist Party for alleged 'decadent' foreign influence; the comic writer Mikhail Zoshchenko – on the editorial board at *Zvezda* – and poet Anna Akhmatova were also expelled from the Writers' Union. A year later Williams wrote one of his first extended published essays on what became known as the 'Soviet Literary Controversy'; it appeared in the late 1940s journal *Politics and Letters*, which he co-edited. See Williams, 'Soviet Literary Controversy in Retrospect', in *Border Country: Raymond Williams in Adult Education*, 41–53.

way. The literature is there as a practice in the society from the beginning, that the society in this sense cannot be seen as fully formed, it is not even fully available for analysis until this one of its practices is included. But if we take that emphasis which is import-ant in one direction, we must take its corresponding implication: that we cannot separate literature and art from other kinds of social practice and make them in some way subject to quite special and distinct laws. They may have quite specific features as practices, but they cannot be separated from the ordinary social process. And indeed it seems to me particularly necessary to emphasize that literature does not operate in any one of the sectors I have been trying to describe in this model. It would be easy to say, it is a familiar rhetoric to say, that literature operates in the emergent cultural sector, that these are the new feelings, the new meanings, the new values. One can persuade oneself of this theoretically, by abstract argument, until one comes to read much literature, because it is perfectly clear if one reads over the whole range, and doesn't perform the sleight-of-hand of calling literature only that which one has already selected as embodying certain meanings and values at a certain scale of intensity, that one is bound to rec-ognize that the act of writing, the practices of discourse in writing and speech, the making of novels and poems and plays and the-ories, all this activity takes place in all these sectors, by no means only in the emergent, which is always, in fact, quite rare.

A great deal of it is of a residual kind; this has been deeply true of much English literature in the last half-century. Some of its fundamental meanings and values have belonged to the cultural achievements of earlier and in fact past stages of society. And lit-erature has in fact been continually redefined and narrowed down by some of the most radical critics of society until, like the pro-verbial bird, it has flown in ever decreasing circles until it finally and fundamentally disappears, and people say, so deep has been the residual emphasis in literary practice, that there is now no literature. In fact, of course, most writing, in any given period, is a contribution to the corporate culture. Indeed many of the specific qualities of literature, its capacity to enact and perform certain meanings and values, to recognize in highly particular ways what would be otherwise merely general truths, enable it to perform this kind of function with great power. To literature, of course, we add in our own society the now even more powerful arts of film, of certain kinds of broadcasting, of certain kinds of visual communication. The theoretical point is, however, clear. If we are looking for the relations between literature and society, we cannot either separate out one practice from a presumably complete and formed body of other practices, nor when we have identified the particular practice can we give it a settled, static, and ahistorical relation to a social formation. My contention is that the arts of writing, the arts of creation and performance, over their whole range, are parts of the cultural process in all the sectors that I have analytically described. They contribute to the corporate culture and are a central articulation of it. They embody residual meanings and values, not all of which are incorporated, though many are. They express also and importantly certain emergent practices and meanings, some of these again are incorporated, and as they reach people, as they begin to move people, then the corporate culture, in certain of the emergent arts of performance, reaches out to transform them or seek to transform them. This happened a great deal in the 1960s with some of the new kinds of art and in the process, of course, the corporate culture itself changes, not necessarily in its central formations, but in many of its articulated features. As indeed it must change if it is to remain, as it must, not only corporate but dominant, if it is still to be felt as in that way central about all the real activities and interests of man.

Now, what implication does this view have for the analysis of works of art? Because this is the point towards which most discussion of cultural theory seems to be directed: the discovery of a method, perhaps even a methodology, by which works of art can be understood and described. I would hesitate in myself subscribing to the view that this is the main purpose of cultural theory, but let us for a moment consider it. What is very striking is that nearly all forms of contemporary critical theory are theories of consumption. That is to say, they are concerned with understanding an object in such a way that it can profitably or correctly be consumed. The earliest stage of consumption theory was the theory of taste, where the link between the practice and the theory was direct in the metaphor. From taste you got the rather more elevated notion of 'sensibility', in which it was the continual consumption by sensibility of elevated or insightful works which was held to be the essential operation, and critical activity was then a function of this sensibility. Then you got more developed theories, in the 1920s with Richards, and later in New Criticism, where the effects were studied directly and the language of the work of art as object became much more overt.[1] 'What effect does this work – *the poem* as it was ordinarily described – have on me?'; 'What impact does it have on me?', as it was later to be put in a much wider area of communication studies. And the notion of the work of art as object, as text, as isolated artifact, became central in all these consumption theories. It was not only that the practices of production were then overlooked, this fused with the notion that most important literature anyway was in the past. And the real social conditions of production were in any case neglected because they were held to be at best secondary. The real relationship was always between the taste, the sensibility, the reader and the object 'in itself as it really is', as people commonly put it. The notion of the work of art as object, however, had a further large theoretical assumption. Because if you ask questions about the work of art seen as object, these are questions about the components of its production. Now there was a use of the formula of base and superstructure which was precisely in line with this. The components of a work of art were, of course, the real activities of the base, and you studied the

---

1   See Williams on I. A. Richards in *Culture and Society* (1958; Harmondsworth: Penguin, 1982), 239–46. 'The handbooks of fictional technique which started coming out of American New Criticism may look impressive', Williams said elsewhere on the critical theory which, by building on Richards, dominated US literary scholarship in the mid-twentieth century, 'but actually cannot even be called formalist, because the Russian Formalists had a much stricter sense of what the literary project was than this quite unrooted academic analysis', *Politics and Letters*, 266.

object to discover these components. Sometimes you even studied the components and then projected the object. But, in any case, the relationship that was understood was between an object and its components. And this was not only true of Marxist theory of a base and a superstructure. It was true of various kinds of psychological theory, whether in the form of archetypes, the images of the collective unconscious, which were the form of myth and symbols, the components of particular works of art, or in the form of particular biography, or psycho-biography and its like, where the components were in the man's life and the work of art was an object in which components of this kind were discovered. Even in some of the more rigorous forms of New Criticism and of structuralist criticism, this essential procedure of regarding the work as an object which has, so to say, to be reduced to its components, even if later it's reconstituted, came to persist.[1]

And I think the true crisis in cultural theory, in our own time, is between the view of the work of art as object and the view of art as a practice. Now, of course, it is at once objected that the work of art is an object: that various works have survived from the past, particular sculptures, particular paintings, particular buildings, which are objects. And this is of course true, but the same way of thinking is applied to works which have no such material existence. There is no *Hamlet* (1609), no *Brothers Karamazov* (1880), no *Wuthering Heights* (1847), in the sense that there is a particular great painting.[2] There is no *Fifth Symphony*,[3] there is no work in

1   For Williams on structuralism, and specifically the literary structuralism associated with Althusser, see 'Crisis in English Studies', in *Writing in Society*, 192–211. He and Garnham also discuss Althusserian Marxism's privileging of the 'text' and 'the work of art as object' during 'Pierre Bourdieu and the Sociology of Culture' in this collection.

2   Out of these three writers – William Shakespeare, Fyodor Dostoyevsky, Emily Brontë – Williams returned repeatedly to the work of Brontë, arguing, for example, that *Wuthering Heights* 'refuses to be reduced to the sum of its other parts. Its interaction, its extraordinary intricacy of opposed and moderated but still absolute feelings, is an active, dynamic process: not balance but dialectic', *The English Novel from Dickens to Lawrence* (1970; St Albans: Paladin, 1974), 53.

3   Ludwig van Beethoven's 1808 symphony.

the whole area of music, dance, performance, which is an object in any way comparable to those works in the visual arts which have survived. And yet the habit of thinking of even such works as objects has persisted because this is a basic theoretical presupposition and the components of the object are thought in much the same way. In fact we have to recognize that in literature, especially in drama, in music, in a very wide area of the performing arts, what we have are not objects but notations. And these notations which have in themselves to be interpreted in an active way, serve to remind us of what is true over an even wider field: that the relationship between the making of a work of art and the reception of a work of art is an active one which is not that of the production of an object and its consumption. It is not, in the simple sense, whatever the medium, the production of an object; it is an activity and a practice, and in its finished forms, although it may in some arts have the character of a material object, it is still a material object subject to reproduction and subject in any case to active perception and interpretation which makes the case of notation, in arts like drama and literature and music, only a special case of a much wider truth. Now what this can show us about the practice of analysis is that we have to break from the notion of isolating the object and then determining its components. On the contrary we have to discover the nature of a practice and then its conditions.

And while in certain particular cases these two processes may in part resemble each other, in many other cases they will be of such radically different kinds. I will conclude with just an observation on the way this distinction relates to the Marxist tradition of the relation between primary social activities and cultural activities. If we suppose that what is produced in cultural activities is this series of objects, we shall set about, as in most forms of critical procedure we now do, to discovering their components and within a Marxist emphasis these components will be in what we've been in the habit of calling the base. We shall isolate certain features which we can, so to say, recognize in component form, or we will ask what processes of transformation or transmutation have these components gone through before they arrived in that state.

Now I think that while the connections between one practice and another, their real location in the whole active social totality that we've been describing, have always to be investigated, we should not look for the components of a product but for the conditions of a practice. That is to say, when we find ourselves looking at a particular work, or group of works, often realizing, as we do so, their essential community as well as their irreducible individuality, we should find ourselves attending first to the reality of their practice and the conditions of the practice as it was then executed. And from this I think we ask essentially different questions. Take for example the way in which an object is related to a genre, in orthodox criticism. We identify it by certain leading features, we then assign it to a larger category, the genre, and then we may find the components of the genre in a particular social history – although in some variants of Marxist criticism not even that is done, and the genre is supposed metaphysically to be in effect eternal.

It is not that way of proceeding that seems to me to be required. The recognition of the relation between a collective mode and an individual project is the recognition of related practices. That is to say, the irreducibly individual projects that particular works are, may come in experience and in analysis to show resemblances which allow us to group them into collective modes. These are by no means always genres. They may exist as resemblances within and across genres. They may be the practice of a group in a period, rather than the practice of a phase in a genre. But as we discover the nature of a particular practice, and the nature of the relation between an individual project and a collective mode, we find that we are involved in what is by no means a predicted or pre-controlled series of extending relationships, within which we can certainly identify certain key features of the corporate culture, of the residual and the emergent processes of incorporation which we often have to be conscious of in approaching any particular work. But we have no built-in procedure of the kind which is indicated by the fixed character of the object. Now this is the kind of claim that has continually to be demonstrated in practice, but in this talk I wanted to look again, however briefly, through the field of propositions that we have received to suggest some reconsiderations and some amendments and to end with an emphasis which seems to me to take us in a radically new direction, that instead of asking about the components of objects, we ask about the conditions of practices.

1973

5

Popular Culture: History and Theory

You must first forgive me for coming from an old-fashioned university where the notion of collaborative discussion of an intellectual project is so bizarre that you must first forgive my inexperience.[1] And also I feel, since you are already well into the discussion of this project, that it is a bit like bringing coals to New-castle – even if one is a collier. However, obviously this interests me because, in a way, it is a very important moment. The interest in what is loosely called 'popular culture' has been so marked since the 1950s, for obviously very crucial reasons, that it really is time – but perhaps it needed this time – to bring it into a focus which is not simply picking up the obviously widespread interest in an ill-defined group of phenomena, but of trying to develop something that is properly an educational discipline.

1   A talk delivered at the Open University on 23 May 1978, original tran-scription by Tony Bennett with new explanatory notes added by the editor. First published in 'Popular Culture No. 2 Bulletin', Open University, August 1978; later in *Cultural Studies*, 32.6, November 2018, 903–28. Williams had been invited by Bennett to address a seminar, convened as part of plans for the ground-breaking Popular Culture course. A lengthy discussion with those who would work on and contribute to the module followed Williams's talk; this was also published in *Cultural Studies*, 32.6. See Bennett, 'Popular Culture 1978: History, Theory, Politics', *Cultural Studies*, 32.6, 2018, 897–902.

The difficulty of doing this in England, specifically I think, is that although it is the case that the English contribution to thinking about popular culture is probably considerably in advance of that in most comparable cultures, for different reasons this is nevertheless an anti-theoretical culture and, in a way, a lot of the work has gone ahead without an awareness even that theoretical questions are involved. The distinction of different theoretical approaches, for example, which is very necessary, is, however, a distinction between things which are in some cases genuine theory – or what is offered as a theory – and other things which are really not much more than empirical generalizations, or even presumptions, which the analyst may disentangle as theory but, if he did, he would probably be disavowed by the authors. This unevenness of theory and the different kinds of approach to what popular culture is, is one of the very first problems.

If I can illustrate this with the notion of culture itself, that uniquely difficult theoretical term. On the one hand, one tendency presents no problems because it presents culture as a body of practices which is neither immediately practical in the sense of producing immediately usable commodities, nor attached to a cult in the sense of being a body of ritual practices attached to a unitary and dominant set of meanings. Culture is a body of practices which has to do with meanings and values within this tendency. It is therefore a body of artistic and intellectual work and a body of related practices which necessarily move into things which are not specifically intellectual or artistic, but which carry meaning and value. This grouping clearly corresponds to the notion of culture as a 'way of life' and, whatever the detailed theoretical problems with this tendency, one knows the area that one is talking about.

However, at the same time, within the definition of culture itself, there is a very strong tendency – and, indeed, in terms of historical development it has priority – in which culture is precisely the development of certain higher faculties which are then, from the beginning and in principle, distinguished from a whole range of other everyday activities. There is the cultivation of a certain kind of rather rare mental, intellectual, artistic, spiritual development so that, even in a term like 'culture', you have what is a radical theoretical divergence but one that it is not too easy, in an atheoretical culture, to bring to that clear definition.

If you add the difficult word 'popular', then you are immediately in difficulties. For, on the one hand, the latter kind of definition of culture would exclude it altogether. Culture would, by definition, not be an activity of a popular kind. Whether or not culture is associated with a particular exclusive or reserved class, by definition, if it were this refining activity of a rather rare kind, it would be excluded from anything that could be called 'popular'. On the other hand, if you associate it with the notion of a body of practices carrying meaning and value, then the question is whether 'popular' means anything more than that in which many people are involved – whether actively or passively – or whether it is simply something that is widely distributed. And it is well known that, following this sort of tendency, people have adopted the notion of popular culture to refer to something in which many people are involved as a distinct entity which can be separated from what is then 'invented' to preserve some of the sense of the terms of the theoretical tendencies embodied in the notion of high culture, and to have the principal distinction between popular culture and high culture, which has been the assumption for so long.

Now, if you look at the bodies of work that bear on the resolution of these questions, some of them are theoretical and some, as I began by saying, are not really much more than generalized observations or assumptions that people bring to the study. It seems to me that there is no way of breaking this knot except historically. If you examine popular culture at any level of empirical observation – what was the audience of a particular art, shall we say, at any particular period – you would find that it is intrinsic that there are radical variations in what kinds of art were enjoyed by what kinds of audience. It is simply not possible to adapt to a supra-historical scheme the notion, that is to say, of a body of highly important work which is always enjoyed by a minority and a body of different work, whether valuable or not, which is enjoyed by a majority. It is simply not possible to adapt to that scheme such varied phenomena as, for example, the Elizabethan and Jacobean theatre, the eighteenth- and nineteenth-century novel or, to move into a more contentious area, the twentieth-century film.[1]

In other words, the application of an *a priori* theoretical distinction between minority and majority art (which carries pre-given distinctions and values) is an act of faith and an act of will – an act of will really against the historical evidence. And one says this even while one is aware how inadequate are the simply populist conclusions which might be drawn from it. The popular nature of the Elizabethan audience for what is, after all, one of the great moments of all in cultural production is a highly specific one and a very brief one and a precarious one. You can't assume that there is some norm in human history and human culture by which all high art is of a generally available kind so long as certain nameable interests do not obstruct it. Some people want to defend that proposition; again, it is an act of faith or an act of will much like the other. In the case of Elizabethan drama, it is as remarkable that it was a very brief moment in which there was a genuinely popular and mixed audience for work we now recognize as some of the highest art ever produced in the world; it is as relevant that it is a brief phenomenon as that it is that kind of phenomenon, the kind of phenomenon that breaks down superficial presumptions that there is a permanent distinction between high and popular art.

Nevertheless, as you begin to look at these historical cases, you realize the need for theory and, there again, you come across this unevenness that I mentioned. Really, I suppose, there are only two contending bodies of theory which you could call truly theoretical, which have been worked out at the level of principles as well as of examples. These are, first, the kind of study of certain societies and cultural institutions and practices which see an intrinsically, historically variable relationship between artistic

---

1   Williams's writing on film encompassed his entire career, from 'Film and the Dramatic Tradition', in *Preface to Film* by Williams and Michael Orrom (1954) to 'Film History' (1983) and 'Cinema and Socialism' (1985), collected in *What I Came to Say* (1989) and *Politics of Modernism* (1989), respectively.

and cultural practice and the rest of social life, which presumes no regular relations between these, whether of a minority or a majority kind. That's one body of theory, and the other body of theory is that which supposes that all cultures are at any time, in any epoch, basically the production of the dominant class and that whatever interests or attitudes or values may be, so to say, co-opted from an area beyond that dominant class, popular culture is always, and must be, the culture of the dominant class transmitted in an accessible form. I may be wrong, but my sense of *theory* is that really only those two interpretations are in the field. That is not to say that certain very important positions aren't held which are quite different from both of those. But these, I think, are not really at the level of theory. I mean, I don't think there is really much theorization at the level of the proposition that important culture is always that of a minority and that popular culture is always a kind of threat to the standards of that minority culture. It's a very well-known, deeply held, elegantly argued, richly exemplified tradition, but it is not a theory. It has never been argued theoretically that this is so. The nearest to a theoretical approach in that way, I suppose, was T. S. Eliot,[1] but it is not a theory in the same sense.

So, I would have thought that you cannot, at the level of teaching in this sort of area, simply review theoretical positions and compare them with each other pedagogically, as it were, if only because the positions are so different in kind. Some really are theoretical, some are just a bundle of empirical generalizations, others again are prejudices and presumptions. A strict theoretical comparison would not, it seems to me, be necessarily the right thing to do. But, once one begins to realize the very varied area of historical fact to which some of these theories and generalizations speak, then, I think, I at least can distinguish something which

---

1   Williams's original impetus for the decade-long research which became *Culture and Society* was reading Eliot's *Notes Towards the Definition of Culture* (1948), followed by discussion of the book alongside the work of F. R. Leavis, Clive Bell, and Matthew Arnold in one of his adult education classes in 1949. He offers an extended analysis of Eliot in his chapter on the poet in *Culture and Society*, 224–38.

marks out an area that ought to be distinct and coherent which leaves all the theoretical issues open to argument but which does not require their prior solution.

This may be optimistic, but it seems to me to be so, and my position is that there is a radical, qualitative change in the relation between anything that can be called 'high culture' and anything which could be called 'popular culture' somewhere in the English eighteenth and nineteenth centuries.[1] The period varies in different societies; that is where it is in England. However, the reasons for that being the period of qualitative change involve one in all sorts of theoretical problems. It is a period of very rapidly expanding and shifting class relations; it is a period of highly developed technology, including cultural technology; it is a period of development of democratic political institutions which are quite closely involved with some of these developments. The explanatory causes leave plenty of room for debate, but the qualitative change there does seem to me to be real and I think it is the first time, in fact, that people begin to talk about popular culture as an issue. This does not mean, of course, that before this period there was some kind of unified culture. But I would argue strongly that there is a qualitative difference between the relations between popular culture and other kinds of culture from, say, the early nineteenth century in England on, and the relations before that date between the culture of the court or the culture of an organized metropolis and, on the other hand, the culture of the country or the folk or the various manifestations in which this other activity is defined. I mean that there is a radically qualitative difference in the relations between popular culture and whatever its opposite or alternative is and folk culture and court culture which have

---

1   In *Keywords*, Williams describes 'popular culture' as 'not identified by *the people* but by others, and it still carries two older senses: inferior kinds of work (cf. popular literature, popular press as distinguished from *quality press*); and work deliberately setting out to win favour (popular journalism as distinguished from *democratic journalism*, or popular entertainment); as well as the more modern sense of well-liked by many people, with which of course, in many cases, the earlier senses overlap' (237).

precise social locations which influence each other but which, nevertheless, are quite differently situated socially from anything which we have known since that transforming early nineteenth-century situation.

I suppose one ought immediately to specify some of the ways in which this is qualitatively new. First, I would have thought, is that popular culture from this period is self-evidently novel. It is continually productive rather than reproductive. It's an obvious characteristic of folk culture that it is highly reproductive and, in that sense, traditional just because it has those precise social roots. In a very different kind of society, the popular culture *is produced*; it includes as much novelty, as a matter of fact, as anything you could provisionally call the high culture. It includes new institutions, new relationships of cultural use in new cultural forms. These are as clear as the new forms and any new relationships in what might be distinguished as the high cultural field.

I mean, to take a couple of examples, that the melodrama in the nineteenth century is as much a new form as anything that happens in nineteenth-century culture.[1] This has nothing to do with its value or its ultimate importance in human history, but it is radically different from some reproduced traditional cultural activity within folk culture. The melodrama is written in new ways, for new audiences, in new institutions. There is nothing like it in the culture used by the majority of the people in earlier periods. At the same time, and this is really what I think deepens one's sense of the qualitative change, the relation between the melodrama and what is happening at the level of what some people separate out as the high culture is itself a very complex one. The relation between Dickens and the melodrama would be a very obvious example.[2] In the same way, the music hall is not some timeless

---

1   'Melodrama touched every nerve of nineteenth-century society, but usually only to play on the nerves and to resolve crisis in an external and providential dramatic world', notes Williams in 'Social Environment and Theatrical Environment: The Case of English Naturalism', *Culture and Materialism*, 125–47.

2   In 'Social Environment and Theatrical Environment', Williams also

phenomenon of the natural cheerfulness and health and vitality of the people. The music hall is a very precise product of a very specific open situation of a novel kind and incidentally of changes at the level of the official theatre in the distinction between legitimate and illegitimate theatre and the way those were changing through changes in the law. And the material that poured into the music hall, although it has many precedents, also includes quite novel elements which relate to this unprecedented situation of people living in social relations, human settlements, and therefore general cultural situations which were, the majority of them, quite unprecedented.[1]

In other words, the location of popular culture as a proposition, as a meaningful description rather than a kind of residual category for things which have not made the grade as serious culture, is, in that sense, historically related to a set of precise conditions which had major elements of novelty and which included novel cultural production. If this is so, I would have thought that what particularly followed from it is that a useful approach to educational discussion of popular culture is that one should be at least as much concerned with these novelties and their conditions as with – as tended to happen in the first stage of the study of popular culture – their presumed 'effects' or with their implied contrast with more received and recognizable traditional forms. It really was desperate that for fifteen or twenty years nobody could look at television, that extraordinary source of novelty of form, without wondering whether it was damaging the children.[2] It was always the question whether it was damaging the children which was the polite form of the question of whether it was damaging anyone else – a much

---

notes how melodrama took from as well as adapted Dickensian depictions of city destitution and child poverty (137).

1 The significance of music hall is discussed in 'Popular Forms of Writing' in this collection.

2 Williams's book, *Television: Technology and Cultural Form* (1974), did much to move critical discussions beyond such limiting approaches. See also *Raymond Williams on Television: Selected Writings* (1989), a collection consisting primarily of his television column for *The Listener*.

harder question to ask. People talked about 'effects' before they had even begun to look at causes and you got a certain prejudicial tone towards this from the beginning that you were examining an evidently deleterious phenomenon which you must study as to its 'effects' by reference to some actually assumed norm.

I don't want to go into too much detail, but it is very instructive to follow the story of the study of violence on television. The problem is not that there is not a great deal of mimed violence on television, but that there is really a lot of room for argument about its forms and its meanings. But what was very curious was that people were studying this as if the introduction of violence and the meanings of violence into the culture had been really undertaken by this medium, as if either there was no violence in the culture otherwise – which is rather improbable given the dates of the television phenomena – or that there had not been other kinds of dramatizations of violence. What I mean is that, and this is what I meant also by the unevenness of theory, people get on to the deleterious effects of this – and indeed there are many – from the presumption that, because this fell outside the definition of what was known to be culture, that was the necessary way in which to approach it. And the poor victims, as always, were the children – the one body of people you can look upon as open to influence and as needing to be guarded without raising any of the more difficult issues about what collective responsibility in cultural practice might be.

So, the notion of the study of the production and the study of novelty and the study of the conditions of this production and novelty – this, I must say, would be the most valuable emphasis that I would have thought could come through. Like all sorts of things, you will not find that the novelties have no history. But you will find that there are significant moments at which they are changed, either by being in a new set of relations with an audience or by being adapted to a new particular technology, and some of the studies of what happens to certain of these things as they go through these changes are very important.

The example which preoccupies me at the moment, because

I have done some teaching on it, is what one loosely calls police fiction.[1] It is quite clear that it is a really singular phenomenon of this culture that people watch so many mimed crimes – really rather more mimed crimes than detection of crimes the way things are now going. This can be treated at a very crude level as sex and violence on television as in 'what is it doing to the children?' Actually, even from year-to-year on television, there is the production of novel crime fiction forms. In the last two years, let me just give this as a challenging example, we have had the cop who is totally indistinguishable, except for the most basic preliminary information that he is a cop, from any villain, and in particular the detective inspector who behaves like the most way-out private eye. This is a phenomenon of the last two years: the novel production of the law upholder who is visibly and literally the law breaker.[2] Now, I take that just as a local example in what is a very long history of the development of crime, detective, and police fiction in various media since the mid-nineteenth century and it is very much a phenomenon of this new society where one is not merely, in a melancholy way, studying this deleterious eruption of low-grade interest in crime or the possible effects of violence, but studying the production of certain meanings – including certain meanings which are profoundly destructive, in my view, as well as meanings which are very challenging – and studying it as production.

In other words, what seems to me to follow from the identification of this, the 'popular culture' category in this historical sense,

---

1   Williams is referring to the BBC police drama *Target*, which ran for seventeen episodes from 1977 and which he taught at Cambridge as it aired. Comparing the writing to Joseph Conrad and arguing that the series was harder to teach than work by Dostoyevsky, in the discussion that followed his talk Williams described *Target* thus: 'This kind of testing, much of it unconscious, of the notions of law and the notions of criminal behaviour and the notions of enforcement and the notions of the relations between law enforcement and revenge and all similar, related questions really is new', *Cultural Studies*, 32.6, 910.

2   The example Williams uses is Det. Supt. Steve Hackett in *Target*, played by Patrick Mower.

is that one will primarily be studying production and conditions of production. And, that being so, one is studying the body of cultural practices and forms and institutions without the need for apology – I think that is rather important – but with a rather new set of problems. It is quite clear that the problems of value are actually in the end just as difficult as in, for example, a straight literature or history of art course, but where there is at least not the ritualized deference before the art object to carry one over the real difficulties of questions of value as one approaches work of this kind.

I think it would be much better, actually, if we discussed this rather than me go on talking, but I wanted to point in a certain direction.[1] As I say, you have probably already either pointed yourselves towards it or in some quite other, much more thoroughly thought-out direction, and if so, I would be glad to hear. But production and conditions of production, within a historically identifiable body of practices and cultural relations – that is what, I think, a popular culture course now needs to be. That is what would distinguish it from the kinds of treatment it has, in the most general ways, had before. This is what would be the educational challenge, and this is what would seem to immediately encourage a wide variety of skills because there are many skills and disciplines which contribute to that definition.

1978

---

1   The subsequent discussion featured Tony Bennett alongside history lecturer Tony Aldgate, BBC producers Vic Lockwood and Susan Boyd-Bowman, sociologist Ken Thompson, and Williams's friend, literature professor Graham Martin.

6

British Working-Class Literature after 1945

I can look at working-class writing since 1945 in one of two ways.[1] What would be expected in England would be a descriptive catalogue of writing that could in a general way be called working-class literature without much analysis of the category; it would be a highly selective catalogue because, at its most extensive of course, there is such a large body of writing that nobody has read. Further, the novels selected would not necessarily be the most important examples of such literature because the processes of selection are involved in the definition of the category, as well as in much more complicated cultural processes. What I want to do instead is to look at the attempts since the war, in practice and in theory, to define what a working-class literature is and would be and to illustrate certain tendencies within theory and practice from particular examples. I think this is much the most useful way. It is a very active field although it is not yet fully mapped; the only people working on it, of course, are typically not the British. The best bibliographies are in the Soviet Union and East Germany

1   A lecture given at Aarhus University, Denmark, 25 September 1979. The lightly edited transcription – from a recording in the Williams family archive – and explanatory notes are by the editor. First published in *Key Words*, 18, 2020, 45–55.

and yet even they are not doing it completely; they are working with rather traditional, often inadequate categories. Now the first question which I would invite you to think about is this: the relations and distinctions between working life and working-class life. This has, as I shall argue, had a great effect on the method and substance of writing in this area.

Now it is a fact that in early bourgeois fiction, the inclusion of work is quite a marked characteristic, indeed it is one of the distinguishing features of bourgeois fiction by comparison to other kinds of narrative which had preceded it. If you look at the great nineteenth-century realists they involve, over quite a wide area of working life but especially of course over a range of bourgeois occupations (in trade, manufacturing, law, politics, and so on), the inclusion of work as a central experience; it becomes normal. However, at a certain point, and very markedly in late bourgeois fiction, work tends to be marginalized or even not specified. And you get a situation which is very like that before the advent of bourgeois realism. After all, to take English examples, if you read Jane Austen, you have some difficulties in inferring the source of income, the source of the livelihood of the characters. Here is the inheritance novel. Certain general phrases such as 'heir to a large estate', 'well-connected', or certain things of that kind can be inferred. If you track it down you can indeed make a social map of the Jane Austen novel which gives you people's class situation, but you have to work for that, it is not something with which she leads.[1] Even when you have inferred not the work but the social position, the class position, the source of income, then the emphasis of the fiction, what it is consumed by, is elsewhere. Once the social position and the livelihood have been assured, then you get the life, and the novelist deals with how people live. In the interval of bourgeois realism you do have, in limited ways but nevertheless very strongly in some cases, the involvement with that making of economic and social and political relations in the world which is not separated from other human relations. But at a

---

1   See Williams on Austen in *The Country and the City* (1973; St Albans: Paladin, 1975), 140–6.

later stage, and this is true right through to Anthony Trollope and
George Eliot, in a later stage you undoubtedly get a retreat from
this by some of the most talented bourgeois novelists. Their great
manifesto was Virginia Woolf's essay 'Mr Bennett and Mrs Brown'
(1924), which was precisely an attack on the tradition of bourgeois
social description. I mention this because it is crucial to subsequent attempts to write working-class literature. Woolf attacked
Arnold Bennett because he would say 'her father kept a shop in
Harrogate', describe the shop, describe the goods in it, describe
what is on the shelves, describe, describe, describe, she says, iron-
ically.[1] Clearly what is being offered as an alternative to that is that
you describe the individual sensibility and personal relations now
abstracted from that social process without getting into it and, of
course, the historical situation to which that relates is the emergence of a significant late bourgeois group who were primarily,
culturally, involved and active in the arts and in education.[2] They
were themselves at some distance from the central productive and
commercial processes of bourgeois life so in a sense that could be
assumed. You got again something which has come up so much
in theory and which I know from direct experience, and talking
to other writers, is something that many working-class writers are
still so impressed by, in some way over impressed. It is the idea
that fiction is about personal relations or that literature is about
personal relations; for social relations it is said we have sociology,
we have social theory, politics, economics. For literature we have
personal relations and personal relations have then been precisely

---

1   A similar but extended point is made by Williams in his conclusion
to *The English Novel*. He quotes from Woolf's essay: 'Begin by saying that her
father kept a shop in Harrogate. Ascertain the rent. Ascertain the wages of shop
assistants in 1878. Discover what her mother died of. Describe cancer. Describe
calico. Describe...'. And then adds: 'I remember very well when to read that out
in Cambridge would be to find assent, a ripple of assent, in the quite familiar
certainty that we had better things to do. I don't find this now' (153).

2   Williams is referring to the Bloomsbury Group, that circle of intellec-
tuals, writers, and artists who included Virginia and Leonard Woolf, Vanessa
Bell, Lytton Strachey, Clive Bell, and Duncan Grant. See 'The Bloomsbury
Fraction', *Culture and Materialism*, 148–69.

defined as not centred in work. I mean they are what happens, you see this as a very deep bourgeois formation, they are what happens after you have assured your livelihood. You go home and live.

The difficulty, of course, is that for a working-class life, certainly in its older senses and still I would have thought in majority today, that separation is that much more difficult to make. There is no problem in a novel by E. M. Forster or Virginia Woolf about the space that has been cleared for the characters to live inside. It is much more difficult to do this with any plausibility, although indeed it has been attempted, with a working-class family in a very small house, necessarily involved in a whole continuous process which is not only the work but the getting ready to go to work, the coming back, the rush of everyday living, people in very close contact, without the spaces in late bourgeois fiction within which that description of relationships occurred. Now, that still does not mean that you have reached a definition because at a certain point, precisely because of the nature of much working-class work, there is a possible reaction which is very like the late bourgeois separation of work and living. The work is too wholly boring or meaningless to describe, or is taken to be, and so what is specified as working-class life is not that which you might hold centrally to constitute the class which is engaged in a certain type of work for wages, but the consequent life, when you come home or when you have free time. So that it is one striking irony of the continual production of what is called working-class literature since the war that there are still extraordinarily few descriptions of working-class work. I mean this even by comparison with the descriptions of that part of life which is there in bourgeois realism. That is the first point and it becomes important for a second reason which is the whole problem of how the working-class writer in fact emerges. Now, here there have been significant changes since the war, but they can only be appreciated if we look at the earlier situation.

Since you could say there had been a working class and, before that, since there had been a class of landless rural labourers to a much greater extent than any of the orthodox histories pose, there had been men without formal education and without any class position – from which such an activity might be expected – who had written. The body of their work is only still in process of being mapped, it is quite extraordinarily large, even when you take only that small proportion which reached print, and that must be a very small proportion of the things which were actually written and merely stayed inside the family or were lost. But throughout you get a certain set of problems. First of course is the problem of access to that kind of developed literacy and certainly from the period of the emergence of the industrial working class, when the opportunities of popular education in fact declined in England, and the first and second generations of the industrial working class found it less easy to get an education than the rural poor of earlier centuries who, if they had shown an interest, could, usually through the church, get some educational provision. The problems of access were very great, and the access was of course through a class which was not their own; that made a great deal of difference. I do not want to get into a lot of examples because I want to talk about post-war working-class literature, but the great paradigm figure is that of the eighteenth-century labourer, Stephen Duck.[1]

Duck was a farm labourer, an uneducated farm labourer, who began to write having taught himself to read, who was then taken up by the local clergy and given an education which went on to include Latin. He was writing, as a young man, a very original kind of peasant poetry which is, nevertheless, in the formal meters of the educated poetry of his day which often contradicts it. By the time he is thirty and has continued to be successful, and in that sense integrated with the normal literary class, Duck is writing pseudo-Horatian odes, he is writing allegories of rural life, he is writing precisely that which the public expected that kind of writer to write. The fact that he was, or had been, an uneducated labourer was simply an interesting fact about his biography. If he

---

1   Stephen Duck (1705–1756) was an agricultural labourer who became a court poet. One of his early poems, 'The Thresher's Labour' (1730), is described approvingly in *The Country and The City* as having a simple power, but his work, notably 'On Richmond Park, and Royal Gardens' (1736), evolves into an imitative, deadening, performative style, according to Williams (110–13).

was to be a writer, that was the kind of thing he should write, and he finished up dressed in antique costume outside a rural pavilion in Richmond Gardens; it was a game of aristocratic pastoral. Now if you want a paradigm story, and people laugh at poor old Duck, I mean he is a ludicrous figure as he finishes, it is a tragic story. But it is one case among scores of which I know, probably in fact, maybe not in such extreme ways, but one of many hundreds. In other words, the problems of access for somebody who reaches adult life still without the skills of literacy are very severe.

However, there is then the further formal problem which has again been acutely problematic since 1945. By and large it would be true to say of the nineteenth-century British working class, or even the British working class up to 1914, that although some of them tried they never could find a way of handling the novel or the play. The literary form which they could handle was the memoir, the autobiography. Partly because they had a religious tradition of the account of one's life, a certain kind of confession as a form of radical witness; partly because it did not involve them in the very complicated creation of plots. Clearly a novel with an inheritance plot would be no use to such a writer. Novels involving travel and adventure would be no use to such a writer because this they had not had. Novels involving this kind of life would have had to contribute not only an example to establish a form, they would have to create a form, and this understandably was virtually beyond anyone's powers. It might have been possible eventually; once Dickens had been read, for example, you got certain working-class writers making a better shot at doing a novel. Eventually the first significant novel by a working-class writer of that kind appeared, but already this was in the early years of the twentieth century. Robert Tressell's *The Ragged-Trousered Philanthropists* (1914) could not have been written if Dickens had not written;[1] this was a different situation from the working-class writers of the early part of the nineteenth century.

The point is this, that by the period after 1920 – and it is really

---

1   For more on Tressell's novel see Williams, 'The Ragged-Arsed Philan-thropists', *Writing in Society*, 239–56.

much more the period after 1920 than the period after 1945 although it is a continuing, rising process – such men, mostly men although there had been some women, would find their way in nine cases out of ten through the education system again. The people with those developed interests in reading and writing who had gone through these different vicissitudes in the eighteenth and nineteenth century were identified relatively early in the educational process. They were moved through the educational system, often through the higher education system, so that you now have in the modern situation a totally different internal class relation of the writer which bears back very closely on the distinction between working life and working-class life. The majority of working-class novels and plays in Britain have been written by people who were born and grew up in working-class families, and who at one stage or another, often relatively early, were moved on to an educational system which took them away, by the time they were in adult life, from working-class jobs but not working-class life and family connections. And so you get the fairly typical working-class novel of which there have been scores of very good examples, in which there is an intense creation of the nature of working-class family life – the home, the meal, the outings, and so on – but not of this one central experience of the class which is work, which the child of such a family sees at that certain distance but do not themselves share. And especially within the situation in which it is being argued, to anyone who says they are a writer or wants to write or are moving into imaginative literature, that they should write about personal life, about family life, it is said they should not write about work and refer to the social things of that kind. The disability becomes very marked, or is it a disability? That is the question I am putting to you.

I am convinced it is a disability because what then happens are two things; first, the formative experience of working,[1] both as a physical process and of actual work relations, takes much less

---

1   For a discussion of the importance of work in fiction as 'pressing and formative' and as a 'primary kind of consciousness', see 'The Welsh Industrial Novel', collected in *Culture and Materialism*, 213–29.

importance than it should in any definition of a working class
and its kind of literature; second, the relations with other classes
are not present, other social classes tend similarly to be excluded.
So, you could define one kind of working-class novel as a kind of
attractive regional novel, not a class novel but a regional novel.[1]
These are people as one might read about some small community on the margins of the normally-written-about world. They
have their specific habits, they talk in their specific ways, their
life is recreated in convincing detail. But whether they are some
particular islanders or whether they are a working-class family in
the backstreets of a Lancashire mill town is no significant difference because what is created both by the fact of the memories of
childhood and by the fact of the exclusion of the writer from that
part of the class experience which was the work is that comparatively enclosed world of the childhood memory and of the family.
Indeed, a working-class novel is bound to be only a regional novel
it seems to me, if it is not showing the relations of the working
class with other classes. After all, the classes in any significant
sense exist in their social relationships, not only internally but
with each other, whereas if you take working class as a kind of
category, a kind of caste attribute, as if it were something that
was merely local and regional and not this dynamic and problematic social process, then you get that sort of literature. It is not to
say that that kind of literature is not welcome, but there is a real
problem as to whether you would call it working class. Most of
the descriptions of working-class literature have been in terms of
that kind of work and I think that there is a certain sadness about
it among the writers who have practised this form, because of
the sort of enclosure it seems in the end to involve. A very good
example has just been republished, a novel of Welsh working-class
life of just that sort, by a man with just that history; it is a novel
called *Times Like These* (1936) by Gwyn Jones.

---

1   An extended analysis of working-class writing as regional fiction is
conducted by Williams in 'Region and Class in the Novel', *Writing in Society*,
229–38.

Gwyn Jones,[1] who characteristically became Professor of Welsh Literature at Cardiff but who had grown up in a mining valley in the Rhondda, marvellously recreates what family life within a mining community is like but with nothing outside it. And of course this is very curious for such a writer, because his world is limited to the working-class family in the working-class community and its streets; it does not really go outside them although it shows people having to go away or wanting to get away or find some different life. Yet all the time this writer is of course such a different person, I mean he is already inhabiting a different social universe, so that there is no question that there are problems of self-identification for the writer in such a situation. If you will forgive me of talking of my own experience for a moment; my own first novel, *Border Country* (1960), I wrote seven times.[2] I do not claim any virtue for the seven. The point of writing it that many times was that the first five came out as I have been describing. The theoretical point I am making is one that I learnt in the process of writing. Of course, there is something endlessly interesting in someone's recollections of childhood if it happens to be a working-class childhood; it has a lot of rich material, you can write it, but what is the dynamic? Either that is the world from which you are now closed off and you produce that kind of form. Or, which is the way it keeps coming out with increasing emphasis in this period of educational mobility, there is some significant person who gets away from it, who is moving away. It is the D. H. Lawrence phenomenon after all, this intense description of working-class life from which a bright young man moves away. So, there are the old

---

1   Gwyn Jones (1907–1999) was a major theorist and practitioner of Welsh writing in English. The published version of Williams's 'The Welsh Industrial Novel' essay is based on the inaugural Gwyn Jones Lecture he gave in April 1978 at Cardiff.

2   See 'The Tenses of Imagination' in *Writing in Society* (259–68) for a detailed analysis of Williams's own writing practice, in particular his 'Welsh Trilogy': *Border Country* (1960), *Second Generation* (1964), and *The Fight for Manod* (1979). See also Dai Smith's *Raymond Williams: A Warrior's Tale* (2008) for an extensive analysis of the earlier versions of *Border Country*.

folks and they are the working class and there are the new folks
who are us and we respect them and we love them and we can
describe them. What is false about this, and nobody will ever see
those first five versions, is not that you cannot write it, it is that the
form gives you one or other of those meanings. The old folks back
home, who you isolate and enclose as a class, are still there. This
class has not ceased to exist or become the past because some individual has gone away from it or been educated away from it. This
class is still there. Moreover, it will change in the ordinary course
of historical change or you transfer the significance from the class
and its group relations to a significant individual who has moved
away. The fact of them being from a working-class family is then
an interesting biographical fact but it has no social significance.
Of course, it is not just what the writer does. I struggled with this
until I could find a form in which the life of a working-class father
and such a son could both stand equally in the novel. The problem
was the relation between the two experiences, and the move back
as well as the move away, and that life had to be experienced not
just as family background, which is the way the form pushes it,
but as something where it is not known what is going to happen.
This is, after all, a fairly familiar experience of a waged labourer
in a period of economic depression and difficulty. It is not the
stable thing which the form continually, by these processes, tends
to create. And eventually, whether successfully or not, I deliberately refused that form in order to have the move back as well as
the move out. It was important to have the father's life standing
independently of whatever happened to the son, although the fact
that other things happened to the son means that the relationship
was problematic.

The question is not only one of what the writer can do with
the form, it is then of what is acceptable, both in quite the literal
sense of acceptable for publishers but also in the way cultural
process happens. When you get feedback from people who tell
you which bits they think you have done well and which bits they
think you have done badly, anyone but an arrogant idiot listens
to such comments. It is right that human beings should listen

to such comments from people they meet but a more sinister process can occur. I say sinister advisedly because at a moment of social transition and crisis such as this, the feedback you are getting can be – particularly from the people you are likely to be meeting who discuss such issues despite giving it, often charmingly, with the best will in the world – fatal to the negotiation of these problems. After all, you are negotiating more subtly and with many more opportunities than those which poor old Stephen Duck experienced. Nobody now need end up in fancy dress at a fake shepherd's hut in Richmond Gardens. He had no choice; he would have starved if he did not take the kind of employment they offered him. Nobody need end up there but the processes of being involved and being nudged this way and that as to how really one should write, these processes are very strong and of course they take their form from the prevailing dominant fiction. So that one wholly acceptable form, wholly acceptable since Lawrence, has been the gifted young man or young woman who has come from a working-class family or otherwise poor family and has made it in some way, made it educationally, made it by marrying the boss's daughter, made it by getting to London and becoming a good painter, made it by marrying a German aristocrat and going to New Mexico. The form is deep because, after all, this is bourgeois idyll, is it not? I mean, the lower he starts, the better the rise. There is absolutely no resistance to this in the culture and people can think 'my god, I am telling them now, I'm telling them how tough it was in the old days and how we had bread dipped in hot water and how we did not have boots'; the response is often 'more please, give us more, because you will then be able to justify the class system because you got out of it didn't you? You have made it with the proper people, so describe it, please, because it will be a very good example to others, how with gifts and energy or without too much scruple you got out.' If that is working-class literature, and it has been the most widely acclaimed of what is called working-class literature, then it is a very curious thing.

It is more curious because it seems as if a change of consciousness has occurred. Not just a change within these individuals, breaking out of the class, but to a very significant part of the class as a whole, whether they have actually succeeded themselves in doing it or whether they regard the escape as the only significant way to live even if they have not managed it themselves. It is an open question whether this is what has happened in the period since 1945 to the working class, and there is no simple answer to that question. However, the form corresponds if you read the change that way. If one reads a very interesting and original work like that of David Storey, for example, who is in direct line from Lawrence, you can see it in literary form.[1] Somebody is working in a form that is already there, that others have practised, and the work gains in strength, richness, and maturity. It is very different from people working out the early examples of some new form. Storey with Lawrence behind him is a very significant writer but he is a writer of this kind that I am describing. *Flight into Camden* (1961), as it eventually emerges, is precisely that; it is not that there is not fidelity to the life that has been led, but the significant trajectory of the form is the individual moving away from it.

There is an alternative and I think an interesting one, and in a way more of a novelty in this period since 1945. It has not many precedents in working-class literature although it had its precedents elsewhere. The alternative is well represented by a novel like *Saturday Night and Sunday Morning* (1958) by Alan Sillitoe;[2] this, after all, in its own way, just as decisively rejects certain sectors of working-class life as previous working-class writers had tried to include them. Work now is seen from a working-class position not as something you do not have to do, as in a Virginia Woolf novel or something of that kind, but as so intolerably boring and meaningless that clearly the significance of life is precisely Saturday night

---

1   David Storey (1933–2017) – a playwright and novelist – was the author of, amongst other works, *This Sporting Life* (1960) and *Radcliffe* (1963). He won the Booker Prize for *Saville* (1976).

2   Alan Sillitoe (1928–2010) – a novelist and short-story writer – is, as Williams suggests, credited with forging a new form of working-class writing, notably with his collection *The Loneliness of the Long-Distance Runner* (1959) and the million-selling paperback *Saturday Night and Sunday Morning*.

and Sunday morning. It is precisely when you do not have to work, when you have got your money and when you can have the good time, that you can have the good life. It is very convincingly done and there have been a whole series of examples like it, imitations of it, indeed it became one of the dominant motifs of the 1960s. The emergence of the new kind of working-class hero who was not, as in the proletarian fiction of the 1930s, the tough organizer who led the strike, the strong man who could do a great amount of physical labour, or any of these characteristic, traditional working-class heroes. The new working-class hero was young, randy, liked the drink, the girls, the betting, the sport, and middle-class readers were delighted by the appearance of this figure. That this vitality was defined in terms of sexual vigour had a lot to do with the popularity of the motif. Here were people who had no middle-class repressions, they had no scruples about enjoying themselves, this was the way it was presented and they raised hell every weekend. As a footnote to the form but not really included in it, they were quite right to raise hell at the weekend because look what they did all week, they did this boring job. What would you do if you did that boring job but you did not raise hell at the weekend?

I want to be absolutely clear; this is a very important form, it captures a lot of that kind of resilience and gaiety. However, it crucially misses one very important factor inside working-class experience which in this respect is radically different from the middle-class work lifestyle. The good time in the real working-class occupation is when you are young and physically active and vigorous; you are not like your middle-class equivalent acquiring a training and living on low income in the hope that as you become more qualified you move up the scale and eventually establish yourself somewhere in middle-age as the professional person who then enjoys themselves. Your high wages, your chance of the most physically demanding jobs, come to you as a young worker. And, indeed, if you look at the curve of working-class manual earnings even today you will find that is still the way it goes: the peak is reached somewhere in the early thirties, after which it declines. The celebration of this reckless and attractive vigour of the young man, if pulled out of the general context of working-class life and if not taking into consideration their life twenty, thirty, forty years on, does not handle later difficulties, the keeping up of that kind of work through physical ageing and through what is often declining income. That part of the experience, at once a natural life process and a pre-destined social process, is not there although it is crucial to the class experience, while this other, very attractive emphasis has been made. And of course, it is once again acceptable, highly acceptable to readers who, because the whole society was moving and loosening, feeling it had been too constricted, too cautious, too prudent, welcomed the appearance of these new, reckless, and potent figures. Here were the young working class who were very easy to celebrate, but by identifying them socially you were cancelling some other social fact about them. The curiosity is if you then take those two forms, the escape, the significant escape from working-class life which may include substantial description of that which has been escaped from, and the working-class weekend novel, I mean the young, active, away from work, physical enjoyment, you have in fact described the majority, I think, as far as I know, of post-war British working-class writing.[1] In that respect, the majority situation is not very different from that which was there immediately before 1945: the very difficult problems of mobility and of changes inside the working class itself, particularly the very marked changes to diminution of manual occupations, the rise of the great majority of the semi- or quarter-skilled routine minor factory operations, very different from that old working class which was being described in mining, ship-building, the land, and so on. But those areas, to an important extent, have not been described and it is a cultural question of some real significance to address why that is so.

1979

---

1   Elsewhere, Williams makes a passing reference to Storey and Sillitoe in *The English Novel*, 152. He also had them in mind when discussing the 'new forms of the fifties' in *Politics and Letters*, 272.

7

Pierre Bourdieu and the Sociology of Culture

(with Nicholas Garnham)

The influence of Pierre Bourdieu upon Anglo-Saxon thought and research has been to date extremely fragmentary, restricted to the discipline of anthropology and to the sub-discipline of the sociology of education.[1] These influences are marked by the publication in English of *Outline of a Theory of Practice* (1972) and *Reproduction in Education, Society and Culture* (1970), respectively. Other aspects, however, of what has been recently described as 'a theoretical system that may be the most elegant and comprehensive since Talcott Parsons's' have been largely ignored.[2] This is especially true of the work in the history and sociology of culture carried out by Bourdieu and his colleagues at the Centre de Sociologie

---

1 First published as 'Pierre Bourdieu and the Sociology of Culture: An Introduction' (co-authored by Nicholas Garnham), *Media, Culture and Society*, 2.3, July 1980, 209–23. Original references included and expanded along with new explanatory notes added by the editor.

2 Paul DiMaggio, 'Review: On Pierre Bourdieu', *American Journal of Sociology*, 84.6, 1979, 1462. Talcott Parsons (1902–1979) was an American functionalist sociologist whose book *The Structure of Social Action* (1937) outlines a theoretical system of social action founded on the voluntaristic principle.

Européenne in Paris and published in that Centre's journal *Actes de la Recherche en Sciences Sociales*. Neglect of this aspect of Bourdieu's work is not only damaging in its own right within cultural studies, but this fragmentary and partial absorption of what is a rich and unified body of theory and related empirical work across a range of fields from the ethnography of Algeria to art, science, religion, language, political science, and education to the epistemology and methodology of the social sciences in general can lead to a danger of seriously misreading the theory. A notable example of this danger can be found in the recent attempt by Halsey and his colleagues to refute Bourdieu's theory of cultural capital.[1]

Thus this introductory article takes the opportunity offered by the recent appearance in France of *La Distinction* (1979), a book that sums up work, spanning over a decade and a half, in the sociology of French culture, to present a necessarily sketchy outline of the structure of Bourdieu's thought.[2] Such an outline is intended both to serve as a contextualizing background to the readings from Bourdieu's theoretical and empirical work that follow, readings whose necessarily restricted scope could lead to just those misreadings and misunderstandings to which we have pointed, and to indicate what in particular Bourdieu's work has to offer us at this moment in what he would call the field of British media and cultural studies, for as his own theory would predict the entry of this particular symbolic production into a different

---

1   See A. H. Halsey, A. F. Heath, and J. M. Ridge, *Origins and Destinations: Family, Class and Education in Modern Britain* (Oxford: Clarendon Press, 1980). For instance, they refute the suggestion that cultural capital and educational qualifications are one and the same: 'the state selective schools (much more than the private schools) were doing far more than "reproducing" cultural capital; they were creating it too. They were bringing an academic or technical training to a very substantial number of boys from homes that were not in any formal sense educated' (77).

2   The essay introduces Bourdieu's book *Distinction* which only appeared in English in 1984, translated by Richard Nice. Garnham and Williams had access to Nice's translation, with two sections from *Distinction* – 'The Aristocracy of Culture' and 'A Diagram of Social Position and Life-style' – appearing in the same issue of *Media, Culture and Society*.

field from that in which it was produced will necessarily give it a specifically different function.

The development of British media and cultural studies over the last decade or so has been characterized by two successive stages, stages that Bourdieu's own theory helps us to explain. The first saw the rise out of literary studies of a culturalist Marxism in opposition to both the subjectivism of Leavisite literary criticism and to that empirical, ahistorical sociology of mass communication and popular culture whose intellectual and ideological roots lay in American sociology. The early work of the Birmingham Centre for Contemporary Cultural Studies marks that development. The second stage saw the development (and here the work of *Screen* is exemplary), under the influence first of Althusser and then of Jacques Lacan, of a theoreticist Marxism which directed consideration of the problem of ideology away from economic and class determinants, seen as vulgarly economistic or sociologistic, and towards the 'text' as the privileged site for a relatively autonomous signifying practice and for the deciphering by means of symptomatic readings of the ideological effectivity of those practices.[1] In the last couple of years this Althusserian current has been challenged by those reasserting from within an older Marxist tradition the value of empirical work in both sociology and history as against theoreticism and the need to restress the social efficacy and explanatory power of economic and class determinants.[2]

---

1   According to Paddy Scannell (one of the founding figures of media studies), *Media, Culture and Society* was set up as a counter to *Screen*, which in the late 1970s was primarily edited by Mark Nash. 'In taking a stance against Althusserian Marxism we were not so much defining ourselves against Birmingham [the Centre for Contemporary Cultural Studies] as against *Screen*', says Scannell, who notes that *Media, Culture and Society* was broader in scope and less 'theoretically dogmatic' than the influential film studies journal. See 'An Interview with Professor Paddy Scannell', *Westminster Papers in Communication and Culture*, 4.1, 2007, 5. For Garnham's critique of the approach taken by *Screen* in the late 1970s, see his article 'Subjectivity, Ideology, Class and Historical Materialism', *Screen*, 20.1, 1979.

2   Williams and Garnham recommend Thompson's *The Poverty of Theory* (1978), 'Histories of Culture/Theories of Ideology: Notes on an Impasse' by

The potential value of Bourdieu's work at this specific moment within British media and cultural studies is that, in a movement of critique in the classic Marxist sense, he confronts and dialectically supersedes these partial and opposed positions. Thus he develops a theory of ideology (or rather of symbolic power since in general he reserves the term ideology for more explicit and coherent bodies of thought) based upon both concrete historical research and upon the use of the classical techniques of empirical sociology such as the statistical analysis of survey data. At the same time he develops his critique of theoreticism, in particular structuralist Marxism and its associated formalist tendencies, by specifying with accompanying empirical evidence the historical roots and economic and class determinants of the relative autonomy of intellectual practice, a relative autonomy that is in its turn the condition for the efficacy of intellectual practice as, in general, the practice of ideological domination. Bourdieu writes:

> Ideologies owe their structure and their most specific functions to the social conditions of their production and circulation, i.e. to the functions they fulfil, first for the specialists competing for the monopoly of the competences in question (religious, artistic, etc.), and secondarily and incidentally for the non-specialists. When we insist that ideologies are always *doubly determined*, that they owe their most specific characteristics not only to the interests of the classes and class fractions which they express (the 'sociodicy' function) but also to the specific interests of those who produce them and to the specific logic of the field of production (usually transfigured into the ideology of 'creation' and the 'creator'), we obtain the means of escaping crude reduction of ideological products to the interests of the classes they serve (a 'short-circuit' effect common in 'Marxist' critiques), without falling into the

---

Richard Johnson and 'Ideology and the Mass Media: The Question of Determination' by Peter Golding and Graham Murdock, both from *Ideology and Cultural Production* (1979), ed. Michèle Barret, Philip Corrigan, Annette Kuhn, and Janet Wolff, alongside their own work: *Marxism and Literature* (1977) by Williams and Garnham's 'Subjectivity, Ideology, Class and Historical Materialism' essay.

idealist illusion of treating ideological productions as self-sufficient and self-generating totalities amenable to pure, purely internal analysis (semiology).[1]

The work of which *La Distinction* is a summation is thus a frontal assault upon all essentialist theories of cultural appropriation (taste) and cultural production (creativity), upon all notions of absolute, universal cultural values and especially upon the intelligentsia and the ideologies of intellectual and cultural autonomy from economic and political determinants which that intelligentsia has constructed in defence of its material and symbolic interests as 'the dominated fraction of the dominant class'.[2]

It can be argued that the central, indeed defining, problem of historical materialism is that of reproduction. This is a problem at both a material and symbolic level. That is to say it involves explaining not only how in social formations characterized by spatial extension and division of labour the actions of human agents are co-ordinated so as to ensure the inter-generational reproduction of the material conditions of existence (the problem of the mode of production) but also how the set of unequal class relations produced by that co-ordination is itself legitimized such that reproduction takes place relatively free from social conflict (the problem of the mode of domination). This of course also implies its converse, namely the problem of specifying the conditions under which reproduction does not take place leading to the more or less rapid transformation of the social formation (the problem of crisis and revolution).

It is to this general problem that Bourdieu's Theory of Practice is addressed. While Bourdieu has concentrated his attention upon the mode of domination, upon what he calls the exercise of Symbolic Power, his theory is cast in resolutely materialist terms and it is not just the terms borrowed from economics such as capital, profit, market, and investment, which he uses to describe

1   Pierre Bourdieu, 'Symbolic Power', in *Critique of Anthropology*, 4.13/14, 1979, 81–2.

2   Pierre Bourdieu, *Distinction* (1984; London: Routledge, 2010), 489.

and analyse cultural practice, that links his theory to a properly economic analysis in the narrow sense of that term, that is to say to the analysis of the mode of production of material life, which for Bourdieu is always ultimately and not so ultimately determinate.

The second important link between Bourdieu's work and the central tradition of historical materialism is that it is cast in the form of a 'critique' in the classical sense practised by Marx himself. That is to say one must not make the mistake of appropriating Bourdieu's theoretical and empirical analysis of symbolic power to some marginal sub-discipline such as cultural studies or the sociology of culture and knowledge. This analysis lies at the very heart of his wider general theory, just as theories of fetishization and ideology do in Marx's work, because it provides the very conditions of its own potential scientificity. Bourdieu sees sociology as by definition the science of the social conditions determining human practices and thus the sociology of symbolic power is the science of the social conditions determining intellectual practice, conditions that are always concretely and specifically historical and the exposure of which is in the movement of critique, the condition for achieving an always partial because always socially conditioned escape from ideology into scientific practice and in that movement revealing the historically defined limits of available truth. This is further always a political act because it is the misrecognition of these conditions and limits that is the condition for the exercise of symbolic power to reinforce the tendency to reproduce the existing structure of class relations.[1] He writes: 'The theory of knowledge is a dimension of political theory because the specifically symbolic power to improve the principles of the construction of reality – in particular, social reality – is a major dimension of political power.'[2]

---

1   See Pierre Bourdieu, 'The Specificity of the Scientific Field and the Social Conditions of the Progress of Reason', *Social Science Information*, 14.6, December 1975, 19–47.

2   Pierre Bourdieu, *Outline of a Theory of Practice* (Cambridge: Cambridge University Press, 1977), 166.

Bourdieu describes clearly in the preface to his most recent book [*Le Sens Pratique*, or *The Logic of Practice*] how his own thought has grown out of and in reaction to those successively dominant influences in French thought Jean-Paul Sartre and Claude Lévi-Strauss. In particular he conducts a continual, ambiguous dance of intellectual repulsion and attraction with Sartre. Hence his choice of Gustave Flaubert as an exemplary case in his study of French cultural production:

> It is by no means easy to recall the social effects produced in the French intellectual field by the work of Claude Lévi-Strauss and the concrete mediations through which a new conception of intellectual activity imposed itself upon a whole generation, a conception which was opposed in an entirely dialectical fashion to that figure of the 'total' intellectual, decisively turned towards the political, of which Jean-Paul Sartre was the incarnation. This exemplary confrontation undoubtedly contributed not a little to encouraging in many of those who were at that time turning to the social sciences, an ambition to reconcile theoretical and practical aims, scientific and ethical or political vocations, which are so often split, to fulfil their task as researchers, a sort of militant craft, as far from pure science as it is from the prophetic, in a humbler and more responsible way.[1]

Within Bourdieu's theoretical discourse the terms Subjectivism and Objectivism point to these two poles of post-war French intellectual life. His work in sociology has developed as a specific critique of these two schools of thought which he sees as two successive dialectical moments in the development of a truly scientific theory of practice which in its turn is the condition for an escape from the unconscious cycle of reproduction. Subjectivism, or as he calls it 'the phenomenal form of knowledge', by which he refers to such tendencies as social psychology, ethnomethodology as well as existentialism and phenomenology, focuses upon the individual actor and upon the experiential reality of social action.

---

1 Pierre Bourdieu, *The Logic of Practice* (Cambridge: Polity, 1990), 1–2. Translated by Richard Nice from the original version, *Le Sens Pratique* (Paris: Les Éditions de Minuit, 1980).

It is, according to Bourdieu, a characteristic tendency of sociology which studies its own society and within which therefore the observer is himself or herself also a participant. Objectivism on the other hand, by which in particular Bourdieu refers to all types of structuralism and functionalism, but especially to Lévi-Strauss and Althusser, goes beyond the immediate experience of the individual actor to identify the 'social facts', the observable regularities of social action, but in so doing has a tendency to fetishize the structures, making the agents mere performers of preordained scores or bearers of the structure. This Bourdieu sees as a tendency to which anthropologists are especially prone as observers of societies of which they are not a part. While Subjectivism cannot recognize the social determinants of human action, the Objectivists have a tendency to succumb to that blindness to which intellectuals are particularly prone, indeed it is the ideology specific to wielders of symbolic power, namely the failure to recognize in the idealization of the structure and its logic an expression of their failure to recognize the social conditions of their own practice by failing to recognize the socially and historically specific conditions determining all human practice.

Inextricably intertwined in Bourdieu's work are the discourses of sociology and history. That is to say in developing his Theory of Practice or 'science of the economy of human practices', he sets himself the task of overcoming the opposition between Subjectivism and Objectivism by explaining the relationship between on the one hand the observed regularities of social action, the structure, and on the other the experiential reality of free, purposeful, reasoning human actors. However, in addition, his theory requires that any solution to this sociological problem must at the same time provide a properly historical explanation by specifying the social conditions under which the structure will be reproduced or conversely will be more or less rapidly transformed. Nor are these seen as two separate problems, for one of Bourdieu's main criticisms of traditional sociology, whether Subjectivist or Objectivist, is what he calls its 'Genesis Amnesia',[1] for as with Keynes in

---

1   Bourdieu, *Outline of a Theory*, 79.

economics Bourdieu is concerned to stress that any satisfactory explanation of human action must take full account of the fact that all human action, unlike its reconstruction in science, takes place irreversibly in time.[1] Thus for Bourdieu all human actors are involved in strategies in situations of which the outcome is uncertain because these strategies are opposed by the strategies of other actors. The problem therefore is to specify the mechanism by which, unbeknownst in principle to the actors (for if they knew they would alter their strategy to take account of this knowledge), these strategies of improvisation are objectively co-ordinated.[2]

The regulating mechanism Bourdieu proposes is the habitus. This he describes as 'the strategy-generating principle enabling agents to cope with unforeseen and ever-changing situations',[3] 'a system of lasting, transposable dispositions which, integrating past experiences, functions at every moment as a *matrix of perceptions, appreciations, and actions* and makes possible the achievement of infinitely diversified tasks, thanks to the analogical transfer of schemes permitting the solution of similarly shaped problems'.[4] The habitus is not just a random series of dispositions but operates according to a relatively coherent logic, what Bourdieu calls the logic of practice. This logic is shaped primarily in early childhood within the family by the internalization of a given set of determinate objective conditions both directly material and material as mediated through the habitus and thus the practices of surrounding adults, especially the parents. While later experience will alter the structure of the habitus's logic of practice, these alterations from school or work will be appropriated according to the structural logic of the existing habitus.[5]

---

1   Ibid., 5–6.
2   Ibid., 1–30.
3   Ibid., 72.
4   Ibid., 82–3.
5   Drawing attention to pages 77–8 of *Outline of a Theory*, Williams and Garnham add: 'The primacy and relative inertia of early-childhood influence on the habitus leads to what Bourdieu calls the hysteresis effect and explains his concern with intergenerational as well as inter-class differences and struggles [see Bourdieu, 'The Production of Belief: Contribution to an Economy of

This logic of practice, since it must be operated unconsciously and since it cannot be explicitly inculcated, must be both an impoverished logic in the sense of working with simple categorical distinctions and also flexible so that it can be applied as the structuring principle of practice across a wide range of situations. Thus the logic of practice operates with such simple dichotomous distinctions as high/low, inside/outside, near/far, male/female, good/bad, black/white, rare/common, distinguished/vulgar, etc., principles of categorization that develop in the immediate environment of the young child but can be subsequently applied across a wide range of fields and situations as unconscious regulating principles.[1]

Moreover the habitus is a unified phenomenon. It produces an ethos that relates all the practices produced by a habitus to a unifying set of principles. The habitus is also by definition not an individual phenomenon. That is to say it is internalized and operationalized by individuals but not to regulate solitary acts but precisely interaction. Thus the habitus is a family, group, and especially class phenomenon, a logic derived from a common set of material conditions of existence to regulate the practice of a set of individuals in common response to those conditions. Indeed Bourdieu's definition of class is based on the habitus.[2]

Thus individual practice as regulated by the logic of practice is always a structural variant of group and especially class practice. However, since the habitus regulates practice according to what Bourdieu calls a probabilistic logic – that is to say practice in a given present situation is conditioned by expectation of the outcome of a given course of action which in its turn is based, through the habitus, on the experience of past outcomes – while class origin is overdetermining of the structure of the habitus, practice is also determined by trajectory. Broadly by this Bourdieu

---

Symbolic Goods', in *Media, Culture and Society*, 2.3, July 1980]. In particular he uses it to explain the conservative and nostalgic tendencies in much progressive politics as well as its reactionary alternatives.'

1   See Bourdieu, *Outline of a Theory*, 96–158.
2   Ibid., 81–7.

refers to upward or downward social mobility of either the family, the class fraction or the class in a hierarchy of determinations from class to family. Crudely, upward mobility will give an optimistic view of possible outcomes and downward mobility a pessimistic view, each of which will determine a different set of practical orientations towards the various fields of social struggle. Bourdieu's classic example of the effect of expectations on practice is that of working-class attitudes to involvement in formal education. The point about these expectations is that like other aspects of the logic of practice they reflect not just random individual reactions to the social environment but on the contrary they are realistic assessments in terms of the habitus of the objective probabilities offered by a given state of the social field to an actor in a given class position.[1]

So when Bourdieu turns to the specific field of cultural consumption, or rather appropriation, the regularities his survey data reveals in taste patterns across a wide range of fields from food, clothing, interior decor, and make-up to sport and popular and high art are markers or indices of the habitus of classes and class fractions, and what Bourdieu is concerned to reveal is not a particular pattern of consumption or appropriation, since in a different state of the field other markers could be used for the same relational positions, but the logic which explains this particular relationship between a range of cultural goods and practices and a range of class habitus. Bourdieu's analysis of the concrete specificities of contemporary French cultural practice is thus part of his wider theory of symbolic power, its empirical validation and refinement and at the same time a political intervention in symbolic class struggle:

> Art is the site par excellence of the denial of the social world. But the
> same unconscious intention of denial is the underlying principle of

---

1   See Pierre Bourdieu, 'The School as a Conservative Force: Scholastic and Natural Inequalities', in *Contemporary Research in the Sociology of Education*, ed. John Eggleston (London: Methuen, 1974); and 'The Social Space and Its Transformations', in *Distinction*, 93–164.

a number of discourses whose overt purpose is to talk of the social world and which as a consequence can be written and read with a double meaning. (How many philosophers, sociologists, philologists came to philosophy, sociology or philology as places which because they are not properly fitted into social space allow one to escape definition? All those in effect utopians who do not wish to know where they are, are not the best placed to know about the social space in which they are placed. Would we have otherwise so many readings and 'lectores', materialists without material, thoughts without instruments of thought, thus without an object, and so few observations and as a consequence 'auctores'?). We cannot advance and expand the science of the social world unless we force a turn of the tide by neutralizing this neutralization and by denying denial in all its forms of which the denial of reality inherent in the exaggerated radicalism of certain revolutionary discourses is by no means the least significant. Against a discourse that is neither true nor false, neither verifiable nor falsifiable, neither theoretical nor empirical which like Racine speaks not of cows but of lowing, cannot speak of Daz or of the singlets of the working class but only of mode of production and of proletariat or of the rôles and attitudes of the 'lower middle class', it is not enough to criticize, it is necessary to show, objects and even people, to touch things with one's fingers – which does not mean pointing a finger at them – and to make people who are used to speaking what they think they think and so no longer think about what they say to make such people enter a popular bistro or a rugby ground, a golf course or a private club.[1]

Bourdieu in the Durkheimian tradition sees symbolic systems, as such, as arbitrary, undetermined taxonomies, structuring structures in the sense that they do not reflect or represent a reality, but themselves structure that reality. Moreover, as in the Saussurean model of language, such systems are based upon 'difference' or 'distinction'. However, he criticizes the idealism of the Durkheimian/ Saussurean tradition by stressing that these systems, although

---

1   Pierre Bourdieu, *La Distinction* (Paris: Les Éditions de Minuit, 1979), 596–7. This version is slightly different from the passage which appears in *Distinction*, 511.

arbitrary in themselves, are not arbitrary in their social function which is to represent, but in a misrecognized form, the structure of class relations, and indeed it is their very arbitrariness that allows them to do this since if they were not arbitrary they could not be the object of class struggle. They represent class relations and in the same movement disguise that representation because their logic is that of 'distinction'. In English as in French the double meaning of that word, both a categorical and a social term, precisely mirrors the function of symbolic power.

Thus symbolic systems serve to reinforce class relations as internalized in the habitus since in the internalizing movement of appropriation their specific logic confirms the general logic of class-determined practice. The internalization of the specific logic of symbolic systems or rather, since it is unified, the symbolic system, confirms a hierarchically organized range of distinctions such as rare/common, distinguished/vulgar, disinterested/interested, freedom from necessity/necessity, etc.

For Bourdieu all societies are characterized by a struggle between groups and/or classes and class fractions to maximize their interests in order to ensure their reproduction. The social formation is seen as a hierarchically organized series of fields within which human agents are engaged in specific struggles to maximize their control over the social resources specific to that field – the intellectual field, the educational field, the economic field, etc. – and within which the position of a social agent is relational, that is to say a shifting position determined by the totality of the lines of force specific to that field. The fields are hierarchically organized in a structure overdetermined by the field of class struggle over the production and distribution of material resources and each subordinate field reproduces within its own structural logic, the logic of the field of class struggle. Bourdieu writes:

> the field which cannot be reduced to a single aggregate of isolated
> agents or to the sum of elements merely juxtaposed is, like a magnetic
> field, made up of a system of power lines. In other words the consti-
> tuting agents or system of agents may be described as so many forces

which, by their existence, opposition or combination, determine its specific structure at a given moment of time. In return each of these is defined by its particular position within this field from which it derives positional properties which cannot be assimilated to intrinsic properties.[1]

Social groups and classes enter in each generation a historically given structured state of these fields and they develop and deploy their strategies of struggle on the basis of a historically given level of material, social, and cultural endowment which may, in a given historical state of the field, be transformed into capital. Although the symbolic field like all fields is a field of class struggle and what is at stake is legitimizing or delegitimizing power, there is a tendency for the symbolic field to legitimize a given state of material class relations by means of the specific mechanism of misrecognition by which symbolic systems represent in a transformed, 'euphemized', 'disinterested' form the balance of forces and hierarchical structure of the field of material class relations.[2]

Bourdieu is also working with a model of historical development. He argues, based upon his anthropological field work with the Kabyle in Algeria,[3] that in pre-industrial, so-called primitive social formations characterized by limited spatial extension, limited division of labour, and simple reproduction, the material and symbolic, the mode of production and the mode of domination, cannot be separated. In such societies, with a low level of material resources, symbolic power has a direct economic function (e.g. in labour mobilization) and symbolic violence is the preferred mode for the exercise of power because overt differences in wealth could not be tolerated. Moreover, since, lacking

---

1   Pierre Bourdieu, 'Champ de Pouvoir, Champ Intellectuel et Habitus de Classe', *Scolies*, 1, 1971, 161. Published in English as 'Field of Power, Literary Field and Habitus', in *The Field of Cultural Production: Essays on Art and Literature* (Cambridge: Polity, 1993).

2   See Bourdieu, *Outline of a Theory*, 159–97, and *Distinction*, 223–54.

3   See Pierre Bourdieu, 'The Sentiment of Honour in Kabyle Society', in *Honour and Shame: The Values of Mediterranean Society*, ed. J. G. Peristiany (London: Weidenfeld and Nicholson, 1965), 191–241.

the objectification of power in institutions such as a market or a church, and associated instruments of objectification such as writing, power relations have constantly to be reasserted in direct human interaction, the overt direct exercise of material force would be too expensive in material resources to allow for simple reproduction. Such societies exist in a state of Doxa, where the symbolic system is both common to all and taken-for-granted because existing at an implicit level as a logic of practice rather than as an explicit discourse.[1]

In the next stage of historical development, Bourdieu argues, economic development leads to the growth of an autonomous economic sphere related to the development of exchange relations and in the same movement breaks the thraldom of the Doxa and creates a relatively autonomous symbolic sphere which, by making the symbolic system more explicit, creates class struggle in the symbolic sphere between Orthodoxy and its necessary corollary Heterodoxy. At the same time there is created a specialized group of symbolic producers with an interest in securing a monopoly of the objectified instruments of symbolic struggle, especially written language, an interest that pits them against the dominant economic class in a struggle over what Bourdieu describes as the hierarchization of the principles of hierarchization. At the same time this specialized group shares a mutual interest with the dominant economic class in maintaining the overall set of material class relations both because cultural capital must ultimately be transformable into economic capital or material resources and because the dominant economic class now requires the services of the producers of symbolic goods in the imposition and maintenance of orthodoxy. Because of this mutual interest the symbolic system tends to reproduce the given state of class relations. However, once Heterodoxy has been created, both political consciousness and science become possible and class struggle and its relation to science can never be totally exorcized from the symbolic field. Nonetheless, in a transitional stage historically, Bourdieu argues,

---

1   See Bourdieu, *Outline of a Theory*, 171–83.

the creation of a market economy and of competitive capitalism did lead to the more open exercise of material class power.

However, this in its turn led to more overt revolutionary and reformist opposition such that the dominant class was forced, in order to maintain its dominance, to progressively shift back to the use of symbolic power as the preferred mode of domination.[1] It is with the specific modalities of this third contemporary phase and with its historical roots in the nineteenth century that Bourdieu is now principally concerned. Human agents enter the field of struggle that is the social formation with historically given endowments, either in an incorporated state within the habitus as dispositions and competences, or in an objectified state, as material goods. It is these endowments that Bourdieu refers to as capital, for the purposes of this exposition divided into economic and cultural capital. Each agent enters the struggle with the aim of reproducing the capital of his or her group and if possible augmenting it. To this end he or she pursues strategies of investment which involve choosing the sub-fields and the modes of intervention in those sub-fields likely to yield the highest profit on a given investment, one of the objects of struggle being the relative returns to a given investment in a given field *vis-à-vis* investments in other fields.[2] As Bourdieu puts it, he treats 'all practices, including those purporting to be disinterested or gratuitous, and hence non-economic, as economic practices directed towards the maximizing of material or symbolic profit'.[3]

This general struggle is ultimately determined by economic struggle in the field of class relations because while there is convertibility between economic and cultural capital in both directions (at differing rates of exchange according to a given state of the struggle in each field and in the social field as a whole) it is the convertibility of cultural into economic capital that ultimately defines it as capital and determines not only the overall structure

---

1   Ibid., 183–9.

2   See Bourdieu, *Outline of a Theory*, 171–97; and 'The Invention of the Artist's Life', *Yale French Studies*, 73, 1987, 75–103.

3   Bourdieu, *Outline of a Theory*, 183.

of the social field but also, in a transformed form, that of the sub-fields, because economic capital being more easily transferable from generation to generation is a more efficient reproductive mechanism. This is why the educational system plays such an important role within Bourdieu's theory, because historically the development of such a system, as a system of certification, created a market in cultural capital within which certificates acted as money both in terms of a common, abstract socially guaranteed medium of exchange between cultural capitals and, crucially, between cultural capital and the labour market and thus access to economic capital.[1]

Cultural practice, as with all practices in general, involves appropriation rather than mere consumption. If one can use the analogy of food, the act of ingestion is merely the necessary condition for the process of digestion which enables the organism to extract those ingredients it requires for physical reproduction and reject the rest. In certain conditions digestion will not take place at all. Thus while it remains important that cultural stratification is in part determined directly by the unequal distribution of economic capital and thus of cultural goods (i.e. the working class cannot afford picture collections, large personal libraries, frequent visits to the theatre and opera, etc.), in terms of the legitimation function of cultural practice the ways in which these objective class distinctions are internalized within the habitus as differing dispositions, differing attitudes towards culture, and differing abilities to utilize cultural objects and practices, and thus result in a different logic of cultural practice, are more important. This is why Bourdieu has been particularly concerned to analyse the class determinants of the use of and attitudes towards relatively widely available cultural practices such as museums and photography.[2]

The cultural field serves as a marker and thus a reinforcer of class relations for two reasons. First because a field occupied

---

1   Ibid., 183–97.

2   Bourdieu, *Distinction*, 269–70. For the relationship between the notion of cultural competence and the political role of opinion polls see Bourdieu's chapter on 'Culture and Politics' in *Distinction*, 398–467.

by objects and practices with minimal use value, indeed in the sub-field of art with a positive rejection of use value, is a field in which *par excellence* the struggle is governed by a pure logic of difference or distinction, a pure logic of positionality. Secondly because the specifically historical creation of art as a special category of social object and social practice defined by its difference from and distance from everyday material reality and indeed its superiority to it, together with its matching ideology, namely the post-Kantian aesthetics of 'pure' form and 'disinterestedness', are an expression of and objectively actually depend upon the relative distance from economic necessity provided by the bourgeois possession of economic capital. Works of art, Bourdieu argues, require for their appropriation first an aesthetic disposition, that is to say an internalized willingness to play the game of art, to see the world from a distance, to bracket off a range of objects and practices from the immediate urgency of the struggle for social reproduction and that this disposition is the determinate expression in an incorporated form in the habitus of the material conditions of existence of the dominant class, the bourgeoisie. Further specific competences are required, that is to say a knowledge of the codes specific to a given art form, competences that are not innate but can only be acquired either through inculcation in the setting of the family through experience of a range of artistic objects and practices and/or through formal inculcation in school. Bourdieu argues that distinct patterns of cultural consumption are associated with these different modes of acquisition of cultural competence, modes of acquisition that oppose culturally but also in a social hierarchy relate to the age of the family's economic capital, the old bourgeoisie who acquire their cultural competence in the family so that it appears to be second nature, a natural gift for discrimination, and those who acquire their cultural competence through school and are exposed to all the cultural scorn and insecurity directed at the autodidact, an insecurity that leads them to stick closely to the hierarchies of cultural legitimacy while the children of the old bourgeoisie can express the assurance of their natural taste in a contempt for such hierarchies and by legitimizing new forms of cultural practice such as cinema and jazz.

One of the main ways in which the convertibility of economic and cultural capital is assured is via control over that scarce resource: time. This control takes two forms. First the ability to invest economically in educational time whether in the family, for instance by an educated mother not working and devoting her time to the cultural development of her children, or in school, in order to pass on or acquire cultural capital in the form of dispositions and competences. It is this relation between economic and cultural capital that is reflected in differential class access to different levels of education and to the certification that accompanies it, which in its turn legitimates the stratification of cultural practice linked to achieved level of education, for instance newspaper readership. But secondly and more originally Bourdieu argues that it has been characteristic of the development of cultural practice in the narrowly artistic sense to maximize the complexity of coding (expressed in common parlance as the level of 'difficulty') both textually and inter-textually (thus requiring a wider and wider range of cultural reference, art being increasingly about other works of art) and this development has meant that art necessarily requires for its appropriation high levels of consumption time (for instance in order to see films from the point of view of auteur theory one has to see all the films by that auteur). Since cultural consumption time is differentially available between classes and between fractions of the dominant class, this development steadily reinforces class divisions while legitimizing these divisions by labelling those excluded from the cultural discourse as stupid, philistine, etc.

But the investment of consumption time is not an absolute governed simply by its availability. Since time is always a scarce resource the decision to invest time in a given mode of cultural appropriation will depend upon the relations of force within a given field or set of fields which in their turn will determine the returns that can be expected from a given investment. Those expectations will in their turn, as in all fields of practice, be determined by the habitus. Thus for instance whether a given agent chooses to cultivate literary, musical or artistic competences in general as opposed to sporting or technical competences will depend upon the market objectively open for the investment of his capital and the relative valuation within these markets of these competences. Thus whether someone chooses to acquire and mobilize in social intercourse knowledge of the field of football or of Western European art, of trainspotting or avant-garde cinema, competences between which it is crucial to restress no hierarchical valuations are being or can be made, will depend upon the cultural and economic endowments with which he or she enters the social field, the fields objectively and realistically open for investment given the position of class origin from which he or she starts and the relative weight of various fields. Thus it may be possible to acquire relatively rapidly and mobilize against weak opposition a competence in film criticism, whereas if one entered the field of fine art scholarship with weak cultural capital one would be doomed to marginality and failure. In this context, for example, the recent much discussed differences between Britain and some of her industrial competitors in terms of the differential social and therefore economic profit resulting from investment by an individual and by a class in cultural rather than technical competences is very relevant.[1]

Thus the logic of the cultural field operates in such a way as to create, reproduce, and legitimate (reproduce because legitimate) a set of class relations structured around two great divides, those between the dominant and dominated classes and within the dominant class between the dominant and dominated fractions. The dominant class, roughly equivalent to what the Oxford Social Mobility Study calls the service class,[2] is those possessing high amounts of economic and cultural capital and the dominated class those possessing exiguous amounts of both; Bourdieu sometimes refers to them as working class (*classe ouvrière*) and

---

1   For Bourdieu on inherited capital, acquired capital, and cultural investment see *Distinction*, 73–89.

2   See Halsey, Heath, and Ridge, *Origins and Destinations*.

sometimes as *les classes populaires* (including the peasantry as a distinct class). The primary distinction operated by the dominant culture and the cultural practices it legitimates (and by so doing those practices it delegitimates) is of culture as all that which is different from, distanced from the experiences and practices of the dominated class, from all that is 'common', 'vulgar', 'popular'. In response, at the deepest level of the class ethos the dominated class reject the dominant culture in a movement of pure negation. However, in opposition they construct, at an implicit level, as what Bourdieu calls the aesthetic of the culture of necessity, an aesthetic that relegates form at the expense of subject and function, that refuses to judge works of art or cultural practices on their own terms but judges them according to the social and ethical values of the class ethos, that values participation and immediate semi-sensual gratification at the expense of disinterested and distanced contemplation. Bourdieu clearly sees his work as part of an essentially political effort to legitimize this implicit aesthetic against all current formalisms whether of the right or left, against both what he calls the racism of class which dismisses working-class taste as beyond redemption by culture and against a naïve populism that tries to assimilate that taste to the norms of legitimate culture, seeing miners banners as works of art. He is particularly severe upon the left 'deconstructionists' whose theories and practices he sees as the latest and most effective of the ideologies of those monopolizers of cultural capital, the dominated fraction of the dominant class, ideologies that always serve to reinforce through misrecognition the dominance of the dominant class.[1]

> Brechtian 'distanciation' can be seen as the movement of withdrawal by which the intellectual affirms, at the very heart of popular art, his distance from popular art, a distance that renders popular art intellectually acceptable, that is to say acceptable to intellectuals and, more profoundly, his distance from the people, a distance that this bracketing of the people by intellectuals presupposes.[2]

---

1   See Bourdieu's 'Postscript: Towards a "Vulgar" Critique of "Pure" Critiques', *Distinction*, 487–502.

2   This quote translated from *La Distinction* appears in the 1984 English

The two fractions into which the dominant class is divided are defined in terms of the relative weight in their patrimony of economic and cultural capital. Broadly Bourdieu sees a historical development whereby the dominant class has divided into two specialized groups, the dominant one concerned with material reproduction in the sphere of production, the dominated concerned with the legitimation of material reproduction through the exercise of symbolic power. While for reasons already given, the specialized producers of symbolic goods will ultimately always remain subordinate to economic capital, they nonetheless are involved in a struggle with the dominant fraction over the relative legitimacy and therefore value of cultural as opposed to economic capital. Thus intellectuals in the widest sense of that term will always struggle to maximize the autonomy of the cultural field and to raise the social value of the specific competences involved in part by constantly trying to raise the scarcity of those competences. It is for this reason that while intellectuals may mobilize wider concepts of political democracy or economic equality in their struggle against economic capital they will always resist as a body moves towards cultural democracy. It is the specificities of this contradiction in particular that require analysis in any given historical conjuncture if one is to understand the political position and role of intellectuals.[1]

It is precisely by stressing their 'disinterestedness' in the sense of their distance from crude material values that they maximize their interest in terms of the value at which they can ultimately convert their cultural capital into economic capital or alternatively

---

version as: 'By the same token, Brecht's "alienation effect" might be the gap whereby, within popular art itself, the intellectual asserts his distance from popular art, which makes popular art acceptable, i.e. acceptable to intellectuals, and, at a deeper level, his distance from the people, the distance presupposed by the intellectuals' leadership of the people' (note 7, page 592).

1   See Pierre Bourdieu, 'The Specificity of the Scientific Field', and 'Marriage Strategies as Strategies of Social Reproduction', in *Family and Society*, ed. Robert Forster and Orest Ranum (Baltimore: John Hopkins University Press, 1976), 117–44.

ensure the reproduction of their cultural capital, in particular through their control of the education system and increasingly of the state bureaucracy in general. For the problem that Bourdieu is concerned with is not merely that of establishing a determinate relationship between class and cultural appropriation in a given state of the field of cultural consumption nor between cultural production and class in a given state of the field of cultural production. The problem is more difficult and complex than that for what his general theory of practice as well as his specific theory of symbolic power require him to explain is how the free, apparently autonomous practices of the agents involved in the two different fields and thus whose actions are governed by a different specific logic of practice, how they so interact as to not just produce but reproduce the class patterns of cultural practice in general and by so doing tend to reproduce the given set of class relations in general.

Bourdieu argues on the basis of detailed studies of the class origins, cultural practices, and associated ideologies (i.e. critical theories) of French intellectuals in the nineteenth and twentieth centuries and of the corresponding consumption patterns among the dominant class as a whole, that the struggle between the fractions takes the form of a struggle between intellectuals for dominance within their specific subfield (i.e. painting, literature, social science, the academic world, etc.) and for the dominance of their subfield within the intellectual field as a whole. It is this constant struggle that explains sociologically and historically that process of constant renewal, or at least change, that the Russian Formalists identified as the dynamic principle of art itself. The notion of 'making new'.[1]

Thus a new entrant, especially a new generation of potential symbolic producers, a potentiality already heavily class determined, faces a field in which the dominant positions are already occupied. This hierarchy of dominance is ultimately determined

---

1   See Bourdieu, 'The Specificity of the Scientific Field', and 'Marriage Strategies as Strategies of Social Reproduction'.

by the economic market for symbolic goods provided by the dominant fraction and thus by the rate at which different forms of cultural capital can be transferred into economic capital. The field is thus arranged along two axes. One axis relates to the direct transfer of cultural capital into economic capital via an immediate transfer in the cultural market, i.e. by painting pictures for rich buyers, writing novels or plays which appeal to the dominant fraction or by entering sub-disciplines which the dominant fraction values highly and to which it thus gives high salaries, research grants, and consultancies (medicine and the natural sciences rather than the social sciences or humanities and within medicine heart surgery rather than geriatrics, for example). However, too obvious a success in the market or what is worse too obvious a desire for such success leads to cultural delegitimization because of the overall struggle between cultural and economic capital. Thus the other axis relates to the maximization of cultural capital which translates the principle which structures the economic class field, namely wealth and the distance from necessity that wealth both allows and represents, into rarity and cultural purity. Thus along this axis the avant-garde is more highly valued than mainstream, so-called 'bourgeois' art, pure science than applied science, fine art than graphic art, until recently at least left-wing rather than right-wing politics and so on.[1]

Facing this specifically structured field, which presents a variety of investment possibilities, are a cohort of potential producers themselves structured according to the laws of the formation of the habitus by the same objective set of class relations that structure the field of symbolic production. Firstly entry to the field at all is structured on class lines by the range of dispositions resulting from the objective assessment of the likelihood of success from any given class starting point. Thus a working-class agent is simply less likely to see him or herself as a painter or novelist (or at least as a professional painter or novelist) than a member of the bourgeoisie because such a career requires a high investment

---

1 For Bourdieu on 'cultural pedigree' see *Distinction*, 55–89.

of cultural capital, which implies for a member of the working class a high investment of time in education to acquire the necessary competences. However, since economic success also requires the ability to fit the disposition for cultural appropriation of the bourgeoisie (e.g. surgeons or conductors or successful novelists and playwrights require objectively bourgeois social attributes), a working-class entrant will be forced in the direction of attempting to maximize the return on acquired cultural capital, which is indeed the point of entry into the dominant class for members of the dominated class, by choosing to enter fields which maximize the possible return while minimizing the possible risks. However, in general the strategy of maximizing cultural capital is both economically risky and expensive since it requires in the early years of practice an ostentatious refusal of direct economic interest and is directed against those who are occupying the culturally most powerful positions within the symbolic field. Thus Bourdieu argues, particularly in relation to Flaubert and the 'art-for-art's sake' movement, that the strategy of maximizing cultural capital, although it often takes on necessarily, as part of the strategy, the lineaments of political radicalism, of opposition to the bourgeoisie, requires existing membership of the dominant fraction of the dominant class to be a viable strategy. Thus Bourdieu argues specifically against Sartre's psychological analysis of Flaubert's artistic development, arguing that this cannot explain the properly sociological fact that all the leading practitioners and theorists of 'art for art's sake' came from the provincial bourgeoisie, thus disposing them to challenge the dominant cultural forms of the Parisian bourgeoisie, while at the same time they all had private means to sustain an uneconomic cultural strategy. He also argues that Flaubert's position as a younger son was typical and that there is a consistent class strategy of using the symbolic field much as the church and the army were used by the aristocracy to ensure a comfortable, high status career for younger sons and increasingly daughters without dissipating the family's economic capital.[1] As a

---

1   See Bourdieu, 'The Invention of the Artist's Life'.

new twist to this strategy he sees the growth of new media-related professions and marginal service industries – such as restaurants, craft shops, and health clinics – as related to the need, because of the relative democratization of education, to create jobs for members of the old bourgeoisie where inherited as opposed to acquired cultural capital can be put to most profitable uses.

Thus both direct economic pressures and the cultural investment required for successful competition for cultural dominance ensure a tendency for the class structure of the dominant class to reproduce itself and its control over symbolic production since those entering the field will possess a habitus which either predisposes them to support the dominant ideology, i.e. members of the dominant fraction directly entering dominant positions or upward mobile members of the petty bourgeoisie forced to invest their small amount of hard-earned cultural capital in the lower echelons of economically favoured positions ensuring a relatively risk free but low return on their investment. On the other hand, what opposition there is is transmuted into the terms of the practical logic of cultural struggle which values rarity and cultural distinction with its associated modes of cultural appropriation, requiring high levels of cultural competence and capital, and thus excluding objectively the dominated class from consumption while legitimizing class distinction as cultural distinction.

Bourdieu's work raises a number of questions for us. First and most obvious is the need, within the terms of the theory, for comparative work to analyse the similarities and differences inscribed in different histories of the strategies of domination and resistance employed by the dominant and dominated classes and between fractions of the dominant class in Britain as opposed to France. The recent work by Mulhern on 'The Moment of "Scrutiny"' is exemplary in this regard.[1]

---

1   See Francis Mulhern, *The Moment of 'Scrutiny'* (London: New Left Books, 1979). 'Mulhern, by raising the question of the historic significance of literary criticism, raises [...] the question of its continuing role in the national culture at a radical level', argued John Goode, who added that Mulhern's study of Leavisite criticism was 'the most important intervention in this domain of

Another research problem is that raised by Murdock and Golding, Garnham, and Miège,[1] namely the effect on the operation of symbolic power of the increased intervention of economic capital directly into the field of the production of symbolic goods via the so-called culture industries and the ways this might affect the field of force in the struggle between the fractions of the dominant class in a situation in which the economic interests of the dominant fraction directly threaten the cultural interests of the dominated fraction.

Then there is the question of Bourdieu's politics. Paul DiMaggio recently described his position as that of a Durkheimian anthropologist rather than a Marxist revolutionary, and the French Marxists, who are so often the target of his attacks, have in return accused him of a relativistic pessimism. If to be as objective as possible about the possibilities of a major and immediate transformation of the social formation of advanced capitalism is to be pessimistic, then Bourdieu is, rightly in our view, pessimistic. However, it has to be stated that unlike many who would criticize this position he is: (a) resolutely committed to a materialist theory of class struggle and of the position of symbolic struggle within that wider struggle; (b) especially in *La Distinction* he exhibits a very rare attribute on the left, namely a positive and unpatronizing valuation of the cultural values and aspirations of the working class which at the same time never lapses into naïve populism or workerism; (c) that his theory, while focused on the problem of symbolic power, allows fully for the concrete analysis of the specific contradictions between the objective social conditions determined by the mode of production and the consciousness and practices of classes and class fractions, contradictions that

---

socialist cultural theory since *Culture and Society* appeared in 1958'. Goode, 'The Moment of "Scrutiny"', *New Left Review*, I/122, July–Aug 1980, 90.

1   Here, alongside Garnham's own work, attention is drawn to the work of Graham Murdock and Peter Golding (authors of 'For a Political Economy of Mass Communications' published in *The Socialist Register* in March 1973) as well as Bernard Miège, whose article 'The Cultural Commodity' was translated by Garnham for *Media, Culture and Society* in July 1979.

might offer the concrete possibility of revolutionary mobilization and action. However, it has to be said that there seems to us
(and this is very much a question of tone, nuance, and attitude)
to be a functionalist/determinist residue in Bourdieu's concept
of reproduction which leads him to place less emphasis on the
possibilities of real change and innovation than either his theory
or his empirical research makes necessary. In our view it is necessary to distinguish within the process of reproduction between
'replication' and 'reformation'.[1] Reformation points us towards
the spaces that are opened up in conjunctural situations in which
the dominant class is objectively weakened and which thus offers
opportunities for real innovation in the social structure, for shifts
in the structure of power in the field of class relations which, while
falling short of 'revolution' in the classical sense, are nonetheless of
real and substantial historical importance and are objectively 'revolutionary' within a longer historical rhythm. For instance it seems
to us that Bourdieu points to just such a potential for 'reformation' in his analysis of the contradictions produced by the current
state of class relations in the field of education and employment
in France. Here he argues that the dominant class, as part of the
wider historical movement towards the use of symbolic power as
the preferred mode of domination, has increasingly shifted from
economic to cultural capital as its preferred mode of accumula-
tion (for instance gaining privileged access to economic power
via control of the higher reaches of the state and state-economic
bureaucracy which in its turn is controlled by means of privileged
access to the dominant institutions of higher education – the so-
called Grandes Écoles). This shift, however, because of the relative
inefficiency of cultural capital for reproduction purposes, unless
it can be translated back into economic capital, presents the dominant class with a major problem. As a result of the increased
'democratization' of education in response to reformist pressures,
pressures which had in part to be met in order to retain the legitimizing power of schooling as a reproduction mechanism, the

1   See Williams on 'Reproduction', in *Culture*, 181–205.

working-class's educational expectations have been raised and at the same time, because of the necessary linkage between school and the job market, its expectations of the better job associated with that attained educational level. These expectations are not being and cannot be met because in order to retain schooling as an operation of hierarchization through which they retain control of the new centres of economic power and thus legitimate that control, the dominant class are forced objectively to devalue educational qualifications, while at the same time the objective developments in the field of material production are yielding to massive de-skilling and the proletarianization of sectors of traditional mental labour. This is a problem, some would argue, that is already calling forth a strategy of domination increasingly reliant on direct rather than symbolic violence. What is not clear is the extent to which Bourdieu himself would draw these conclusions from his own concrete analysis.

Finally there is the epistemological problem of the social conditions of Bourdieu's own intellectual practice. This of course relates to the problem of social change, of 'reformation'. If Bourdieu's is a progressive political intervention, as he clearly believes and with which we agree, does the structure of the symbolic field according to his own theory doom the intervention to recuperation and futility or on the other hand are there conditions under which the logic proper to the symbolic field can produce contradictions at the symbolic level such that they no longer tend to reproduce the given set of class relations?

1980

8

Popular Forms of Writing

The notice at the station tonight said 'due to adverse weather conditions' and with the theme of this talk in mind it was worth reflecting on the phrase; we take it absolutely for granted now, 'due to adverse weather conditions', we don't ask why didn't they put 'because of bad weather' or just 'snow'.[1] That phrase, 'adverse weather conditions', has replaced our direct language; we have all learned to use it, especially when we're being either official or posh. This is the first area I want to talk about because, before we can talk about popular writing, which is distinctly a modern problem in societies like our own, we have to think for a little while about the relations between speaking and writing which turn out to be historically important and still to have their effect on the problems of popular writing today.

It is a very obvious point but it is fundamental when you reflect on it, that all the oral forms – both the oldest and most common of all: people speaking and listening including in organized ways – come in the natural process of ordinary growing up, what the station announcer would have called socialization

1   A talk given at Centerprise, Hackney, 8 January 1982. The lightly edited transcription – from a recording in the Williams family archive – and explanatory notes are by the editor.

I suppose. We all, except for the occasional physical disability, learn to listen and speak, without being given any specific cultural privilege.[1] From the beginning, those cultural resources are in some degree made available to us and in highly developed ways, even within relatively deprived communities or classes and those materially deprived you can still have that rich resource of speaking and hearing available to you. Because writing has dominated cultural activity, especially since print, we've failed to see the cultural shift, the inherent cultural division that is there – whatever the general policy of a society – by the fact that what is thought of as the central cultural medium has to be acquired, it doesn't come in the ordinary process of growing up. You have to be given access to it, you need fairly considerable training in writing and reading, and so from the beginning there is a cultural specialization, and the relations between that and speaking, which we all have as a resource, are historically very complicated because even when there is the decision to make these faculties general, it is still very differentially distributed. Further, the relations between the kind of language that gets imbedded in print and taken as the standard of the language can have very differential relations to the way other groups in the society actually speak. When it comes to difficult matters of description and expression, these effects can be very important. So before we get to popular forms of writing at all, we have to recognize that there's an inbuilt bias within writing against what we broadly mean by popular expression because the historical balance has been shifted that way.

This is so, especially in the case of writing, because if you go back to Harriet Martineau and others writing around the turn of the nineteenth century you get this response to the new demand for literacy by what I suppose was then half to two-thirds of the British population who couldn't write or read.[2] There was a case for

---

1   Williams also touches on writing as a distinct, systematic skill in his brief introduction – simply titled 'Writing' – to *Writing in Society*, 1–7, and expands on the social development and acquisition of speech, language, and writing in *Culture*, specifically the chapter 'Means of Production', 87–118.

2   Harriet Martineau (1802–1876) was a prominent Victorian writer

teaching the poor to read, because then they could read the Bible and get moral instruction and learn to be content with their lot and so on; later on, people pointed out that they could also read notices and instructions. But when somebody said, 'I'm writing', that response wasn't there, not at all, 'what would such people have to write?', they said. And this inbuilt bias in education in those early days although, of course, now greatly changed, shows the way in which the distribution of this key resource gets socially controlled by comparison with what is after all the largest part of the history of imaginative composition in language; it is composition in the resource we all acquire in the normal process of human development which is speaking and hearing. And, just to complete this rough preliminary outline, the key importance I think of the electronic media is that although imposing their own new kinds of control, they are not able to impose a control at the very level of access. I mean there is no way in which you have to go to somebody to be instructed and trained in particular ways to listen to the radio or watch a speaker on television. Although other controls come into play, the fact that we're back to some of the basic social resources, rather than having to go through the education process before we begin expression, is I think in the medium term – who can think now about the short term, it's barely thinkable about – ought to be very constructive. But still we are talking about writing and rightly so, because the new media they are using, these general resources of speaking and listening and so on, are still heavily dependent on central cultural production which is still in print and in writing. The cultural forms have become so set towards print, and writing does seem the preferred medium.

Of course, because the history is like that, we don't know as much as we should about the long, immense body of popular imaginative composition which didn't pass through print. What

and journalist. She wrote extensively for *The Daily News* and first came to prominence with her studies of figures such as Jeremy Bentham, Adam Smith, and David Ricardo in *Illustrations of Political Economy* (1832–34). An early and leading sociologist, Martineau also wrote novels, travel books, and campaigned for the rights of women and the abolition of slavery.

people call, retrospectively, oral literature, although that's a contradiction if you ever wanted one, I mean after all, most of the
poetry in the world, most of the drama in the world, most of
popular imaginative composition wasn't written down, it was
spoken and performed and passed on through oral storytellers.
We have quite considerable records of what that was like but every
one of them has passed through a print medium, and because of
the limited distribution of the ability to read and write, it often
passed through a very selective kind of mind and was often being
pulled back towards certain norms.[1] If you look at the way the old
Celtic oral tales, for instance, went through the priests who wrote
them down and even when you got the good priest, as it were, or
the good monk who was writing down as near as he could remember them, you see all that sort of shift. We don't really know much
about it in this country until we come to drama, the genuinely
popular drama of the Middle Ages and of the late sixteenth, early
seventeenth century, the great drama, where there is a distinction
that I want to explore. It is a distinction not for its own sake, that's
merely the history, but because I think it still has some effect. I
want to take the example of a kind of speech, a kind of writing of
speech which was genuinely popular; it was all written and told
by the dramatist, which was differently orientated from the formal
and the polite.

Now this is very widely misunderstood and there's been
heavy ideological interpretation by most scholars. If you take for
example the porter in *Macbeth* (1606): look up accounts of why
the porter comes on, swearing and cursing about having to get
up in the middle of the night to answer the door.[2] 'Knock, knock.
Who's there?' is one of the phrases that right through the oral

---

1   Williams offers an historical perspective on such developments and
the importance of technological advances in 'Communications, Technologies
and Social Institutions', in *What I Came to Say* (London: Hutchinson, 1989),
172–92.

2   For more on the use of monologue in *Macbeth*, and an extended discussion of Shakespeare's plays, see Williams's essay 'On Dramatic Dialogue and
Monologue' in *Writing in Society*, 50–7.

tradition has persisted. Most scholars say, 'Well it's comic relief,' all the textbooks say, 'It's comic relief,' you've had enough of blood for a while so bring on some knockabout low-class character for comic relief and then you go on with the real play and the important people. You get the same sort of interpretation for the gravedigger in *Hamlet* (1603), he's a funny sort of clownish character who sets off the prince's eloquence, and there's the jailer in *Cymbeline* (1611). So there's a whole series of such characters. We do know a lot more about this now but immediately as we got to know about it, the linguists gave it a description which would put anyone off, they called it anti-language, which is precisely what it isn't. It is language, it's not anti-language. In fact I'm trying to get a different term adopted which is counter-language – that is what it really is.[1] The point is that it is not written for relief, it is written for tension. And those characters, and these are by no means the only ones, have not only a different idiom but an idiom which is put into a certain critical relation with the more formal and polite speech of the courts and the highly educated and the privileged who dominate the actions of the drama. I'm not saying there isn't a class bias inherent in the constructions of the plays, there is, and it is almost impossible that it could have been otherwise. Nevertheless, it is one of the remarkable things about that drama and precisely because it was being played to a very heterogeneous audience, what you could genuinely call a popular audience in the cities anyway, that the position of these characters, which you can even get down to where they stood on the stage in relation to the more formal characters, was an identification with the audience. People were in a sense speaking in the terms of the majority of the audience about the things that were going on further upstage in a much more elevated way. It

---

1   'Counter-language' is a term Williams introduced during his lectures and seminars at Cambridge in the early 1980s. In 'On Dramatic Dialogue and Monologue', he explains it thus: 'the evident linguistic shift, to a traditional colloquial mode, is not empty "relief" but a deliberate shift of dramatic perspective: a connecting communal mode, played very close to the audience, in which the action is seen from a different base', *Writing in Society*, 50–1.

is clear that this is what's happening with the porter in *Macbeth*, but perhaps the best example is Thersites in *Troilus and Cressida* (1602) where Troilus and Ulysses watching Cressida's betrayal are doing almost everything but call it what it is. They are discussing in very elevated language what's happening when it's obvious to anyone who looks what's happening, and when Thersites says 'now they are clapping and clawing each other' you get this immediate move into this rougher, popular language. He is standing at the front of the stage, half-turned to the audience and half-turned to them while they are upstage in this much more formal position, speaking in a different language. Now, I am not saying, it would be absurd, that Shakespeare is choosing a popular language tradition as an alternative to the formal, that is not what happens. But the two elements are included and if you look at what happened as that popular drama audience of that period narrowed and became a much more class-based and selective audience, it was that element of the language that was excluded from writing. People increasingly thought that the proper language of literature, the proper language of polite writing, had to exclude that much more vigorous, colloquial language not done for its own sake, done because those characters stood as a sort of bridge between the audience and these more formal events.

That was a culture only just coming out of a majority oral phase in which a lot of the great composition is after all in drama and in the sermons – oral forms in a largely pre-literate society. Steadily, however, you get the increased authority of print and probably an actual narrowing of the extent of literacy in the course of the later seventeenth and eighteenth centuries. Probably the amount of literacy went down at the same time the confidence, not to say the arrogance, of those who controlled the printed word and through it controlled education went up. After all, it was in the eighteenth century that the notion was developed that there was one true English which was put into the new dictionaries and into the manuals. These were often full of errors by the way, errors of the pronunciation coaches, the spelling coaches who were bounded in the eighteenth century to teach the new bourgeoisie how to read and how to talk proper, having made their money. The whole notion of a correct language and of one use, and this totally anti-linguistic notion of an English which existed over against all the dialects, is still the biggest problem in popular writing in our own time. It is most difficult for people entering a world of print: the notion that somewhere, and actually there is no great secret about where it is, there is a real English and everywhere else there are subordinate varieties of it. This is the time when the word 'dialect' changed to suggest 'subordinate' and an 'eccentric variety' of a language;[1] it is the same time when 'region' got the notion of a 'subordinate' part of somewhere rather than just that place where other people live.[2] The authority of print and the authority of correctness got so heavily established that the problem of people writing from a different social base was full of difficulties even when it had been to some extent theoretically understood. But then of course it wasn't theoretically understood until really well into our own century; I mean I wouldn't like to bet now how many people would dissent from the proposition that there is a form of correct English which isn't just one particular way of speaking it or writing it but is something much more than that, the real thing that you've got to learn.

---

1   'It is indeed in the stabilization of a "national" language, and then within that centralizing process of a "standard", that wholly native, authentic and longstanding variations become designated as culturally subordinate', writes Williams, in his entry on 'dialect' in *Keywords*. 'The language, seen neutrally, exists as this body of variations. But within the process of cultural domination, what is projected is not only a selected authoritative version, from which all other variations can be judged to be inferior or actually incorrect, but also a virtually metaphysical notion of the language as existing in other than its actual variations' (105–6).

2   Williams makes a similar comparison between dialect and region in *Keywords*, commenting specifically on 'regional' as a cultural term: 'It can, like dialect, be used to indicate a "subordinate" or "inferior" form, as in "regional accent", which implies that there is somewhere (and not only in a class) a "national accent". But in "regional novel" there can be simple acknowledgment of a distinct place and way of life, though probably more often this is also a limiting judgment' (265).

Of course, since the educational system has been controlled from that belief, we have had now in universal education more than a century of people coming with these resources I was talking about at the beginning, resources of speaking and listening which we acquire in the ordinary processes of growing up, coming with them for an education which is going to give knowledge and enlarge the mind, stimulate, and give opportunities for practice, only to be told – based on their most basic possession and resource – that they're inadequate. And because we are all inadequate and because none of us can speak English well enough and none of us can write well enough, it is very easy to agree until it's too late to see the trick that is being practised on you. The inadequacy doesn't come from those exceptional cases of a few exceptional teachers or from the sense that there would be a better way of doing it which is worked out in relation to the actual material in hand; it comes from this notion, which is supposedly supported by scholarship, that there is a 'correct' way. But the tensions around that 'correct' way are enormous. If you explore the rise of the most approved accent in English and the way people learn it or adapt to it and at the same time have for well over a century and a half been getting a lot of their fun out of parodying it and writing pastiche of it, you get a curious amalgam of resentment and deference around the notion of correct English which goes right into the heart of the whole problem of British sensibility. The energies locked up in that complication of resentment and deference I think are very considerable.

Now, in fact, this bears on something which is coming very much towards our own time, because you do happen to get from the second half of the eighteenth century quite a lot of people, working men and women, beginning to write, and indeed in a certain way some of them are taken up and patronized, even in some cases petted. It is usually a bad history, if you look at what happened to Stephen Duck who was a thrasher and a quite considerable poet in the mid-eighteenth century.[1] He got helped

---

1   See 'British Working-Class Literature after 1945' in this collection,

initially by being given books, which was kind, but in the end he was turned into a sort of footman attendant on some royal pavilion as a way of giving him money, by which time he had been put in that subordinate position and instead of writing the material of his early poems he was anxiously aping the fashionable poets of the time. This happened in case after case. I don't think there's anybody who escapes it until John Clare in the 1820s and even then Clare only fully escapes it by the time the society has decided he's insane.[1] The tension on Clare was enormous: Clare without orthodox punctuation, without orthodox spelling, with a tremendous sense of the natural rhythms of the language, still sticking to his material. It was the thing Duck and others couldn't do and didn't do. Of course, that was not the only basis for the diagnosis of insanity, but it shows some of the stresses that are there. In other words, in a medium which is already dominated by a standard form which is being imposed by people with other interests and other experiences and notions of what is the correct way to write, it is no use saying from some theoretical distance, either now or historically, that people ought to have resisted, ought to have been themselves, ought to have written as they spoke, ought to have kept to their own material. You can't say that, the job is too tough. It's too near the roots, you need all your energy to be able to do anything of it at all and if your energy is continually being sapped by the confusion of the fact that it's difficult anyway, which it is for anyone who is taking it seriously, and this particular difficulty which is the contrary, then there can't be any sort of adverse sense or direct criticism as we look at what happened to those poets. On the contrary, it is with great respect. But because of the respect,

---

during which Williams also discusses Stephen Duck, an agricultural labourer who became a court poet.

1   John Clare (1793–1864) – poet, farm labourer, and naturalist – was first committed to an asylum in Epping Forest in 1837, dying at a Northampton asylum at the age of seventy. Williams, along with his daughter Merryn, edited *John Clare: Selected Poetry and Prose* (1986) and described the poet as 'in every way a deeply significant figure', one able to capture the 'inwardness of [...] social transformation', *The Country and the City*, 166.

one doesn't disguise the result, we look straight at it, they would have wanted us to.

With this anxious adaptation towards what's thought to be correct, what's thought to be the proper literary form and what's thought to be the proper material of a poem, you see it even in the popular radical verse from the 1780s through to the middle of the nineteenth century, yet often with admirable sentiments. The language is often this acquired language, only that which is thought to be the entry into print, the necessary part of the entry. And you get more coming through, although it is a difficult case in theatre and in particular in that area between melodrama and music hall. Here you have popular writers who made much closer approaches to writing about what they wanted to write about and writing about it in a language near themselves and their hoped-for audience rather than what you'd find in print. You can overstate this; we shouldn't idealize the music hall, which is a typical mix of absolutely incorporated culture of people playing the fashionable tricks and imitating society gentleman and ladies. At the other extreme, it is the absolutely authentic writing, including especially the comedians coming out of a popular life and carrying on that which the popular tradition has never been without: a constant supply of the jokes and the catchphrases of the day which are extraordinarily vigorous compared with the level of the official culture. But music hall is a mixed case, so I think really is melo-drama. Some people now try to say that melodrama was the really popular radical form. It was popular in the sense that a much wider part of the people went to it and, undoubtedly, it engages people by writing about themes that interested them: melodrama plots are full of social injustice, of the poor being cheated by landlords, by officers, by the aristocracy, indeed the standard themes are that. At the same time, however, you don't only perceive that source of villainy, in melodrama you always magically escape from that villain. This does make most melodrama in the end an extremely conformist mode because you've identified the wicked officer and the wicked aristocrat and usually identified the heroine, the girl betrayed by one of them. But, what is crucial, is that you don't go through with that difficulty, you don't say this is where we are, you don't say what should we do about it. The whole point about the form which became so popular was that a letter or a birthmark or whatever turned up and you were really the long-lost daughter of an aristocrat and you shouldn't have been treated that way. This is a sell-out, over fifty years, a sell-out over and over because all your emotions have been engaged on the side of the poor girl who has been used and betrayed by the rich man and then at the end she wasn't a poor girl after all and she may even, if things haven't got too far, marry him, and the rest of the poor girls, well that will be a subject for another play but then the same thing will happen with the next poor girl.

There's some danger now – I say this about some of my colleagues and old students who have idealized the radical melodrama – it's full of radical stuff in the early acts, it's only if you read the last act that you realize what a deeply conformist thing it is. Amongst the people sitting in those audiences through the nineteenth century, the desire for magical solutions was very strong. This is one of the things that you come onto in twentieth-century commercial popular culture, it's always what's underestimated, if one's lucky enough not to have the pressures on oneself too hard. It is a great thing to sit in a theatre or a cinema and see problems melt away. If only, without any illusions, they won't be there when you go home. You still feel that you've had an evening which has relieved you in some way, encouraged you, perhaps you too are the long-lost daughter of an aristocrat. Perhaps you too would be the best prize fighter of the day. All these dreams of where you name the problem and then the magical solution, that is a genuine element of popular drama. We should never merely idealize it as that's the real danger, we should face the fact that it engages this in language and theme and then sells it out.

As a matter of fact, we have to trace that to what happened in journalism and is still happening. William Cobbett takes on *The Times* in the early nineteenth century and writes a plain, abusive English – that's what one must call it because abusive it is, at a level which still makes your hair curl when you don't know the objects.

The thought of a Cobbett now, you know, being able to say the things Cobbett regularly said and when he's been put in prison comes out saying twice as hard, taking on *The Times* and beating it in the early nineteenth century, getting a bigger readership.[1] By the middle and end of the century those papers have become capitalized at levels which are not accessible to some radical independent or group; the level of mechanical investment is much higher and the radical papers have been marginalized, they are just then the papers of the political underground as compared to what has become the widely read and the so-called 'popular' press. Popular at this point having changed its meaning from 'of the people, for the people' to widely bought *by* the people and provided for them by others.[2] That is the history of the nineteenth century and it is still largely the history of our own, and in the course of it, this very skilful business of knowing enough, either by study and imitation or by having come from a poor family yourself, knowing enough of the language, knowing enough of the colloquial and the demotic, knowing enough of the slang, to be able to write for the boss as if he was not the boss. This is one of the histories of modern commercial popular journalism. Who could

---

1   William Cobbett (1763–1835) was a political writer imprisoned for two years in 1810 for sedition after criticizing the flogging of common soldiers in Ely. Cobbett faced a second prison spell in 1831; he was prosecuted for incitement and subversion, with the case reaching trial before being dropped. In his study of the renowned pamphleteer, Williams quotes from Cobbett's article on the 1830 labourers' revolt which led to the second prosecution: 'Will this Ministry *shed their blood*? ... The bloody old *Times* newspaper, which is the organ, and, perhaps, in great part the *property*, of this hellish crew, says, that the labourers "*are starving*, and that they have been *cruelly oppressed*; but that *some* of them must be made to suffer the *severest penalty* of the law". So that this bloody crew would have men *put to death* for using the *only means* left to save themselves from starvation!', quoted in Williams, *Cobbett* (Oxford: Oxford University Press, 1983), 51.

2   See Williams's entry for 'popular' in *Keywords*, 236–8. For an extended discussion of the meanings of 'popular' as they pertain to journalism and the history of British newspapers, see his chapter on 'The Growth of the Popular Press', in *The Long Revolution*, 195–236, and 'The Press and Popular Culture: An Historical Perspective', collected in *What I Came to Say*, 120–31.

compete with some really successful right-wing journalist who's really studied that? Someone who gets through hard by having learnt the tricks of simulating ordinary talk, man to man. Richard Hoggart studied this in the 1950s; it was a very important moment when this was pinned down – immediately they asked Hoggart to advise them how to do it better.[1] He is a man of principal and he refused but there are lots that haven't refused.

How distant, how narrow, and then often how stilted can sound the language of the political activist by comparison with the man who can really write three metaphors a sentence about football. You get to feel, if you are a certain kind of writer, that you are in the wrong trade, you too should be writing three metaphors a sentence about the processes of capitalist incorporation except that the three metaphors a sentence for that come pretty hard. And anyway most of the ones you'd be using would be playing into people's false perceptions of that whereas you can hit out a false perception about any of these other things with a century's practice behind you. What happened then in melodrama happened also in popular writing and then there was this one area which both has been and, I think, still is an area where much of this can be avoided. I think at the level of argument, when you got deeply imbedded falsehoods in a society, it is extraordinarily difficult except at certain moments of crisis when people's feelings are really roused and when certain issues have become very clear and open and public, and it's not too complex a situation, at such

---

1   In his 1957 review of *The Uses of Literacy*, Williams was more critical of Hoggart, albeit on different grounds: 'he has admitted (though with apologies and partial disclaimers) the extremely damaging and quite untrue identification of "popular culture" (commercial newspapers, magazines, entertainments, etc.) with "working-class culture". In fact the main source of this "popular culture" lies outside the working class altogether, for it was instituted, financed and operated by the commercial *bourgeoisie*, and remains typically capitalist in its methods of production and distribution.' See 'Fiction and the Writing Public', originally published in *Essays in Criticism*, collected in *What I Came to Say*, 27. For the two men in conversation, and a sense of the differences between them, both biographically and politically, see 'Working Class Attitudes', *New Left Review*, I/1, Jan–Feb 1960.

moments you can get the language of argument which is not fake popular but genuinely popular. Suddenly you find that people are writing and speaking in ways which do connect with the ordinary language and yet which do not reduce, simplify, or traduce the issues but still you've got, all the time, an immense body of argument alongside it, or pseudo argument, which is able to get there much quicker precisely because it is formed around the existing prejudices and mystifications.

I had this as a student when we used to get a very hard training for any left organization, if you were writing a pamphlet it must be good, hard-hitting, popular language, none of this student stuff, not like you'd write your essays, people used to say.[1] So we'd go and write our hard-hitting, popular pamphlets about things we didn't know a lot about and of course we developed a style of being hard-hitting and popular which I hope no one ever looks up in the files. That stuff dates; the vocabulary of political abuse and what you call your opponents and what you call your friends, it can't be done in that way at the level of argument. You have to be very tough in defending the true complexity of issues against the false appeal to writing the simple hard-hitting piece about something pretty complicated like a capitalist crisis or whatever it may be. It still happens, a lot of the best people want to do it. I had a highly intellectual research student who would not go on with his research because he was determined to write an agitational pamphlet for the post office workers who were on strike. And since his style was Lukácsian, I used to really look forward to this pamphlet. When he produced a draft, of course the postal office workers didn't want it. The impetus is good and it can be done, we've seen with Cobbett that it can be done, but if it can't be done, there is no need in my opinion to have this endless guilt about it.

---

1   As a member of the Communist Party of Great Britain (CPGB) and a student in the English Faculty, Williams joined the Writers' Group at Cambridge. '[W]e were often called on to do rush jobs in propaganda', he recalls of his work for the CPGB. 'You were often in there writing about topics you did not know very much about, as a professional with words. The pamphlets were issued from on top, unsigned', *Politics and Letters*, 42–3.

At least by this stage in the culture in those complex arguments, the reality of the issues is what matters; that is the responsibility. It isn't as if endless simplification of every colour were not all the time available; my experience is that most people know perfectly well what it is and are perfectly sick of it – just to join in because it's a good thing is a kind of betrayal although it's often undertaken for the best of motives.

There is this other area which is really in the end much more important because it's much nearer to where most people live: the areas of imaginative prose, plays, poems. Here the situation is now very different from that nineteenth-century situation I was describing, although still with its problems. One of the extraordinary things is when you see how many working-class writers there are in the nineteenth century and think why hardly any of them wrote novels. What we are now finding is how many of them wrote autobiographies. It wasn't lack of writing skill, a lot of the autobiographies are extremely well written and Samuel Bamford's autobiographical writing, after all, is as good as Elizabeth Gaskell's in fiction.[1] Alexander Somerville's autobiography has extraordinary power.[2] And there are many others who are not so well

---

1   Samuel Bamford (1788–1872) – radical and political organizer – recounts his life across the biographical writings collected in *Account of the Arrest and Imprisonment of Samuel Bamford* (1817), *Passages in the Life of a Radical* (1840–44), and *Early Days* (1849), documenting, amongst many other events, his arrest at Peterloo and subsequent year in prison. For an analysis of the work of Elizabeth Gaskell (1810–1865), see Williams's chapter 'The Industrial Novels' from *Culture and Society*, in which he describes *Mary Barton* (1848) as containing, in its early chapters, 'the most moving response in literature to the industrial suffering of the 1840s' (99).

2   Alexander Somerville (1811–1885) was a radical journalist whose *The Autobiography of a Working Man* (1848) recalls his life as a child growing up in poverty and later as a soldier. In 'Notes on English Prose: 1780–1950', Williams compares Somerville's writing to Dickens, noting 'a common pressure: restless, crowded, vivid: a social world of a radically different kind from that which was still there, and still important, as a basis for the composed, quiet and connected prose of the formally educated tradition. Whenever such a change happens, it is easy for those who are used to the existing conventions to see only the rough edges, hear only the loudness and crudeness, of this different

known. But the novel was not tackled and for a particular reason. The plot was the one thing an honest working-class writer was shy of because most of the novels were about inheriting money – which might be dreamt about: dreaming of the pools for instance – or a particular kind of distant romance which had not much to do with people living in very crowded close quarters. How could a Victorian romance or ordinary relationship of the kind that got into novels be transferred to the size of house most people were living in? You'd have to be immensely inventive and nobody was inventive enough to say, 'well I could write a plot rather like that but shift the locale'. It in fact took about three generations, if it's yet been done. It can be done, after all it's some comfort to think back to 1840 when most middle-class people thought their own lives were much too dull to be put into a novel and all novels should be about the aristocracy. They succeeded so well in the end that for a novel not to be about the middle class now is almost a literary sin. So I suppose everybody's turn will come, but the fact that working-class writers went to the autobiography rather than the novel was interesting for this reason, that there's a model and this is what I mean by popular form.

Writing is hard enough and it usually only gets done at all if there is a form, whether people are aware of it or not. Not a model to be followed slavishly but the problem of writing depends on available forms which at least at some level can be taken for granted so that you're not, in the process of writing, actually having to invent forms. This is only very rarely done and for people with the difficulties we were earlier talking about, about the level of language, it is an exceptionally difficult thing to do. It's been a tough thing because the two stories that came through which were alternatives were the story about a very enclosed working-class or otherwise poor, disadvantaged community. The South Wales and some of the Northern proletarian novels of the 1930s, for example. They are very enclosed, intensely authentic, very faithful to the detail of

---

manner', *Writing in Society*, 89. See also Williams's analysis of Somerville in *The Country and the City*, 229–31.

that life, usually centred around some crisis in their community's life of a strike or depression or war. But the interesting thing about them, and I mean it's still a highly available form under which a lot more were written, is that in a way one of the problems of that community is, by the nature of the form, not present: the problems of the people keeping them there. What you can't do in that kind of proletarian novel is have any class *but* the proletariat. And this type of novel has, as a matter of fact, become more difficult: when capitalists lived up the hill in the big house and you could see them from the workplace at least you could set up one kind of relationship. When the people who sack you now are in a boardroom in Detroit or in Tokyo or somewhere in the City of London, it's a very genuine problem; you say 'well, who cares about them, we all know what the bosses do', so you write about your own people, your own life. They are absolutely right to do so, the immense discouragement which virtually every cultural authority in the country puts out about doing any such thing has to be simply sent on its way. This writing has to be done. But there is that problem of the form; it can very easily become enclosed, it can create a certain idealization as if nobody else existed. And it can even try to become more and more pure, until if someone has got a job in a council office, they've moved out of the working-class community;[1] whereas, it's precisely in our time when there are these problems of mobility and overlaps within families over a quite complicated social spectrum. This characteristic aspect of the form comes from a very close rendering, often from a child's point-of-view or from an adolescent's point-of-view from which you then go away. It produces the curious effect of thinking that everybody gets born into the working class and everybody goes away from it – that what's left behind is the old folks at home but not people still in generations of the class reproducing itself and the people still there and the work still being done.[2] Those were

---

1   A passing allusion to John Braine's novel *Room at the Top* (1957) in which the protagonist Joe Lampton leaves the fictional working-class Dufton to work as a local government accountant in Warley.

2   Williams makes the same point in 'British Working-Class Literature

the forms that, however, were the way through by comparison with the inheritance novel and the romance in the nineteenth century and have produced what is still, if ever you could persuade the academic establishment to acknowledge it, a very important body of popular imaginative writing from those popular areas in the twentieth century. It is certainly enough to make it quite clear that the thing can be done because it was done by people as disadvantaged and having to struggle as hard as you could well imagine.

I think that they can still be written, those forms, and there is the other form of access into the television play and into the new kinds of very active alternative theatre which are now proving very open, particularly to this kind of counter-language which I was mentioning at the beginning. A lot of it can be done in theatre. It is at the level of the novel which I think is still very important, while those old forms will continue on being written because there are still vast areas which have not been written and lots of experience of going away and going back are still to be told. We are in the process now of having to face forms which are dealing with something more complex and still under these pressures because one of the effects of education having been to some extent improved is that we can all say 'adverse weather conditions'; we not only can say it, we know what it means. The result is that you are dealing now with a different situation from the porter in *Macbeth* situation, where the way a porter talks and a king talks can be, not only in conventional writing but in reality, separate because these are separated classes. There's now this extraordinary sharing of levels of the language, with a very uneven, multi-layered, and often as it were geologically faulted set of connections inside them which means that although there can be experiments in the wholly alternative and counter-language, and this has been done across different ethnic groups, a lot of the mainstream problems

---

after 1945' as well as in 'Region and Class in the Novel', *Writing in Society*, 235. Of course, it is also something he grappled with in his own fiction, notably in *Border Country* (1960). For an extended discussion of such concerns, see Phil O'Brien and Nicola Wilson, 'Introduction: Raymond Williams and Working-Class Writing', *Key Words*, 18, 2020, 5–21.

are dealing with this multi-layered complex situation. Here the popular impulse has still to be there but it must not be just a case of providing alternative, low-life images for the entertainment of the bourgeoisie. It's one thing they've always rather liked: the lower, the better, be real scum and it's okay. However, be different and say 'we live here, this is what we're like, and we're not charmingly wicked or feckless, like your fantasies, we are not like that, we are just ourselves, we happen to live here, we've got these problems' – do that and they'll tell you to go away, you're boring. It's just that point where they tell you you're boring – I've faced this so often for a long time, not in lecture situations but by talking to people – or you're harping on the same old theme, that's the pressure point, that's where you've got to stick. It is on that where you don't give a damn if you're the colourful poor, you don't give a damn if you're an interesting region, because you don't see it in that way. I mean things have to be written and spoken about where you are and because you're there and because of who you are and you need absolutely no external reason. They write about themselves without any excuse. One is not writing regional novels or community novels; nobody ever calls the thing centred in Manhattan or Chelsea a regional or community novel, but they are as much and as little so as these alternatives.

1982

9

The Future of Socialism

The traditional time for really serious reflection when we put hard questions to ourselves is the small hours; we are a bit early for that but perhaps late enough after a hard day.[1] Nevertheless, the object of this meeting is precisely to put questions to ourselves that are not always possible to attend to in the necessary hurry of day-to-day, month-to-month, year-to-year politics. I think there is genuinely a crisis about the nature of socialism which has emerged partly because of the way that capitalism itself has developed and partly because of certain developments on the left. Certainly, now in Western Europe, there is a widespread desertion from socialism by people who have been its allies over a generation. It is more marked, I suppose, in France and Italy than it has been here but it is still very significant. And, moreover, there is something which

---

1 A talk delivered as part of a *New Socialist* panel (titled 'The Future of Socialism', an echo of Anthony Crosland's revisionist analysis of 1956) with Tony Benn, at a Labour Party Conference fringe event, Heathlands Hotel, Bournemouth, 30 September 1985. The transcript – which has been edited for publication – is held in the Raymond Williams Collection, Richard Burton Archives, Swansea University, WWE/2/1/7/3/7. Explanatory notes by the editor. The last page is missing from the archive and, although the transcript captures Williams's move towards a conclusion, his final few remarks on 'democracy' and 'self-management' are absent.

is the substance of my first point, a very notable rise of something that you can properly call anti-capitalism, which is vigorous, in many respects campaigning, but which is not socialist or is at best uneasily socialist. So the first thing I want to discuss is the nature of that anti-capitalism and why it hesitates before socialism and what we as socialists can say to it.

As a matter of fact, anti-capitalism has always obviously been a major component of socialism: people who saw that the capitalist economic system was inhuman and in natural terms destructive; people who therefore emphasized notions of co-operative activity, of more protective attitudes towards the environment, of kinder human relations. Within nineteenth-century development, and for much of the twentieth century, that found its place within a broad socialist movement which felt that these were its own perspectives, which was moving towards a kinder, more caring, more co-operating, less harsh and competitive society.

Yet one can't overlook the fact now that certain campaigns – the varied ecology campaigns are the first example, some elements of the peace campaigns are the next, important elements of the women's movement are a third – who are as vigorously anti-capitalist and against the whole shape or the dominant order as any of us but who, not all of them, but a number of them, a significant number of them, hesitate before socialism and sometimes even more than that see socialism itself as part of what they are against.[1] I mean, take the ecology campaign. They say that the capitalist stress on production and growth as the solution to poverty, never mind what kind of production, never mind what kind of growth, never mind what kinds of damage certain kinds of production and growth do to people and to the natural world, that that has been so widely adopted by dominant tendencies in the socialist movement that they say they can't distinguish between a socialist and a capitalist emphasis. And so you get certain positions in Western

1   In 1986, Williams returned to such questions in his article 'Hesitations before Socialism' for *New Socialist*, later collected in *Resources of Hope*, 288–94. For more on the coalescing of peace, ecology, and feminism as a way of forging 'radically new kinds of politics', see Williams, *Towards 2000*, 248–60 (248).

Europe, I don't apply this to Green politics, which, although one wing may be socialist, has another wing which is distinctly seeking to surpass socialism and to regard socialists as trapped in an old kind of order which they are trying to move beyond, or the peace movements, which have certainly moved towards saying this. Here, of course, one gets into very difficult areas of the nature of Soviet and East European societies, that they can, at the level of the deployment of nuclear weapons and the predominance of military strategic thinking of that inhuman kind, move to a level of political perspective in which the distinctions between socialist and capitalist policies are minimal.

People see their problem as moving to a kind of peace-making which is beyond the perspectives not only of the capitalist and imperialist states of the West but beyond the actually existing socialist states of the East.[1] It's a difficult argument there because many West European socialists would want to make their quali-fications about those East European societies. But, nevertheless, this is a further example of people who are terribly against the existing order, who can lead themselves to be more absolutely against it than many of us who are socialists and who are looking for some, not always very clearly defined, state of society which they certainly don't call socialism. Or again, in many parts of the women's movement, there is the critique of that socialist tradition which is founded largely on the male wage earner, through that kind of definition of the labour and trade union movement where the socialist tradition is seen as a kind of tunnel vision from the point of view of the male manual worker, wage earner, which has never admitted the problems of the different nature of women's work, women's aspirations, women's problems in their relations with men. Now, again, they are attacking the whole bourgeois order as they more commonly put it than the capitalist, but they don't have any time for capitalism. But many of them say that they can't see, either in socialist practice or in what they hear of

1   See Williams, 'Beyond Actually Existing Socialism', collected in *Culture and Materialism*, 252–73.

socialist theory, the solution to their urgent concern in a notion of socialism.

In other words, we are in this very curious situation that there is a very widespread refusal of capitalism which is not converting itself into the kind of socialist affiliation which at earlier stages it did. And this for socialists is a matter that has to be very seriously addressed. Not that I am going to suggest that this is an obvious area that we can discuss, not an area that we can address by merely repeating the position which pre-existed the emergence of this tendency. I don't think we can any longer say to the ecologists in a simple way that the Labour movement was founded to end poverty among working people; that the only way to end poverty among working people is to produce more so that there is more to distribute, therefore the socialist answer to this problem is the final answer. I don't think we can any longer say that because we have learnt – indeed the early socialists were often much clearer about this than we have been – that it cannot be a matter only of how much in aggregate we produce because first it is always a question of what to produce and is always also, as socialists were the first to emphasize, not only what is produced but what are the relations of production to the system of distribution. What the nature of a given productive system does is a way of setting up relations between people which decide who gets what. In other words, in that long period, which anyone who knows the history of working people understands and sympathizes with deeply from the inside, when faced by desperate and dividable poverty, the instinctive answer is to say, 'Produce more; we need more.' Then we really have now to recognize that simply doing that is, as the ecologists now say, not a solution even to the problem of poverty. We have learnt that even in the richest societies – and you can't imagine anything reasonably richer than say California – the more you produce the less in some ways do you reduce poverty; you produce new kinds of poverty and you produce new kinds of damage to human beings which simply have to be included in the argument at a much earlier stage.[1]

1   Williams spent late 1972 and the early part of 1973 at Stanford Univer-

In all these cases, to patronize these anti-capitalist movements, as on the whole socialists have tended to do, as immature movements which are on their way towards socialism but are still a bit muddled, is to misunderstand the nature of the present crisis.

There is much for socialists to learn from each of these cases and no doubt we can take this argument in whatever direction people want. But I would like to focus on two particular examples which seem to me where we have either got to win the intellectual and political argument in relation to these movements and to the whole situation or to accept the conclusions of our former comrades – the people who are deserting socialism all over the West – that socialism is an idea that missed its time. And the first is the whole question of democracy. I think that unless we win this argument then in the West, at least, we are fundamentally blocked. The current association between the most aggressive kind of capitalism and democracy is an outrage, I mean it is an intellectual and a practical outrage, that people like Thatcher and Reagan can claim to be speaking for democracy and can apply the rhetoric of democracy against socialism, against the idea of socialism. But this is partly because we ourselves have never fully thought this through.[1] I think first that in our own situation we were for a very long time content to receive definitions of democracy from previous political practice by other parties. We acquired a rhetoric about parliament for example which conceded too much in the

sity as a visiting professor of political science: 'When I was teaching political economy in California, which sounds like a joke in itself, we didn't go anywhere around by car, we went on the buses and on the trains, and I have never seen such poverty, at least in any comparable country. [...] And right in the middle of it – although conveniently not seen by the people who say, "oh, it's a terrible life but it sure produces the goods" – right in the middle of it are desperately poor people, desperately poor and unhappy and stressed people. And this is not an accident, any more than it is an accident that in a rich society like this one still is, there are people desperately poor.' See 'Ecology and the Labour Movement', a talk delivered to the Socialist Environment and Resources Association (SERA), Letchworth, June 1984, Raymond Williams Society Blog at raymondwilliams.co.uk.

1   See Williams, 'Democracy and Parliament', collected in *Resources of Hope*, 256–80.

sense that the challenges we made to the whole economic order were rebutted by the appeal to political democracy in parliament. You still hear this every day. It's a difficult argument because, necessarily, socialists are intervening in social relationships in a fundamental way which does break the habits on which parliamentary democracy has depended. It does challenge assumptions about the limited sharing of power on which parliamentary democracy has been able to function. The assertion of new kinds of 'rights' does come up against what people have learnt as democracy in a kind of textbook version so that it has been in one way too easy for the right to present us as the enemies of democracy. We have had to carry the heavy burden, which I suppose it's fair that we should have to carry, of socialist revolutions in countries which had no experience of democracy of any kind and which, whether under enormous external pressures or because of deformities and betrayals within their own movement, however you interpret it, nobody can say, 'Look there for democracy', as something which is superior to our practice. And because this is so, we have been put on the defensive and it's my belief that unless we can break this alliance between what is, to speak plainly, an aggressive imperialism in the West and the notion of liberal democracy, an association which has become natural in many minds that those two things are intimately associated, unless we can break that link the prospects for advance are limited.

Now, what I want to argue is that we can break it. But that to do so we have to think our way beyond the notions of representative democracy which we have inherited in a way because we wanted to say: we are the completion of this system. We are what it has been moving towards. We are the final stage of the democratic tradition. We are, but only by changing it, only by radically changing it.

It strikes me very much that representative democracy was actually introduced as an alternative to direct democracy. In fact, if you look at the people who theorized it first, they said it is too dangerous for the people to govern themselves; people are too unstable, insufficiently informed. Whereas if we have a process in which we select the wisest, the best informed among them, if we have representatives, then we can have democracy without destroying the social order, without limiting civilization. And because we all know that in complex societies you need representatives, you can't all go to all meetings all the time, we have tended to go along with that definition of democracy, that democracy is the representative. Now the only way in which we can actually get past the present block, in which there is this association between capitalists and the free market and the democratic right, is to have something in conceptual socialist democracy which is qualitatively better and qualitatively different from the notion of representation. And I find talking to friends in the labour movement that this is still something people are unwilling to accept.[1] Because, in a way, the tradition has been too well learned and it is still the case that if there is, for example, a strike, who speaks? When the engagement with the public is to happen, who speaks: the leader, the representative, the chairman, the general secretary? It was very striking during the coal strike that whenever a working miner or striking miner spoke directly there was a totally different quality of communication from the best of the representatives.[2] And this is because – it should be evident to all socialists that we are in this difficulty I have been trying to describe – our whole case is that people within a world with which they have mixed their labouring, in a physical world where they have learnt what

---

1   During his 1984 SERA talk, Williams describes such difficulties: 'I was born into the labour movement. My own life perspective was entirely formed by this sense of an avoidable poverty and therefore of the need for the remedy, the justice, the correction of proportion which was the labour movement's own definition of itself. And I think that if you come from outside that, as with part of my mind I now can, and simply say: this is a social order which is going to reproduce poverty inside growth; this is a social order which in substituting production, the notion of production, for the notion of livelihood, is going to find that in the end it *cannot* serve all its people – you do sound like a visitor from another planet sometimes'. See 'Ecology and the Labour Movement', Raymond Williams Society Blog.

2   For Williams on the British Miners' Strike of 1984/85, see 'Mining the Meaning: Key Words in the Miners' Strike', collected in *Resources of Hope*, 120–7.

they are talking about the hard way, what they can say – even if by abstract standards it is tentative stumbling and not what the media are accustomed to hear, not the smooth performance – has that unmistakable quality of truth telling. It has that unmistakable quality of a man or a woman speaking from life experience. There are a few, the best of them, the representatives of the working class and the labour movement who can articulate that. But they have to learn to do it. The other comes of itself and yet it is so quickly checked by socialists who say we must put forward our representative. There is a classic study of the American New Left, of the student movement who didn't believe in leaders, who didn't believe in having a spokesperson who spoke for the movement.[1] And they found that the media insisted that they must have a representative, they must have a spokesperson. To go and say 'why are you carrying a placard outside this building?' was not reasonable. You had to have somebody that you could ring up and say 'we will do an interview with you, who is your representative?' And they found that the media were selecting the leaders of the movement and that the movement then started addressing itself to the leader; although they hadn't had leaders, they then found they got them because the media in that sense had created them. Now this is just a small practical example of what is a big theoretical problem. If we are to have a notion of socialist democracy which is beyond representation how in practice are we going to do it? How in practice are we going to manage our affairs so that people are really not only making decisions for themselves but speaking for themselves? It is in this direction that the ideas of a socialist democracy which is qualitatively superior to anything that we have known in bourgeois democracy is to be found, but it is not easy. It is where we have to share experience. And some of the rhetoric against what is called bourgeois democracy, under those slogans that get thrown around, is actually very damaging.

---

1   See Todd Gitlin, *The Whole World Is Watching: Mass Media in the Making and Unmaking of the New Left* (Berkeley: University of California Press, 1980).

Bourgeois democracy means one precise thing. It has got one precise meaning which is that there is a political electoral system so that you can choose a government within its terms, but that this co-exists with the endurance of wholly unequal economic power. In other words, it is democracy as far as it goes within the electoral system but it is inside a system where power and wealth and resources are shared so unequally that the one at least cancels out, or limits, or sometimes at worst absolutely blocks, the other. And that is the precise meaning of bourgeois democracy: the co-existence of what is genuinely democratic, as far as it goes, but which cancels itself because of the unchanged economic relation. Yet listen to some of our friends, and bourgeois democracy is the whole apparatus of the right to individual dissent; the right to free dissenting expression. That these are held to be challenges to the necessary unity of the class or the party, nothing could be more dangerous, because those societies which have experienced bourgeois democracy – even at times like this when it is actually being limited and being pressed in on – will only move towards socialism if it is something which is visibly, practically more democratic. They are not going to turn to notions of a simple collective will or the taking of decisions and the making of declarations by the duly appointed authorities or the authorized representatives. In other words, for socialists, we either move towards this very practical everyday and equal democracy or we lose this crucial argument. And this is one of the blocks I know from talking to so many people in these positions, one of the blocks which make people who are anti-capitalist hesitate before socialism.

The second point is this, and then I will finish because I mustn't talk too long.[1] We are still only at the beginning of learning something that is the exciting challenge of the next phase of socialism.

---

1   The panel with Benn ran from 10pm until past midnight, with the Labour MP recording in his audio diary that Williams spoke for 41 minutes, 'without a note'. 'I spoke for about 20', adds Benn, 'and he spoke for another 30 and I spoke for another 10. Two hours elapsed before the audience were allowed in at all'. Unpublished transcript from Benn's audio diary, courtesy of the Trustees of the Tony Benn Estate and the British Library.

For good reasons, most socialist practice has emphasized the necessity of strong central planning and control in the hardest case of command authority. Not only has that been the case in practice, in those post-revolutionary societies which had to defend themselves against internal enemies and external assault, who had to nurse their societies through extraordinary shortages which would overwhelm any body of human beings that didn't have clear practical, central direction. It has also of course been the predominant labour tradition that you have your central, expertly informed, public-spirited but, above all, central, strong government. On the other hand, and this is precisely where we have to engage the argument of the anti-capitalists and a whole body of democratic feeling and impulse which is widespread in this society but which hesitates before socialism, the actual thing that people now want is much more say in their own affairs, much more opportunity to run their own concerns, and, to take the phrase which has become established in the tradition, 'much more self-management'. Now I may be unkind, but I think that many contemporary socialists believe in these two things simultaneously and have not yet fully thought through the relations between them. That is to say, and nobody can deny it, if a Labour government is elected in 1987 you will need very powerful and determined central authorities to deal with a counter-offensive, strong, financial, industrial, military, foreign interest. That really cannot be seriously doubted. Not to have that would in effect be to give up before you start. But on the other hand, to have that and to have only that would drain the will, drain the vision, drain the energy of precisely the people who would be needed to support that kind of hard policy. In other words, what we want, and this is where we now have to learn to think in new ways, is an understanding of the relations between the need for a central authority which is capable at least of the necessary defensive action and the widest possible distribution of effective day-to-day power.

Now I think there are such ways but they are not simple ways and they have not been bequeathed to us by the previous socialist tradition; both currents have run very strongly in the labour movement. The next stage, and the stage to get beyond some of the blocks now on the movement towards socialism, is to be able to show in practice how these two things could be combined, because self-management on its own is never likely to be any kind of solution to the way of running society. This is where we can engage with the simple anti-capitalist position from a genuinely socialist position. Self-management is marvellously attractive. To take a simple example. If you are a collective running a hotel on a sun-kissed coast, plenty of people come, there are profits in the enterprise and running the hotel and running the profits and deciding their investment is a charming social exercise.[1] Then think of the self-management of a refuge dump in the bleakest mountain range of the same country. Yes, it can be self-managed, but if that is all that happens in each of those places, that they run their own affairs, then the problems which only socialists can address occur. In any human society, if there is not transfer, if there is not the arrangement for equity between people who are doing favourable and well-rewarding work and people doing unfavourable and ill-rewarded work, if there is not the arrangement for transfer between the physically well-endowed regions and the badly endowed, if there are not arrangements between the active and successful workers and those who are for various reasons unsuccessful or disabled or outside the production process altogether, if those arrangements are not there then there is no socialism.

On the other hand, if there is only the central authority which is seeing to this distribution and, by some calculus of its own, deciding what everybody is worth and passing it out, people will

---

1   Williams also uses the example of a hotel to make the same point in *Politics and Letters*: 'Whether you are a hotel collective on a charmed coast in direct or indirect negotiation with a mining collective in a bleak region – and there will be thousands of such cases, all different – or an attractive autonomous region faced with problems of mobility – some of it desperate, some exploitative – from other regions, you will know soon enough that you need complex procedures of negotiation and resolution at any of these external levels as well as the necessary complexities of internal procedures' (434).

give up, they may even go back to the market or to the crude ideas of society and opportunity which are now popular among people with whom they should not be popular. Because they will say 'at least it is not that central machine running our lives', and, because the central machine is always more visible than the market, it is always much easier to blame. To find those intermediate institutions between the strong defensive authority which any serious socialist project requires and self-management and the relations between self-managing enterprises – this is where we are, this is where we need to think, and in fact the crisis of the relations between central and local government in the last two years of the Thatcher assault have been extraordinarily instructive in this respect, because although it is not self-management of enterprises, it is exactly the same problem of the relations between a central and a local government and how very difficult these relations are to think through, not just in opposing what has been done but in constructive ways of how we would do it much better, qualitatively differently. That was to summarize what I have been saying and apologies for taking so long about it.

We are in a very curious situation. In some ways the left has its back up against a wall. We have been more resolute in this country, despite the series of defeats, than in many other West European countries where the morale is very low. We are living in societies in which, for reasons we must all know, the hatred of capitalism, the conviction that this cannot be a way to organize human life, is spreading and strengthening and deepening and yet in which there is this hesitation before socialism. Let us identify these issues and realize that they do present us with very serious challenges of innovation, challenges of innovation to go beyond our traditional arrangement, and above all let us not rest satisfied with the degree of hostility to capitalism which is all around us. There is quite evident hostility now towards Thatcherism which could in the end not amount to very much unless we have something more than a negation of it, unless we have something constructive on the chief points where people hesitate about socialism.

1985

10

When Was Modernism?

Modern, in its root sense, means 'just now'.[1] But since the time some 500 years ago when groups of people began defining themselves as moderns in comparison and contrast with the ancients and, indeed, invented the Middle Ages to create a proper distance between them, modern has also taken on a historical dimension. That is to say that at any time, modern in the last 500 years has been 'just now' but has also been this constantly extending period after some date which usually settles around the Renaissance. Since that time certain words derived from it – 'modernist' itself, 'modernism', 'modernize' – have been regularly used on the whole until the nineteenth century relatively unfavourably; as 'a state of alteration, perhaps of improvement', as Jane Austen was to put it in one novel.[2] There was a sense that something was being brought

---

1 A Lewis Fry Memorial Lecture delivered on 17 March 1987 at the University of Bristol. The lightly edited transcription – from a recording in the Williams family archive – and explanatory notes are by the editor. It is the 'When Was Modernism?' lecture as it was given by Williams, not the previously published version which was reconstructed by Fred Inglis – who describes it as 'my version' – from his own notes and those of Williams before inclusion in the posthumous collection *Politics of Modernism* (1989).

2 Williams is quoting from Austen's novel *Persuasion*: 'The Musgroves, like their house, were in a state of alteration, perhaps of improvement. The

up to date but whether this was anything better was always a question. It wasn't until the nineteenth century when it began to acquire, in the wake of the industrial revolution, much more positive uses. From then on there are certain decades where the description modern or new seems almost obligatory for certain groups of a cultural kind making their way.[1]

The 1840s is such a period, when John Ruskin publishes *Modern Painters*, meaning principally J. M. W. Turner.[2] The 1890s is also such a period, when the number of periodicals founded with modern or new in the title is remarkable. The 1930s was another period of that kind. The 1960s again. The problem is that these moderns, these versions of the modern, continually recede into history and there is a tension between the sense which is offered to be conveyed by these self-descriptions of 'just now' – immediacy, up-to-date, very often the reformed, innovating, the experimental – and the steadily accumulating period which in this and other contexts are defined as modern. 'Contemporary' sometimes rivals it but contemporary can mean 'just then'; you can have contemporaries of William Shakespeare or contemporaries

father and mother were in the old English style and the young people in the new. [...] Their children had more modern minds and manners', Jane Austen, *Persuasion* (1818; Oxford: Oxford University Press, 2008), 38. Elsewhere, Williams links such notions of 'improvement' in Austen's work to morality: 'What happens in *Emma*, in *Persuasion*, in *Mansfield Park*, is the development of an everyday, uncompromising morality, which is in the end separable from its social base and which, in other hands, can be turned against it', *The Country and the City*, 145. See also Williams on 'improve' in *Keywords*, where he briefly discusses Austen's awareness of the 'contradictory senses' of improvement (161).

1   See also Williams's entry for 'modern' in *Keywords*, 208–9.

2   The first of what became the five-volume *Modern Painters* (1843–60) was written as a defence of Turner, Ruskin insisting on the significance of the proto-impressionism of an artist who for him epitomized the 'modern'. 'Modern landscape painters have looked at nature with totally different eyes, seeking not for what is easiest to imitate, but for what is most important to tell', writes Ruskin. 'Rejecting at once all idea of *bonâ fide* imitation, they think only of conveying the impression of nature into the mind of the spectator', John Ruskin, *Modern Painters* (1843; London: Smith, Elder, and Co, 1844), 89.

of William the Bastard who are not necessarily modern. So contemporary as an indication of 'just now' is always subject to that difficulty. Now my question 'When Was Modernism?' is an adaptation of a title of a book by my friend, professor Gwyn Williams of the University of Wales, *When Was Wales?* (1985).[1] That was a historical question addressed to a very real, very strong but necessarily problematic identity. It was there, when did it happen, how did it happen? My question has a similar spirit but it's going to be centred on one very particular fact: that, from a comparatively recent date, a whole area of work in the arts was confidently described as modernist and, in product, as modernism. It was described to the point where you have the very curious linguistic situation that what has followed that work has to be called postmodern. So that a post- 'just now' situation, which has been operative for the last twenty years, is a linguistic curiosity at least but it is also I think historically very instructive.

Modern got settled in a description of certain innovations in literature, painting, music, and drama as having begun somewhere around 1890 and – then the arguments about dates begin – ending somewhere around 1940, 1950. But what is so curious is that this modern has gone on being modern even if on some accounts it has been over for half a century. It is this curious phenomenon that I want to explore. It is like that other related phrase, avantgarde, which is a very important component of modernism but I think, as I will try to argue, quite distinct from it.[2] The avantgarde is originally a military metaphor for the vanguard outriding

---

1   Gwyn Alf Williams (1925–1995) was a leading socialist historian of Wales, particularly of industrial South Wales, an influential broadcaster, and an authority on the French Revolution and Antonio Gramsci. *When Was Wales? A History of the Welsh* was reviewed for *The Guardian* by Williams, who described it as 'the best general history of the Welsh now available'. See Raymond Williams, 'The Shadow of the Dragon', collected in *Who Speaks for Wales? Nation, Culture, Identity*, ed. Daniel Williams (Cardiff: University of Wales Press, 2003), 68.

2   For an extended analysis of these distinctions, see Williams 'The Politics of the Avant-Garde' and 'Language and the Avant-Garde', both collected in *Politics of Modernism*, 49–63; 65–80.

206   CULTURE AND POLITICS

the main force, through to a political metaphor from the 1830s of
the vanguard of social progress and development, and then into
a specialization of artistic movements from, I suppose, the 1890s
but very confidently from 1910. And the point that has to be made
about the avant-garde which still makes it a distinguishable definition from modernism is that the avant-garde was never a cultural
movement alone. I think that in recent usage this point has been
forgotten, in fact for interesting social reasons. The avant-garde,
typically the futurists or the surrealists, always proposed new
methods in the arts but they also proposed them as means to or
consequent upon very radical changes in society or, to be even
more ambitious, in human nature, the apprehension of life itself.
The avant-garde really was something that was going to change
the nature of life. And the fact that those movements have not
been so common since, say, 1945 is a distinct historical development – something is lost I think if we go on calling avant-garde
what is merely an experimental method in one of the arts. This
will be one of the problems I shall keep raising and returning to.
Avant-garde means more than experimental. Avant-garde really
meant, as a metaphor from which it was derived, the notion of a
general direction of change of which certain changes in the arts
were the outriders, the heralds, the witnesses. Modern might have
been like that but if, for example, you'd gone up to some highly
educated gentleman in 1900 and said 'sir, can you tell me what
you understand by modernism?', he'd have said, 'well it refers to
a well-known theological tendency in the Catholic church where
a particular group are trying to redefine the relations between
dogma and the new science'. Modernism in fact in these specific
senses – meaning some actual body of work and ideas as distinct
from earlier seventeenth-, eighteenth-, and nineteenth-century
senses where it simply meant bringing something up-to-date,
a new style – begins in English and, I think more generally, in
Europe as a theological concept. I am not sure, I don't think anyone
can yet be sure, because the amount of material to be searched
is immense, when it really becomes specialized in courses and
studies of literature, drama, and painting to particular methods

which new artists are using. Certainly it is not common, this I can say with confidence, before the 1950s, and its place of origin in that immensely influential use is as you might expect New York. In fact, the announcement in New York that what had been significant in the arts and culture of the previous fifty years was properly understood as modernism was an announcement which beat by only a few years the consequent announcement that it had ended and we are now in the epoch of postmodernism. As we shall see, the people who were making innovations in these different arts were very conscious that they were making something new, and they might occasionally use the word modern in relation to their work, but they did not see themselves as modernists or part of modernism. The sense that has been given is largely retrospective and this has importance because in that retrospective generalization ideological points have been made but made surreptitiously, not declared as values and arguments but offered as a kind of history which carries certain inevitable conclusions. To those people above all one must address the question: 'When Was Modernism?' Is it for example in the novel, those radical innovations which one can identify with the names of Nikolai Gogol or Gustave Flaubert or Charles Dickens, which would have us around the middle of the nineteenth century? Or is it those innovations which one associates with the names of say Marcel Proust, James Joyce, and Franz Kafka? I know what the New York generalization of the 1950s tells us – Proust, Joyce, Kafka – but that is the sort of unresolved point which we will be exploring. In painting, is the new, radical break the impressionists for example? Which would take us back in certain ways to John Constable, who was seen in the 1830s as painting in certain radical new ways which offended contemporary sensibility. Or is it to be dated precisely at post-impressionism, the move away from representation, cubism, and so on? In verse, is it to be dated to the symbolists of the 1870s or 1880s? Or is it to be dated to those many schools of poets, futurists, constructivists, and imagists who precisely rejected symbolism as an outdated form? Symbolism itself had been seen as a radical break, remember. In drama, is it the extraordinary innovation of Henrik Ibsen, or the equally extraordinary but different innovation of August Strindberg?[1] They were seen in their time as carriers of the new. Ibsen was so regarded as the carrier of the new that even the newly fashionable cigarette got a brand named after him; Strindberg was regarded as the archetypal radical, careless, anti-traditional dramatist. Is it to be dated from them, those who describe themselves as naturalists, at least until the turn of the century? Or is it to be dated from what is now called the revolt against naturalism which can be reduced with a certain simplification to the period of the expressionists and a certain centring on the name of Bertolt Brecht?[2]

These are not questions designed only to raise difficulties but they go to the heart of this particular definition of modernism which has become cultural orthodoxy. And I will, if I may, try to extract from each of those points of reference the underlying positions which choosing one or other date implies. For example, take the selection which goes back to Proust, Kafka, and Joyce, to the post-impressionists, to the anti-symbolists, surrealists or constructivists, and to the anti-naturalist dramatists, Brecht, and the expressionists. In that grouping, what is seen as the underlying set of definitions is this. First, the modern discovery, as it is put, of the unconscious: the quite new realization of the nature of unconscious attachments, obsessions, the revelation in dreams, the availability to art of material which it was held had not previously been available to it or fully used. What is held to underly this

---

1   Williams completed his Tripos at Cambridge with a thesis on Ibsen; it was later included in *Drama from Ibsen to Eliot* (1952). He also wrote on Strindberg in *Modern Tragedy* (1966). 'The reason for the intense significance that Ibsen possessed for me then', Williams revealed in *Politics and Letters*, reflecting on his return from the trauma of fighting in Europe during World War Two, 'was that he was the author who spoke nearest to my sense of my own condition at the time' (62).

2   Williams – who would extend *Drama from Ibsen to Eliot* in 1968 to include Brecht – describes the German playwright's work as 'a very powerful kind of critical negation whose effect really depended on the presence of what it was negating', *Politics and Letters*, 216. For more on Brecht, see Williams, 'Theatre as a Political Forum', collected in *Politics of Modernism*, 81–94.

shift, according to this selection, is the realization that language is not natural, that language is an artificial system, that its apparent naturalization in the life of society is merely an illusion of customary experience. The nature of language and its relation to what it is offering to describe (whether objects or experiences) is much more deeply buried than previous linguistic theories had supposed. From this it followed that significant language in the arts was a language which in itself dealt with that problem of distance. Indeed, in that extraordinary, influential definition of the early formalists, that the key to the presence of art in a piece of writing was an element of estrangement in the use of language; that it was a use of language which announced itself in its true nature rather than allowing itself to be sunk into the illusion of natural language. Representation is the next element: the assumption that the purpose of art, in a range of possible styles, to represent objects or images was believed to be an illusion. The purpose of painting, although the definitions vary, was now newly declared to be painting – that it was the use of the medium itself rather than the representation of anything that was not the medium that was now realized to be the necessary business of art. From this, you also get a comparable shift in literature, from the notion of narrative. It is now that people begin in practice and soon enough in theory to ask questions about storytelling which had certainly occurred to many people before but which they did not suppose were all that difficult to answer. People suddenly said, 'who is supposed to know enough to be able to tell this story?' 'From what source does this author gain their omniscience?' 'Can we accept their good faith in presenting these facts as they are laid before them?' Evidently, we cannot. The centring on that kind of narrative is an act of illusion offering itself as realism. By contrast, what has to be introduced into any account of an action or experience is its inherently problematic nature and the inherently problematic stance of anybody who offers to tell you about it.

I remember the time when graduate students first put these questions most insistently to me, asking by what right does anyone tell me a story and reflecting on the long history of human storytelling when the only right anybody ever got to storytelling was the right to be listened to. This was always a proof of practice – whether you were listened to, whether you accepted the story as being told – not whether there was a question of authority inherent in the fact of narrative itself. And from these things, in literature especially, what came to be admired was the self-reflexive text which has now happened in so many of the arts that it has become an orthodoxy, that is to say the text or the picture which in the very process of composition is reflecting on the processes of its composition.

This has been taken very far and it belongs in this complex of attitudes which I hope I have now sufficiently, briefly outlined: the new emphasis on the unconscious, the denaturalization of language, the rejection of representation, the questionability of narrative, and with that the notion of the authentic work of art as self-reflective. Now, the works which correspond to all those positions, works which in fact one can find over a long period but which have been there in both considerable quantity and high quality in the last seventy or eighty years, is indispensably of our time. Nothing I am going on to say is any questioning of the value of those works on any *a priori* principle. What I do want to argue is the extent to which the grouping of those particular positions – especially since it was retrospective and particularly since as a matter of fact it applies much more closely to some of these artists who are celebrated than to others – is often simplifying the positions of a number of them who are grouped under this general label. This generalization becomes a statement out of the 1950s, specifically out of the 1950s of the United States, and especially New York, rather than as an account of the modern movement in the arts as it is also more generally called. One could take the great breaks that one can see happening everywhere in painting, in fiction, in drama, in music, in architecture, from the last third of the nineteenth century, and deduce a quite different set of common values. It depends of course where you put the dates, particularly if you look at what many of those artists themselves were saying.

The first thing that was very widely said was that the existing forms were too fixed and too rigid and what was needed was a revolt against these fixed forms. Second, that all together, too much power was invested in social and cultural authorities who laid down rules for the practice of particular arts. So that you get an attack on the academies in painting, until academic becomes a term of abuse from this position. You get the attack on rules, you get the attack on the constraints of the market, for example. For novelists, the key decade was the 1850s when it became possible to write a novel which did not almost automatically have to be in three volumes and therefore of a certain size; there was more flexibility from the 1850s in purely commercial arrangements and people could write novels of different lengths.[1] An attack on all authorities of this kind, including very powerful attacks on the role of state and church in the censorship of the arts, meant that many of the most celebrated battles were against some censorship or attempt at censorship by an authority of this kind. It was almost obligatory for almost any innovating artist from the last third of the nineteenth century on to declare themself as anti-bourgeois. I mean it is almost an article of faith. One has immediately to add that before that is linked in some post-war situation to a left or Marxist position, that the critique of the bourgeoisie came from both ends of the spectrum. It came in fact from a position above the bourgeoisie, whether the people concerned were actually above it or only aspired to be or identified themselves in that way: the identification of the artist as naturally aristocratic, the identification of the artist as above the bourgeois preoccupation with money and wealthy position. That characteristic aristocratic critique of the bourgeoisie as narrow-minded, provincial, centred on money and position, having no sense of the movement of the

1   The three-volume novel system came to an end in 1894 with the announcement by circulating libraries Mudie's and W. H. Smith's of a change to their purchasing policy, reducing the amount they were prepared to pay for a single volume and imposing new restrictions on cheaper republications. Williams's essay on 'Forms of English Fiction in 1848', collected in *Writing in Society*, is also relevant here.

human spirit. And, curiously, you go across to the other end of the political spectrum and all those things are said again with the addition that the bourgeoisie is precisely the class which raises problems about the morality of certain works of art; it is also the class which in its control of the commerce of art tries to enforce commercial considerations on the practice of arts which should be serving the people. It is very important to remember that these positions are different, but you will hardly find an innovating artist who does not begin by saying, 'I am not writing for the bourgeoisie,' or it might even be a definition of value that it will shock the bourgeoisie, or at least, 'We are not producing things for bourgeois theatres.' You don't hear about that in the 1950s definition from New York. Why will be an interesting question I shall return to.

In other words, what is the modern break? Is it a revolt against certain fixed forms, against the role of cultural authorities, against the cultural dominance of a body of public opinion which was itself only a part of the society? Was that the modern break, and all the methods that have followed from it have at least those sources in common? Or is it solely what has been generalized as the orthodoxy, the discovery of the unconscious, the denaturalization of language, the rejection of representation and narrative? To try to answer those questions we have to dig through two historical levels. The first, which is normally left out of the account in these retrospective summaries, is that this was a period of the most radical change in the media of art, the media of cultural production, one might now say of any time, I suppose, including the period of the invention of printing. The coming of photography, then of moving pictures, the coming of broadcasting, of recorded sound, television – the development of these techniques into whole technologies of cultural production in cinema and the broadcasting institutions, the widespread reproduction of works of art, all those changes altered the conditions in which artists were working to a quite extraordinary extent. And, in a sense, there would have been radical shifts in actual, material, artistic practice whether or not any of these social or philosophical or pseudo-philosophical positions had also been operative. The second fact, which leads us into what is to me the most interesting area, is that indeed, in part in relation to these changes in the nature of medium, there is a new phenomenon in the actual social organization of artists.[1] In certain earlier periods artists had got together for specific purposes which hadn't previously been seen since the pre-modern guilds. People got into defensive positions, particularly in certain declining media, or you got specialized groupings trying to promote a particular kind of art, watercolour, or certain kinds of engraving. You got artists organizing to protect copyright, in a new position of greatly expanded reproduction. But there is now a qualitative change – it is generally qualitative – in the emergence of what are no longer really schools but movements of a kind.

This makes the study of the history of any of these arts a baffling exercise in memory, if you think what you have mainly to do is memorize that succession of movements which announce themselves as futurists, imagists, Dadaists, surrealists, whatever may be. You have a whole succession of movements, and artists grouped around them, that come together, sometimes with a common manifesto of certain new works they are going to do; sometimes the manifesto is simply an exhibition or a new periodical, *salon de refusé*, or the new age. A grouping of artists, often not many, often of personal friends, characteristically these movements don't last very long; they are subject to extreme internal fission, in the case of the surrealists, for example, within ten years people were actually being expelled.[2] Yet, immediately, it is not the principle of grouping around some shared method or intention

---

1 Williams offers an examination of the social history of artists, their organization, and the historical processes of cultural production across two chapters in *The Long Revolution*: 'The Social History of English Writers' and 'The Social History of Dramatic Forms', 254–70; 271–99.

2 Salvador Dalí was symbolically expelled by André Breton and the surrealists due to his alleged sympathy for fascism. For more on such groupings, and the way they often moved decisively left to communism or right to fascism, see Williams, 'The Politics of the Avant-Garde', *Politics of Modernism*, 49–53.

that is abandoned, simply that a new school breaks away, gives itself a new name, announces itself, now this phenomenon is new. And it is of fundamental importance, I think, in understanding the real history in changes in the arts in this period which is generalized as modernist.

Now the next thing is that nearly all these movements have a very specific social location and indeed social composition. There are exceptions of course but overwhelmingly these are movements of the new kinds of the metropolitan, capital city. A capital city had always attracted artists from all over the nation state which it controlled because typically the major means of production and reputation were centred there. But these new capital cities were in the period of imperialism and their range of attraction was very much wider. They are in that true sense, para-national. If you look at the role of Paris from indeed the 1850s, but very strongly from the 1870s and 1880s, if you look at Vienna, if you look at Berlin, if you look even at London, which is not as fully represented as those others but which in certain areas is very marked, you find this new phenomenon that the new is – the new movements, the movements proclaiming themselves as a new departure – finding the point of announcement in these great metropolitan capitals. It is a sign of the great mobility of the period, of the crossing of frontiers which is one of the regular emphases of this kind of art, of the movement indeed beyond the notion of a national art towards an art less dependent on specific national traditions. But then with certain consequences: first, that an unusually high number of the contributors to these movements, and specifically to those movements which were generalized retrospectively in the 1950s as modernism, were literally exiles or, I shall put it the other way round, immigrants. They came to these extraordinarily powerful and miscellaneous metropolitan cities in the period of imperialism, cities which were already to their inhabitants cities of strangers. That phenomenon of the city had been noted as far back as the Romantic movement: remember what a shock it was to William Wordsworth to come to a place of human settlement where as you passed people in the street you did not necessarily know them or know who they belonged or related to.[1] It is something which now seems so naïve that one is tempted to apologize retrospectively for Wordsworth, yet it had been the normal condition of human settlement that one would know at least most of the people one met in and around one's ordinary business. Suddenly the new phenomenon is to see someone who you do know – the main thoroughfares are thronged with people sharing the same conditions but who are strangers.

Now if you take that underlying phenomenon of the city of strangers and impose on it the very particular fact that so many of these artists were themselves exiles or immigrants, you have a very particular situation. Some elements – at least from Joyce or Guillaume Apollinaire through to Samuel Beckett and Eugène Ionesco – of the new practice belong to the situation of the exile in the metropolis, rather than to any more general phenomenon of the modern.[2] And this I think is what explains the very particular interpretation of these movements which happened in the United States and above all in New York. The interpretation was made by people who were living in, what is in a sense, *the* capital, a capital of exiles and immigrants, a country of exiles and immigrants. In other words, what had become a normal situation for discoverable social and historical reasons in the United States is seen as ratifying a particular historical movement which was going on at an earlier period within these great imperial metropolitan capitals, producing over and over that situation.

One has to consider the effects of this on certain presumptions about the nature of art. For example, it is very difficult, once this underlying social situation is recognized, to take in quite the

---

1 Williams is recalling the following lines from *The Prelude*: 'How often, in the overflowing streets/Have I gone forward with the crowd and said/Unto myself, "The face of every one/That passes by me is a mystery!"', William Wordsworth, *The Prelude: A Parallel Text* (1805; 1850; Harmondsworth: Penguin, 1971), 695. See also Williams, 'Metropolitan Perceptions and the Emergence of Modernism', *Politics of Modernism*, 37–48.

2 See 'The Figure in the City' and 'The New Metropolis' in Williams, *The Country and the City*, 280–96; 334–46.

naïve way people have the propositions for example about denaturalization of language. The notion that language is systematic and in the sense it is undeniably an artificial system is wholly to be supported on linguistic grounds, but the whole point is also that any such artificial system is naturalized in the course of an ordinary social life. That it is so naturalized, that it is not in itself natural, has certainly still to be emphasized. However, the extreme position that would have us believe that language, as such, is of its nature denaturalized, that language is simply a system of signs so that the work of a writer is simply a movement within this system of signs, an initiative with the system of a certain kind – that is a notion of great power, of great productivity in certain kinds of work but one which in becoming accepted as a general orthodoxy has a really deep and, I would have thought in the end, destructive absurdity. What is omitted is the process that the city of strangers, the nation of immigrants – not unknown situations in human history – still constitutes an ongoing society. Certain social processes occur and artistic processes among others develop within those social processes; it's a much older position – that they do so in now vastly altered conditions, all that is a wholly acceptable interpretation of modernism. What is not acceptable it seems to me is the proclamation that is true ideology: a) of 'the modern', in a kind of absolute sense; and b) that once having reached a stage of modernity, of that kind, there is nothing beyond it. There is only something which recycles it in slightly altered terms which is what postmodernism has in practice amounted to.[1]

If you are prepared to believe, which some are, that there was something called the discovery of the unconscious, that language

---

1   'Post-modernism for him was a strictly ideological compound from an enemy formation, and long in need of this authoritative rebuttal', Inglis argues in his brief note accompanying the reconstructed version of 'When Was Modernism?', *Politics of Modernism*, 31. Crucially, Inglis misses the nuance of Williams's critique, which comes through more forcefully in the complete version: the naming of a historical process as a specific, enclosed moment in time ('modernism') and then, with the designation of the prefix 'post-', the suggestion that we are now beyond historical process.

is inherently denaturalized, that narrative and representation are not only difficult and changing processes through all the history of fiction, and painting, and sculpture, subject to a very wide variety of modes and styles but that they are intrinsically acts of illusion, that there can be narrative in that sense, that there can be representation in that sense, if you believe that the only serious work is that which inhabits this very specific world, a world of people who have moved out of continuing societies and who are relating only in a way through their own constructions and their own media, then perhaps you could be said to be a modernist. But then consider what that implies. If any of these movements – and they would need different descriptions not only within each of the arts but between different arts – had been called, for example as some more locally were, the abstract movement, or the anti-natural movement, or any of those possible descriptions, we would still be in a very straight and honest world because we would be comparing that method with this. The questions of value between them are endlessly open and diverse, the appropriation of 'modern' for a selection of what have in fact been the modern processes is an act of pure ideology. It attempts to relegate to a pre-history – or to irrelevant provinces in which these key modern processes have not yet occurred but may be hoped to be about to occur, or if they do not occur quickly enough may be helped to move on to occur – the notion that that is so.

That this contrast is made implies an extraordinary redefinition of the nature of art: it removes it for a start from clear and understandable social processes. It ratifies a notion of the artist as an estranged individual working necessarily with the given materials of estrangement. It ratifies ways of seeing fundamental to anyone in the position of exile or immigrant strangeness as if these were fundamental, general human ways of seeing of which the truth has only just been discovered. It ratifies all those things, and all those things with all the implications they have, for the understanding of life in society cannot be conceded to an ideological generation of even this important body of art. Because what happened to the formerly neglected, marginal, indeed accursed artists of modernism, those people who lived in breathless and often ragged ways at the edges of their challenges to authority and orthodoxy, the very people who precisely because they were innovating in so many ways found little public attention – they were roundly and systematically abused – was that they suddenly moved with this generalization into a kind of canon. It was too late for them, too late, for example, for the painters whose works were now traded as international commodities, when because precisely of their actual shift, they could hardly find a sale. Disruptive, radically estranging works were suddenly the material of lecture room and seminar and were examined upon so that a process as established and orthodox as instruction and examination was being applied to something which was at the same time being defined as brilliantly subversive and estranging.

But it was more than that. It was not only that they moved into international commodities, it was that if you see the history of the modern world in the twentieth century, especially in a particular way, you can quite properly see this wave of people who would move from Poland, from Sweden, from Southern Italy, from Ireland, to these international centres of cultural authority, where there was wealth around, where you could find a place just because it was so miscellaneous, where you could get away from the pressure of more local authorities. The very people who moved in that way could be seen as the precursors of a vast international movement of mobility of just that kind. Indeed, to the point where it would be accepted as the normal condition of late twentieth-century life that the notion of communities you did not want to get away from was merely out of date. In every particular case you can understand why those exiles went, but to find it generalized as the desirable and natural human condition is different and, of course, it had a very particular social point. It was saying that those socially worked and diverse forms of painting, storytelling, verse, drama that came out of the very diverse life of peoples across the world, were in a sense the past. This was the point of this definition of modernism: they were the past, modernity was the breaking down of that autonomy in diversity, towards what was offered in fact ludicrously as the new universality. It was a universality that was, however, based on so few centres of power and influence that in its very claim it betrays itself as an ideological move.

And, I suppose, the final indication of that is the ease with which detached elements, and the extraordinary technical innovations of these generations of artists, moved into precisely the pseudo-universal artistic commerce of just this projected society. The methods of montage which looked strange in a film in the early 1920s are now the commonplaces of detergent commercials.[1] The methods of isolated, alienating images, which were strange in the painting of the turn of the century and the early expressionists, you can see now on the hoardings. The methods of narrative continuity, of historical setting which had been there in fiction, replaced by certain jumps, certain centres in isolated personalities who connect only through action, become the staple of a certain kind of successful commercial film. It is the most ironic thing of all that the strangest art in human history, and I think it was the strangest art of the period of this extraordinary innovation, should have become by the last quarter of the twentieth century so accessible, in diluted, adapted, and abstracted forms, to the most popular commercial art with the notion of a pseudo-universality behind it. Precisely because it could be exported, precisely because it didn't come out of any autonomous and diverse life but was a pseudo-international currency which had that kind of trade. Now all that takes one into areas of much more general, difficult, and often of course angry argument, but the central point I've been making is this: one can call any of these methods or positions anything one likes within reason. The more precisely and specifically they are named the more likely we are to understand them beyond the hasty generalizations through which they have been interpreted. The one thing which must not be conceded is the property of the modern, because then that is conceding to a

---

1 See Williams on advertising in *Communications* (1962), *Television: Technology and Cultural Form* (1974), and 'Advertising: The Magic System', collected in *Culture and Materialism*, 170–95.

particular kind of life and a particular interpretation of it: our sense of 'just now', our sense of what is modern. It is in asking 'When Was Modernism?' that I am refusing this because I think there is reason to believe that modernism in that sense, the sense as it was offered of a universal alienation, is something which the human race will either overcome or destroy itself with.

1987

Index